Global *The* Age

For SJO

The Global Age

Global Age

State and Society Beyond Modernity

MARTIN ALBROW

Stanford University Press
Stanford, California
1997

Stanford University Press
Stanford, California
© 1996 Martin Albrow
Originating publisher: Polity Press, Cambridge
   in association with Blackwell Publishers Ltd.
First published in the U.S.A. by
   Stanford University Press, 1996
Printed in Great Britain
Cloth ISBN 0-8047-2869-0
Paper ISBN 0-8047-2870-4
LC 96-69671
This book is printed on acid-free paper.

Contents

Acknowledgements

I owe a big debt to my collaborators in the Roehampton Institute London globalization research cluster: Patricia Alleyne-Dettmers, Laura Buffoni, Jörg Dürrschmidt, John Eade, Graham Fennell, Darren O'Byrne and Neil Washbourne. Their collective enthusiasm and ever-willing readiness to exchange information and ideas has been a marvellous stimulus, though neither individually nor collectively do they bear any responsibility for this book. Our joint efforts have been assembled by John Eade in *Living the Global City* (1996). Of them only Neil has been involved directly by criticizing my drafts in depth and then plying me with corroborative material far beyond my capacity to use. His encouragement and help have been invaluable. I have also greatly appreciated and benefited from my conversations with Jörg, whose contribution has gone far beyond the simply intellectual.

Thanks are due to support from the Institute's Research Committee, and to the Department of Sociology and Social Policy and the Faculty of Social Sciences for allowing me a semester's study leave.

Montserrat Guibernau of the University of Warwick and Sandro Segre of the University of Genoa have each made lengthy, insightful and very helpful comments on a draft of the book. They have helped me to improve it in important respects. I am most grateful to them both and am only sorry that there was no time to engage with every suggestion. I am grateful to Richard Grathoff of the University of Bielefeld for the sheer fun of intellectual friendship as well as for his willingness to take over from me the time consuming labours of editing *International Sociology*.

At Polity Press, Tony Giddens has timed his interventions to perfection and given just the right kind of encouragement. Gill Motley has made reassurance an art and waiting a very positive thing. Ann Bone has shown me that copy-editing is really a useful branch of critical theory. Julia Harsant has cheerfully expedited everything. Annabelle Mundy has shown every care and consideration for an author's last minute thoughts. My thanks to them all.

Susan Owen knows the diversity of meanings, not all of them positive, which this book has had for both of us. It is to her that it is dedicated with gratitude for the support she has given. But our five-year-old son, Thomas Albrow-Owen, has probably got the best approach. He has promised me 'another Global Age book' for Christmas. Finally many thanks to Stephen Albrow for his patient and informative responses to the questions which the older generation is prone to ask about Glastonbury and like things.

Introduction

The balance of evidence suggests a discernible human influence on global climate.

United Nations Intergovernmental Panel on Climate Change, 1995

A sense of rupture with the past pervades the public consciousness of our time. It extends beyond national and ideological differences. The American sociologist Alvin Toffler (1981) announced the dying of industrial civilization and has become a favoured source for Republican Party thinking. In Britain the Marxist 'New Times' project reported a qualitative change so deep as to be an epochal transition (Hall and Jacques 1989).

At the same time, despite all the 'new age' talk ('age of automation', 'atomic age', 'space age', 'electronic age', 'solar age'), the idea that we are still in some sense 'modern' is remarkably persistent. It indicates how successful the thinking of modernity has been in claiming any innovation as its own, even a 'new age'. As a result the postmodern has never escaped modernity. It has only been able to define itself in relation to the modern, and for some is only a phase of it: 'our postmodern modern' for the German philosopher Wolfgang Welsch (1993).

Modernity holds its adherents in a double bind: it promises new futures and at the same time denies any possibility of an alternative to itself. As we know from interpersonal relations, double binds are designed to lock people in by involving them in irresolvable argument. Escape comes by refusing to accept the terms of discussion. We can only do this by moving on beyond both modernity and postmodernity and recognizing a new reality. I am suggesting then that theoretical argument has for some time been trapped by the narcissism of modernity even as the world has moved on.

This book confronts theory with the reality of the Global Age in which we now live. The argument is new, although it was hinted at by Karl Jaspers (1955), who saw how the dropping of the atomic bomb in 1945 implicated the globe as a whole. Edward Tiryakian (1984a) went as far as seeing the 'global crisis as an interregnum of modernity'. Yet, in spite of 'globalization' becoming 'the epithet of choice' (Himmelfarb 1995: ix), those who have recognized it as a major social transformation (notably Beck 1986, Giddens 1990 and Robertson 1992) have still stressed the continuity of modernity.

But people sense epochal change in world events. For me the most compelling announcement comes today (as I write), from the United Nations Panel on Global Warming, which has for the first time unequivocally announced that global warming is happening. There could not be a more dramatic marker of epochal change. If Hiroshima marked the beginning, surely this marks the end of the transitional period into the Global Age. But it also means the Modern Age has passed.

There is a deep contradiction between this experience of epochal change and the language of modernity which leaves our public discourse in an incoherent state. Modern visions of a globalized world tend to see it in some familiar guise: realization of world government; a single world market; a new world order; global culture; late modernity. I contend that none of these provide an adequate account of the flux through which we have moved. We are at one of those moments when we have to recognize that our ideas have stayed still too long and we need a new beginning.

It is not so much that they are partial accounts; any account of a 'change in the world' is, but each carries with it too much of the modern past and too little of the difference we experience. Indeed any talk of the end of modernity sounds so destructive that it evokes the appalling prospect of 'the end of history'. The intention of this book is to address the problem of making the new intelligible without either assimilating it to the world we have lost or announcing the Last Judgement. It offers neither comfort nor apocalypse.

This then is an intervention into the thoughtworld of modernity. It intrudes by asking the reader to think the unthinkable, namely that the Modern Age has actually finished but that *history has not ended*. Instead another age has taken its place, with its own dominant features and shape. We will then, with the advantage of our position in the new age, be able to assess the one which has passed. We also depict the new age in terms which are not specifically modern. For there is an inherent fault in the narrative of modernity itself. It only satisfies the human longing for immortality by securing itself against ever ending. This book is about coming to terms with the present as history, that is as part of a story in which all times are equal in the sight of God. We can write of epochal change in the past. There is no reason to deny the possibility for the present.

This cannot be done without challenging both the language and the interpretation of the facts in the modern theory of globalization. What some have called 'global babble' (beginning with Marshall McLuhan's 'global village', 1962) involves intense controversy about globalization and whether it really does mean anything new. But much of it is talking at cross purposes because of the inappropriateness of an older modern discourse about novelty which sought always to assimilate it to modernity, an ever renewed present arising as a trend out of the past.

It is concern to do justice to the times in which we live which makes it necessary to take history into our account. It is not antiquarian interest which requires a review of modernity as a historical phenomenon. The true 'test of time' is to recognize the Modern Age as a passing stage of history. Simultaneously we acknowledge that humanity has more potential than could ever be contained in one period, however dynamic and expansive it might have been. We don't in this way assimilate the Global Age to the Modern, or indeed any age or culture to any other; rather we disaggregate their achievements to provide us with the full array of human possibilities. Humanity is the subject, neither necessarily the 'modern' nor the 'global' human being.

The first three chapters of this book reassess the problems of writing about the Modern Age. Chapter 1 considers the general requirements for writing the history of the present. These involve rescuing it from the self-narratives of modernity. Chapter 2 shows how narratives of modernity were intrinsic to the Modern Project as a comprehensive frame for living, both material and ideal, over which the nation-state claimed jurisdiction. Chapter 3 points to the culmination of the Modern Project as its simultaneous dissolution and therefore the need to find a new historical narrative.

Chapter 4 sifts the language of the global for the contribution it can make towards a new self-understanding of our times. Chapter 5 reviews accounts of our own times and finds that these misinterpret epochal change by seeking to assimilate globality to a past Modern Age.

Chapters 6 and 7 accept the consequences of treating our time as a new epoch, beyond modernity. They explore the new configurations of phenomena, which have in the past only been seen as features of modernity, or of its impending dissolution, to show their own characteristic non-modern coherence.

Chapter 8 examines the consequences of the Global Age thesis for politics and argues that it requires us to resume conceptualizations of society and the state which were suppressed by modernity. It identifies a new popular construction of the state which I call performative citizenship. Politicians as a result need to heed the relativization of the nation-state and their claims on its citizens which they took for granted in the Modern Age.

Chapter 9 concludes by arguing that the Global Age narrative contains more than an appeal to change the way we think about our own time. It equally needs to be treated as an explanatory hypothesis for cultural shift and social transformation.

New thinking requires new research. It must by now be clear that the mass of research around modernity, on industrialization, democratization, bureaucratization, urbanization, and rationalization, carried with it a sense of a relentless overall process of modernization. Yet none of those 'processes' ever reached a determinate end-point, and all of them have been transmuted into what now appear to be features of a past historical period. They never were processes in the sense of developments governed by scientific laws with necessary outcomes, nor is globalization. The '-ization' suffix of globalization is an indication in itself of the inappropriate attempt to assimilate it to the modern. It leads to accounts which minimize the contemporary transformation. It cannot possibly be adequate for the epochal shift which Ralf Dahrendorf (1975) described as the move from expansion to survival with justice.

Some imagine that globalization is about the expansion of free trade. But even among economists it is well recognized that this is only one aspect of a transformation in the world economy in which changes in production and consumption are central. But accounts of globalization as simply economic betray a narrow economistic outlook, when we are involved in a comprehensive social transformation. Those who imagine that globalization is about trade barriers are seriously unprepared to understand what is happening.

Fundamentally the Global Age involves the supplanting of modernity with globality and this means an overall change in the basis of action and social organization for individuals and groups. There are at least five major ways in which globality has taken us beyond the assumptions of modernity. They include the global environmental consequences of aggregate human activities; the loss of security where weaponry has global destructiveness; the globality of communication systems; the rise of a global economy; and the reflexivity of globalism, where people and groups of all kinds refer to the globe as the frame for their beliefs.

Taken together these represent the greatest challenge yet to the idea of ever expanding modernity, and hence to the nation-state. Moreover this challenge to nation-states encourages their citizens and other agencies to cross and transgress their physical and conceptual boundaries.

The total effect is of a social transformation which threatens the nation-state in a more extensive way than anything since the international working-class movement of the nineteenth century. Modern discourse persistently misreads this. National governments wrestle with the disaggregation of state and nation, seek to reduce government while administering a global rationality and simultaneously lose touch with their populations.

We can agree with Zygmunt Bauman (1992: 65) that postmodern conditions mean we can no longer attach our analytical models to the nation-state. But what are these conditions? Encoding them with 'globalization' in general has been inadequate to grasp the nature of the epochal shift for reasons which the book will set out in detail. We are on much safer ground with 'globality' since it carries no connotation of necessary outcomes. But then the complex, often contradictory, directions in which globality relates to life require us to register the change as epochal. I know of no better way to do this than through 'the Global Age'.

This book draws on many disciplines but its main problem setting arises out of the interplay of sociology, social and political theory, history and the newer field of cultural studies. I hope there will be interested readers in all four disciplinary areas and that they may find room for the new category of epochal theory on their shelves. The broad relevance of epochal theory is not in providing a set of answers to universal problems. It points rather to issues arising out of the conditions of human existence, where the solutions vary in different periods of history and cultures. They include reaching understanding; communication; relations between people; life and death; right and wrong; reward and punishment; power, freedom and consent; humanity and nature.

Answers to these issues are not foundations for our lives in the way that food, warmth and shelter are. But the recurrence of ideas like 'society', 'state', 'community', 'welfare', 'justice' suggests that they are not merely modern fixes, because they never acquire a final meaning. It is a mark of epochal change that they are called in for fundamental reappraisal.

The best term I can find for this as a philosophical position is 'pragmatic universalism'. It rests neither on scientific nor on religious certainties, but on the daily lived experience of human beings and its comparative cultural and historical record. On a scale of late modern thought in which Michel Foucault is at point zero and Alasdair MacIntyre at point ten, I settle around point six. Finding a way between these two wild extremes, a ruthless scientific relativism and living as a quest for meaning in living, is the fate of anyone who seeks to grasp the contemporary world. Max Weber has long provided a model for this kind of intellectual equilibration. His work is one of the most abiding legacies of modernity, but the Global Age obliges us to go beyond it.

I therefore make no apology to Weber or my contemporaries in declaring that the contributions of premodern and non-Western thinkers can illuminate the debate about globalization. In scholarly terms this requires us to rethink our understanding of globalization and globality in terms of epochal theory. At a broader human level it is an invitation to respect all peoples as potential sources of wisdom for our own time. Already the Global Age is the first period in human history when both sexes and all peoples have gone a substantial way towards asserting an equal right to make their contribution to the common stock of human knowledge.

In everyday terms the message is 'Forget modernity'. See what it does to your language and behaviour if you stop worrying whether something is modern or not. Ask what it is you are being persuaded of when you are told that an outlook is modern. Substitute the words 'new', 'contemporary', 'present-day', 'rational' for modern where appropriate. Judge the newness of a product on some ground or other rather than simply welcoming its novelty. Get used to thinking of 'old modern' things. Collect old-fashioned modernist memorabilia if you wish, but remember you are not simply *after* modernity. Escape the stifling hold of the modern on the imagination. We live in our own time and the Global Age opens worlds up to us in unprecedented ways.

Very often someone else's contribution to one's own thinking is greatest where there is disagreement and a roll call of names could be very misleading. I doubt whether there is a single idea in this book which doesn't have antecedents elsewhere, not all of which I know, some of which I have retrieved from a long time back. Yet in the Global Age there is no premium for novelty. Even though I claim that the configuration of ideas is original and has never been advanced before, you should judge their worth by other standards.

1

Resuming the History of Epochs

The most decisive event in inaugurating the Modern Age was the 'discovery of America' in 1492. Similarly epoch making was the event which signalled its impending termination, the dropping of the atomic bombs on Japan in 1945. In between, the story of modernity was of a project to extend human control over space, time, nature and society. The main agent of the project was the nation-state working with and through capitalist and military organization. It gave a distinctive shape to people's lives and the passing of generations. But the culmination of the project in the unification of the world was also its dissolution. With the end of the epoch, postmodern disorientation became widespread even as markers were laid for the coming new age. It was just not recognized at first for what it was. The Cold War, the Three Worlds, the human landing on the moon in 1969, the electronic 'global village', triumph of the United States with the collapse of the Soviet Union in 1991, and finally global warming were not triumphant modernity but signs of the new globality. In the 1980s 'globalization' became the keyword. In the 1990s came the general recognition that the Modern Age was at an end and that the Global Age had already begun.

Anon. AD 2050

1.1 Refusing to be Modern

Why there is an alternative to the forced choice between everlasting modernity and the end of history

The account which heads this chapter will strike some as odd, even self-contradictory. Its anonymous author may be in school now and yet writes like a rather conventional, somewhat old-fashioned historian.

It reads like a modern narrative and yet announces the end of the Modern Age. Does this not undermine the basis for the account? We are left feeling discomfited by a history of our own time written in the way it has been done for past eras.

Yet I would contend that the narrative makes good sense. The difficulties which arise stem not from its self-contradictions, but from the wider and current confusions in contemporary accounts of modernity and postmodernity. It ought to be entirely possible to write of the end of the Modern Age and the beginning of a new one, if that is indeed what has happened. But we haven't even been able to contemplate the possibility of such an account. Modernity has kept a tenacious grip on the imagination of intellectuals, even after it has lost its hold on the world.

Our difficulties have arisen because accounts of the Modern Age have sought to find some foundation for it in a philosophical 'modernity'. Then, as the Modern Age passes away, they assume that the foundations are crumbling and with them the possibility of making any sense of our time. To this extent the proponents of modernity and postmodernity share a common assumption, namely that without founding principles the world makes no sense. They disagree only on whether such principles exist.

Yet epochs, cultures, civilizations have no more arisen out of ideas and principles than religion out of theology, or society from sociology. In contrast, our fictional narrator writes of the epoch as a unique constellation of human striving, impersonal forces, underlying processes and key events at a level of the highest generality. She or he references a configuration of our time, not as a theory or principle, but as real constraints. The talk is of power blocs, of nuclear warfare, of threats to the body. In contrast to the much noticed contemporary proliferation of histories of any and every thing, this is 'grand narrative'.[1]

This book arises out of the discourse of a new epoch. It is bound to reopen issues of the past, because it is in the past that we can identify the growth of the distorted sense of the present. So although our direct concern will be with the transformation since the end of the Second World War, we are bound to take issue with accounts of a much longer past, the Modern Age. We can no longer see modernity as an irresistible movement. For it hasn't turned out that way. We will therefore be seeking both to identify the Global Age, but also to achieve recognition of the Modern Age as a transitory epoch with its peculiar features, which has given way to another.

The new age is not the postmodern, even if it comes after the modern. From Wolfgang Welsch's viewpoint (1993: 6) the postmodern is only the latest radical form of modernity. To John Gray (1995: viii) postmodernity is the self-undermining of modernity. In both cases postmodernity is the expression, however self-destructive, of modernity. The modern retains its hold on the intellectual imagination.

We have to listen to the language of the new age in a wider discourse. It resounds most in 'global' and all its variations: 'globalization', 'globalism', 'globality' and others. They are labels for new perspectives, styles, strategies, forces, interests and values which do not necessarily make novelty a virtue and which in numerous ways replace the directions of modernity. They signal the comprehensive transformation which is what historians have recognized as a change of epoch.

We have not learned truly to write the history of the present. This failure arises from the way modernity survives sufficiently to impede our recognition of historical change in our own time. Most seriously it means that even those who recognize globalization as a profound contemporary transformation seek to assimilate it to modernity. We can see a representative example in one of the most important books of the 1980s, Ulrich Beck's *Risk Society*.

He opened his book (1986/1992: 9) with the statement that the prefix 'post-' had become the key word of our times. He found it was a symptom of a historical break, but yet he located it still within modernity. It expressed a new kind of reflexive modernization beyond industrial society, in which the production of risk became more important than the production of wealth. Even where the risks encompassed the globe as a whole, which is where Beck introduced the idea of globalization, it appeared that modernity could continue its reflexive path.

Yet this misses the limits to reflexivity which the global reference highlights. Reflexivity in any sphere ultimately terminates in the non-reflective, the obstacle or the decision which represents the end of analysis, the time to act. Confronting the globe as a whole is just such a point, where there is such a check to expansive modernity that a real transformation takes place.

Modernity has so transfixed the intellectual imagination that the prospect of its end even promotes the idea of the end of history as such (Fukuyama 1992), or at least the end of the writing of history as the story of humanity (Lyotard 1979, Vattimo 1988). But these famous paradoxes arise from modernity's claim to monopolize novelty. If everything new is by definition modern then it cannot grasp its own end as the beginning of a new epoch. Far from modernity giving history its full dignity, it deprives the past of any meaning except as a prelude to itself, and cannot imagine the future except as its own continuation, or else chaos.

The many announcements of the end of the Modern Age should encourage us to bring questions of historical periodization to the fore again. The problem is, however, that without a new beginning the announcement of the 'end of' a period sounds like the end of all we have loved.[2] For even in their quest for the new, the sense of being at one with the past is what bonded modern people together. In the introduction to the *Cambridge Modern History*, which acquired at the beginning of the twentieth century widespread authority in defining the Modern Age, we can hear its authentic voice, this self-understanding of modernity:

> It is this sense of familiarity which leads us to draw a line and mark out the beginnings of modern history. On the hither side of this line men speak a language which we can readily understand; they are animated by ideas and aspirations which resemble those animating ourselves; the forms in which they express their thoughts and the records of their activity are the same as those still prevailing among us. Any one who works through the records of the fifteenth and sixteenth centuries becomes conscious of an extraordinary change of mental attitude, showing itself on all sides in unexpected ways. (Creighton 1902: 1–2)

The author was writing of what was often called at the time a 'consciousness of kind'. Modern people 'resemble ourselves' and that reference extended in both time and space, back to the fifteenth century but also only to Europe and North America and all that came under their sway. Modernity dominated thought to the extent that it became impossible to gain detachment from it. It was about 'us' and all to which we aspired. And 'we', the smaller part of humanity, represented ourselves as being at the ever advancing cutting edge of History. The Modern Age was no passing phenomenon, it rolled forward relentlessly and triumphantly.

The resumption of historical periodization is only possible if we find a way of writing about our own time as a new period. In other words we have to be as confident as Creighton was for the Modern Age that we can find a vantage point for today that separates us from him. At the same time, and this will become clear in the course of the book, this depends on treating all humanity as equal in the light of the Global Age. We already have intimations of this new recognition of our time. So Fernandez-Armesto's (1995) treatment of the last millennium in the histories of the Americas, Africa and Asia, where they are equal in salience to Europe's for understanding the present, is one which prepares us for the dramatically different vantage point of a new age. He concludes by reflecting on the possible future courses of the new global culture, oscillating between universality and diversity (p. 710), and although he does not challenge the conventional characterization of modernity he effectively relativizes it.

Such an account of the new globality is an implicit invitation to go beyond the postmodern sense of an end of an age and to announce the beginning of a new one, the Global Age. It encourages us to think, not of the way modernity has outstripped all other times and cultures, but, on the contrary, the way in which any appreciation of our own place in historical time must be prepared to give precedence to ideas from other times and other cultures. In this way we demonstrate our appreciation of the significance of the limits of the Modern Age. We show that we see it for what it was, a passing historical episode, without denying its world-historical significance as the expansion of the West. Yet this is still difficult for us to do, and to make it easier we need to understand how modernity laid claim to exclusive rights on the course of history.

1.2 From Universal History to the People's Epic

How the grand narrative ceased to be a divine story and celebrated the self-creation of the Modern Age

The Oxford historian and philosopher R. G. Collingwood (1946: 49–52) attributed the invention of the idea of historical periodization to the early Christians. They had to see history as universal, working according to God's will, divided by a divine event, Christ's coming, and then further divided into periods by epoch-making events. Against that background we can see what the Modern Age did. It turned history into an instrument for the rulers of emerging nation-states. Later it was to represent the nation-state as the achievement of all the people. First it had to instruct the princes who could direct events.

When the seventeenth-century Bishop of Meaux, J.-B. Bossuet, wrote his 'discourse on universal history' for the benefit of the young heir to the throne of France, he began: 'While history might be of no use to other people, princes have to read it' (1681/1887: 1), and presented him with a panorama where the ruler, with the oversight of a nation, surveyed a field where potentially anything in the world could become a matter of concern and cause for action. Far below him was the milieu of ordinary people, protected from the greater perturbations.

The scale and the distance, detail and generality of Bossuet's account provided the logical ground for administrative and social hierarchy. As the concerns of the higher orders extended over an ever widening area of territory, the only logical culmination was a conception of a world order with a single ruler.

The idea which guided his historical narrative equally underpinned the whole of the modern period; namely human control had to expand to take in the whole world.[3] Universal history required the creation of a unified field of human discourse, providing a single frame of events, making one world. This was the Modern Project and universal history was its record, its accompaniment and its achievement. But it was the record of human, not God's, deeds.

The supreme rationalist Voltaire (1694–1778) acknowledged the Christian bishop's method and took it forward in a new exemplary manner. In his *The Age of Louis XIV* he praised Bossuet's narrative art: 'He applied the art of oratory to history itself, a literary genre which would seem incapable of admitting it' (Voltaire 1751/1926: 360–1). Universal history had to be the grand narrative, along with the ordering of time into epochs.[4] Moreover he brought them up to his own time, which meant the potential was there to record new beginnings in the present.[5]

Self-description as a time of new beginnings was a mark of the new age. Already in 1470 'modern music' was being dated as beginning in 1430. There was 'modern' painting in the mid-sixteenth century (Burke 1987: 17). The Modern Age began with a sense of many beginnings, of both innovation and discovery. It was carried especially in references to a 'new world'. Later to be a cliché, at the time it was coined by Amerigo Vespucci in an open letter to Lorenzo de Medici it reflected the conjuncture of two distinct spheres, novelty and earthly existence, which hitherto had inhabited different fields of thought (Ginzburg 1982: 82).

For a world itself to be new meant a challenge from the outside, novelty not simply out of self-directed development in the arts and sciences, but from other human beings who presented real-life alternatives to what had been assumed to be the world. The 'new world' rapidly became an image which opened up the possibility of a new social order, of realizing Utopia on earth. Not just works of art but institutions and ways of life could potentially be otherwise.

Discovery of 'unknown' worlds disturbed the thoughts of ordinary people, like the miller Mennochio (1532–99) from a Friulian village, whose recurrent speculations around dangerous themes of alternatives to the present order, stimulated on his own admission by reading the travels of Sir John Mandeville, made him so uncomfortable to the Church of his time that he was burnt at the stake (Ginzburg 1982: xiii).

The discovery of the 'new world' was a dramatic intensification of the stimulus which contact with foreign lands had already given to European culture. For an intelligent peasant, mayor of his village, the result was 'heresy' and death. For the educated Mayor of Bordeaux, Michel de Montaigne (1533–92), it prompted reflection on the decline of the old world and the corruption it was introducing into the new (Montaigne 1580/1842: 421). For him the simplicity of the new world surpassed the aspirations of the philosophers in demonstrating what a pure Utopia could be like (p. 89). It threw into relief the arbitrariness of one's own country and its customs. It strengthened his conviction about the educational worth of travel. The child should learn against a background of the diversity of the whole world (p. 63).

Reports from the newly named 'America' were already a stimulus to the reflections of Sir Thomas More's *Utopia* (1516/1970), and they inspired, as well as Montaigne, a tradition of libertarian speculation and radical reformers including Rousseau and Thomas Paine (Weatherford 1988: 117–31). It was also a new world to be conquered, to be subjected to the artifices of European forms of government, to be converted to Christianity, to become the arena for the most self-conscious effort yet to create a new civilization, freed from the incubus of the old. The 'new world' was to become later the United States, where modernity has been able to develop with the least encumbrance from the past.

This sense of continual innovation held the age together. It was the continuing basis of its self-narrative. In 1895 Lord Acton began his brief but brilliant tenure of the Chair of Modern History in Cambridge with an inaugural lecture on the study of his subject by declaring that: 'The modern age did not descend from the mediaeval by normal succession, with outward tokens of legitimate descent. Unheralded, it founded a new order of things, under a law of innovation, sapping the ancient reign of continuity' (1906: 3). It continued this way up to his own time. This for him was the main point of its study: 'it is a narrative told of ourselves, the record of a life which is our own, of efforts not yet abandoned to repose, of problems that still entangle the feet and vex the hearts of men' (p. 8).

This sense of contemporary newness has also become the main defence erected by modern ways of thought against the demise of modernity. Can there ever be another epoch when the modern claims to be the ever new? Does it make sense to think of ourselves as anything other than modern? On the face of it, it ought to be easy. If the Modern Age is a period in history, surely like any other it can end. But, to counter that, if the modern is the new, it seems to have the secret of perpetual self-renewal. For modernity, men (much more than women, who only give birth) become gods. To solve this conundrum we have to sift the ingredients of the unique mix of narrative art and scientific theory which enabled modernity to have its cake and eat it too, to found a new historical epoch and yet never be replaced.

1.3 A Science of Historical Periods

How Marx's materialist version of Aristotle's muthos *was only replaced with the baleful prospect of everlasting modernity*

In the early modern period, writing history was still a narrative art. As such it was subordinate to doctrines which sought to find the deeper sense of human accounts of themselves. In the classical Greek theory, history as an account of the facts was definitely inferior to poetry, which explored the profounder reality. But this elevated rather than undermined the idea of the historical epoch. For Aristotle's *Poetics* endowed any story of human affairs with a poetic structure, with beginning, middle and end. It was this, the plot (*muthos*), which made sense of the incidents.

The Aristotelian emphasis on the beginning of the plot resonated perfectly with the modern experience of new discovery. Discovering beginnings became a central concern for modern historical scholarship. It became the obsessive concern of the lonely genius, Giambattista Vico (1668–1744), Professor of Rhetoric in Naples, whose *New Science* went through three editions in 1725, 1730 and 1744 as he sought to solve the mystery of the origins of nations.

'The nature of things is nothing else than their origins at particular times and in particular circumstances' (Vico quoted by Meinecke 1959: 63). Looking for origins, the researcher finds clues in language, everyday sayings and above all in fables and myth. In the products of the human mind are elements of which their producers are not aware. They are therefore importantly not creations of individual authors, but of the experience of a whole community of people, and reaching out beyond them to a common humanity (Said 1975/1978: 347–81). The spirit of the age is therefore diffused throughout its people.

There was another Aristotelian theme which inspired the new historical understanding. The interrelatedness of facts and incidents which is the *muthos* diverts attention from the single author to the collective story. Drawing connections over time and space permits constructions not only between contemporaries, but between them and their forebears. Credit for perceiving the intrinsic link between collective culture and history belongs to a local historian of the city of Osnabruck, Justus Möser (1720–94). He inferred that the principles of composition which establish the connectedness of the locality ('local reason') apply equally to time periods. 'Every period has its style' was his motto (Meinecke 1959: 329) and he made explicit the connection between Aristotelian poetic principles and the authorless text of history.[6]

In brief, at the dawn of high modernity, the period of the Enlightenment, humanity had become the collective author of novelty, of all new beginnings. At the same time, on poetic principles, the story of the author had a beginning, middle and end too. The tension between these two viewpoints remained to the end of the Modern Age. It became the site for the development of the social sciences. In them science devoted to beginnings merged with a narrative of humanity's story. In this respect Karl Marx became the prime representative of modernity's attempt to resolve its intellectual contradictions in his quest for a science of history.

Marx dismissed Möser's 'patriotic visions' in a brief footnote. He accused him of never abandoning 'the respectable, petty-bourgeois "home-baked", ordinary, narrow horizon of the philistine, and which nevertheless remain pure fancy' (Marx and Engels 1975a: 287).[7] Typical Marx polemic, but there was more behind it than abuse. Historical materialism, as Marx and Engels developed it, contained at its heart a theory of historical epochs or periods. It depicted the succession from the ancient world to the medieval, from medieval to modern. It made no attempt to challenge what were by then the generally accepted periods of European history.

But it went much further than that. Each epoch had its Aristotelian beginning, middle and end. Moreover each had its plot, an unfolding story of the development of the means of production and their ever growing disparity with the social relations of the time, so that eventually one type of society passed away to be replaced with another. It was a comprehensive movement covering every aspect of people's lives.

No narrative structure could be more dramatic. It was the basis of the *Communist Manifesto* of 1848 – 'The modern bourgeois society that has sprouted from the ruins of feudal society has not done away with class antagonisms' (Marx and Engels 1976b: 485). 'Modern industry', following the discovery of America, established the world market. The 'modern bourgeoisie' developed with it, establishing its own committee, the 'modern state'.

Modern, modern, modern: Marx and Engels wrote the history of modernity. This was an abiding, core feature of their work, a life's work deliberately undertaken.[8] In *The German Ideology* in 1846 they had set out to supplant the idealist conception of history. For them its basic mistake was to imagine that history could be written from the standpoint of the ideas of the historical actors. It was the illusion of the epoch – 'It takes every epoch at its word and believes that everything it says and imagines about itself is true' (Marx and Engels 1976a: 62).

By contrast their materialist conception explained ideas from material practice. It took people's social relations, the methods by which they produced things, the way these related to nature, their funds of capital, and it showed how each generation took a given situation and modified it for its successors. The historian had to take ideas back to people, not move into the realm of pure spirit (pp. 54–5).

They wrote the history of modernity without a *concept* of the modern. They had no difficulty in accepting the completely conventional use of the term modern, precisely because for them it paralleled the underlying structure of practices which their method revealed. It was not the idea of the modern which modernity embodied, rather that the changes which took place in a certain historical period acquired the label 'modern'. They did so because there were deep real connections of which even the historical actors were not aware.

In other words Marx and Engels had an explicit answer to our Aristotelian question: How do we define the connections which make the narrative plot, the *muthos*? These were not the intangibles of 'style', certainly not Hegel's 'spirit'. They were real underlying connections between people, forces and material things, which could only be explained with good scientific theory. Theirs was a quest for a Holy Grail which has inspired intellectuals, Marxist and non-Marxist alike, throughout the Modern Age. The powerful idea which led them was that it might be possible to find scientific laws, identify basic processes, uncover an underlying reality, which would enable us to determine the course of history. Historical narrative and science would be one.

In one way we can view historical materialism as the highpoint of the theory of historical periodization up till then. Despite its scathing judgements on idealist historians, it took what had become the standard divisions in the historiography of the time and sought to assimilate them to a science. It was, then, a high modernist account of modernity. In another way it was the downfall of epochal theory. For its premonitions of, and actual association with revolution so alarmed the dominant powers that for the rest of the Modern Age much of social science as well as political activity in general was devoted to warding off the threat.

The result was that the prospect of an end of the Modern Age was suppressed in favour of an account which effectively condemned modernity to everlasting purgatory. The decline of the West came to mean the end of civilization as such and the alternative prospect was one of unending toil. In the late modernity of the twentieth century both Oswald Spengler and Max Weber combated Marxist visions of a new age, but the outcome of their debate with each other was a future with no promise except more of the same.

Spengler's *The Decline of the West* (1919–22) captured a public mood at the end of the First World War. Significantly he began by rejecting the threefold ancient, medieval, modern schema of historical periods. He replaced it with an organic conception of the growth, maturity and decline of individual cultures, in which each historical fact was interpreted as an expression of their living nature.

Spengler denied the universality of the Western experience. So he commended Marx for understanding that machine manufacture was the proudest product of the bourgeoisie, but chided him for his adherence to the old three-period schema and his failure to understand that its world dominance was under threat from old cultures like the Russian, Jewish, Indian, Arab and Japanese. For good measure the West was equally bound to decline as money took over from machines, only to be replaced by the sword (vol. 2: 633–5).

It was lurid, intellectualist anti-science, with, however, sufficient imaginative hold on the limits of existing knowledge to suggest bold alternative futures and to rubbish the much more painstaking scholarship within the three-period tradition. Effectively it opened windows on hitherto unimagined possibilities, but in such terms as to invite their closure. In its suggestion that there was no other possibility for the future than resort to the sword, it was the text which accompanied the slaughters of the twentieth century.

It was Max Weber who sought to free modernity from these apocalyptic visions. He rejected both the Marxist science of history and Spengler's narrative of impending disaster.[9] He could not accept an emphasis on material production at the expense of ideas. No more could he agree that a theoretical political economy could ground historical narrative. Instead he spent a lifetime developing a complex theory of history, equally grounded in data, where Western society developed along the lines of an ever expanding and deepening rationalization of every aspect of life.

The rationalization thesis began in an account of the origins of modern capitalism, with its famous thesis of the results of Protestant theology for economic action. It explicitly engaged with the materialist conception of history. But by the end of his short career Weber had developed it into an interpretation of Western development in comparison with the cultures of the East. He began to talk of a specific kind of Western rationalism, with its roots in ancient culture.

Weber insisted on the infinite variety of causal connections in history. He refused primacy for material or any other factors. The precipitating factor in modern capitalism is then a contingent and sudden intrusion, Protestant theology, set in a context of practices and institutions deep-rooted in Western history, in its law, its accounting procedures, its city development.

Lacking a strong causal model of modern social processes, Weber still required some guideline for sifting his multiple casual connections. His use of the idea of rationality as a guiding thread was emphatically modernist at one level, but at another it lent itself to a developmental account whose origins take us back to Greek thought and where the future stretches out as a limitless expansion of more of the same, an intensification (Steigerung) of rationality.[10]

The modern, viewed as the rational rather than as a period in history, becomes a cultural condition of the West, from which there appears to be no escape – the iron cage. It is an intellectualist view of the modern which leaves open only an intellectual response in the form of critique or the romantic escapes which Weber rejected.

As one commentator has suggested, after the Weberian account the best that is left open in a politics of modern culture is some kind of subjective control of the abstract objectivity of the world around (Scaff 1989: 240). Weber remained held in the clutches of a limitless modernity from which the only escape was personal. There would be no more epoch making in human history.

1.4 Towards the History of the Present

Seeking to understand our own times as history in the making

Effectively, then, it was social scientists, in tune with the times, sometimes following, sometimes independently replicating Weber, who promoted the limitless modernity notion. They responded to Marx by discarding his theory of epochal change, making their science into a study of the present as an unbroken continuation of the past. Historians colluded in jettisoning epochal theory and adopting the guise of scientists of past facts.

This was true even of a dedicated advocate of history as the story of the human mind like Collingwood. His *Idea of History* (1946) imbued a generation of historians with the idea that the core of their special science was the gathering of evidence to arrive at solutions. Certainly he agreed they had to tell a tale, but his exemplar was the story 'Who killed John Doe?' not the Tolstoyan epic, and the craft was inference from facts, not the story telling. It enabled him to dismiss with a sweep of the pen comparative interpretations of civilizations like Toynbee's *Study of History* (1939–61) as 'scissors and paste' history: it merely involved pigeon-holing into boxes called 'periods' or 'societies'. The price Collingwood paid to preserve the dignity of history was to reduce narrative art to the detective story.[11] So in spite of acknowledging writing about periods as 'a mark of advanced and mature historical thought' (1946: 50–1), he ignored them as a topic of concern for the professional historian. He accused Toynbee of 'positivism' for his concern to classify civilizations, but he was equally positivistic in stressing scientific inference.

The picture of two major figures in historical studies in the mid-twentieth century each declaring the centrality of the human being, but both vying for the crown of 'science', makes a prime exhibit in the museum of modernity. Since then poetics have been recovered and reoccupy a central place in the interpretation of history. This involves not only narrative structure as a problem, but a wider transformation signalled by invoking 'discourse' and 'construction' (see White 1987).

Collingwood sold history short in the end. He underestimated the power of the past in the lives of ordinary people (see Carr 1986). For the transformation of the modern period was not invented by historians, pigeon-holers or otherwise. It involved a profound sense that the times were changing. The modern period persisted through the repeated reproduction of modernity in peoples' lives, in the assumptions of science, and in political ideology. The frame within which historical research takes place has not been invented by historians, but neither should they take it for granted. Rather their public duty is to make us aware of how it was constructed and how it might change. This is intrinsic to epochal theory.

Following Collingwood's lead, historians have since been inclined to treat periodization as a relatively superficial organizing device. The theory of epochs, or at least of the Modern Age, has been left to theorists of modernism and modernity, students of literature and philosophy, and social scientists. Its strongest support has come from the tenacious Marxist belief in an end of capitalism. Opposed to the Weberian account of limitless modernity, this has given what has remained of epochal theory an ideological dimension which has made it more, rather than less, difficult to make it part of the historian's professional concern.

The dominant approach in this century to the Modern Age by social scientists has been to associate it with capitalism, industrialism or an abstract modernity and to regard the relationship of each to society as the key to understanding the course of events. 'Capitalist society', 'industrial society' and 'modern society' have dominated writing about the Modern Age. Anything which looks like the decline or transformation of capitalism, industrialism or modernity is then seen as presaging a 'post-age' in which society is in a dire state of disarray.

The problem with these accounts from the historian's point of view is that they confuse theory and history. The markers of an epoch cannot be derived from underlying theoretical relationships; the 'discovery' of the New World transformed the field in which those relationships could find free play. Such an event could not be derived from them, any more than, looking in the reverse direction, the nation-state could be seen as a result of the discovery of gunpowder.

For historians there is no reason why key events should operate only in one sector. The impetus for change may originate equally in religion as in the economy, in science as in politics, in disease as in ideas. To this extent Weber's multiple factor account remains intact and is consistent with the subsequent direction of professional history writing. Any sphere of activity can provide the epochal event: a scientific discovery, or a revolution, or a natural disaster, or a slump, or the impact of a prophet. In this sense the historical period is the diachronic chronicle of culture and not a phase of a scientifically determinable process.

The epoch brings with it all the problems associated with describing the extent and limits of culture, with the additional one of identifying origins in time. Just as with culture, so with the historical period: the interplay of sectors or spheres has to be taken as axiomatic. Equally that interplay is neither chaotic nor without sense to the participants. In any one epoch a characteristic arrangement or configuration of factors will take on paramount significance for the people concerned and they will label it accordingly.

The social scientist in effect detracts from the specificity of the Modern Age by reducing it to the economy or to capitalism, or industrialism. No age can be reduced to a single sphere. Moreover, if one sphere has exercised more of a defining quality, it has been the nation-state rather than the economy. This is not to say that capitalism has been unimportant. It has outlived the Modern Age and taken on new forms in the Global Age. On the other hand the nation-state displays its ephemeral historical limitations as it becomes just another form of the organization of power in human affairs.

Social scientists can be criticized for their reductionist approach to historical periods, but they can be credited with taking history seriously. Historians on the other hand often outdo social scientists in respect for facts but have become relativistic about questions of periodization. Yet they draw freely on an intellectual resource which has been a deep assumption of passing generations of people. 'Modern' has been the name for their time. In the way a place name or a personal name identifies a uniqueness, so does a time name. The banality of dates is not sufficient, any more than a map reference or a personal identification number.

This is not a question then of arbitrary classification, pigeon-holing or scissors and paste, which are cheap comments from a lofty height. The knowledge and understanding which enabled Toynbee to be one of the very first to suggest an emerging postmodern age arose out of a profound sense of the specific nature of the modern configuration compared with all others. It meant understanding the present in terms of the presence of history in people's lives.[12]

Epochal narrative is then a resource for a historical understanding of the present, not a relic of outdated scholarship. It reveals the contradictions we have highlighted in the idea of everlasting modernity and the pervasive fear of catastrophe and sees them as symptoms of what is denied, namely that the Modern Age can and indeed has been supplanted.

1.5 Determinism and Modernity

Why there is no formula from which one can deduce the
characteristics of an epoch

The basic error of historical materialism was to seek to derive epochal
change from movements in the abstract relations of capital and labour.
But the same error inhabits social scientific accounts of the Modern
Age when they seek to derive it from an abstract modernity. We can
accept that modernity dominated the Modern Age, expanded control
in space and time, and recognized no limit to itself. Yet the Modern Age
was much more than modernity. It saw religious intolerance, racism,
unspeakable cruelty, enormous population growth, wars of unprecedented destruction, slavery, the destruction of species and habitats.
And even if each of these has also often been associated with rationality, that is technique, discipline, calculation, this does not explain the
demonic features of the age. If, following both Marx and Weber, we
see rationality as central to modernity, we have also, as they did, to
acknowledge contingent features of the Modern Age. To see the whole
age as the product of rationality is a radical pessimism which prompts
the retreat into mysticism which some have taken or foresee (Gray
1995: 184).

A lot depends on how we write history, not least on our understanding of our own time. We should keep our theorizing and our
historical narrative as distinct phases in our attempt to understand it.
Then if we allow for modernity to be the theoretical thrust, we can see
the Modern Age as a much larger and more complex configuration,
comprising among much else that very modernity. In this way we will
avoid resorting to ultimate explanatory factors, like 'technology' or
'ideas' or 'relations of production', while at the same time we won't
go to the opposite extreme, accord no priorities and find no pattern.

Certainly we can identify in modernity how an increasingly complex set of relationships developed between a number of core, or profiling, factors. Marxist and non-Marxist social scientists may have
differed on priorities but not on theoretical strategy. They disclosed how
markets required the division of labour, how specialization advanced
the application of technical knowledge, how science served capital and
social control, how the state guaranteed freedom of contract and citizenship. Throughout, the idea of rationality provided linkage, both in
elaborating analytical abstract theories in economics, political science
or law, and in supplying the common thread of a historical account as
in Max Weber's rationalization process.[13]

But the elaboration over time of the unique pattern of life and social relations which characterized the Modern Age cannot be reduced to a formula based on such factors. So, to take a recent example, when Michael Mann singles out four sources of power, ideological, economic, military and political (or state power), and traces the way these are interwoven over time, he equally acknowledges that we cannot derive the complexity of the historical account simply from these factors. Different nation-states combined elements of the premodern with the modern, and in different ways. There has been no general evolution towards human freedom based on national citizenship (Mann 1993: 251).

We need also to recognize the contingency of historical events which determine the concrete relationships between nations, and the directions which human endeavours take. These shape the developing profile to the age. We can call them 'configurational events'. Examples include, at the beginning of the period, the 'discovery' of the New World (1492) and Luther's attack on the Papacy (1517); in the middle, the Declaration of American Independence (1776) and the French Revolution (1789). The beginning of the end was signalled with the First World War (1914–18) and the Russian Revolution (1917); and terminal decline with the Holocaust (1943–5) and the dropping of the atomic bombs on Hiroshima and Nagasaki (1945).

These events stand out; there are many others associated with them, arguably many just as important. The historians of the age will find in them markers for new directions because they signal the resolution of an older uncertainty, or the final destruction of an old and persisting balance of power. So configurational events mark off epochs and periods within them.[14] Hence it is well grounded to identify three periods within the Modern Age: Early Modern from the late fifteenth century to mid-eighteenth century; High Modern until the early twentieth century; and late Modern thereafter.

The Early Modern saw the expansion of Europe, the crystallization of secular state power and the autonomy of science. Hence 1492 and 1517 are key dates. The High Modern experienced the Industrial Revolution, the formation of the bureaucratic state (hence 1776 and 1789) and imperial expansion. The Late Modern was the period of the mobilization of the masses, the capitalist corporation and the Western domination of the world. It is the connection between the different underlying forces for change which justifies us in singling out configurational events. They are not the arbitrary selections of a heritage committee. Thus the ends of two world wars, 1918 and 1945, are associated each with major advances in technology, the tank and the atomic bomb, and the decisiveness of those events for the fate of nations brings technological development to the fore as a factor in historical change.

The ultimate outcome of the development of the Modern Age was nothing less than the unification of the world, although certainly not into harmonious unity. Mann (1993: 11) calls it a 'global society'. But this has been an outcome rather than a goal, a distinction which will prove to be of considerable importance. For the expansion of the West was not with a view to completeness, but to continued expansion, and the coverage of the globe represents an arbitrary halt imposed from outside, rather than a consummation.

The Modern Age was a unique historical development, in the sense that its profiling factors interacted under specific terrestrial circumstances and with a cultural heritage which could have been different. Thus had there been a single land mass, voyages of discovery could not have precipitated fundamental change. If Roman script had not spread throughout Europe, bureaucratic practices might never have permitted the modern organization to develop.

So the relationship between our profiling factors which gives us the configuration of the Modern Age is both profound, in that it has enduring influence on millions of lives, and contingent, in that it depends on and interacts with outside factors which can produce unexpected change at any time. This is particularly true for the natural environment. The distribution of mineral deposits constrains the pattern of their exploitation, and the human use of carbon compounds precipitates unplanned natural consequences because the atmosphere is constituted in the way it is.

The direction of human history is not encoded in some original source. It is not encoded at all.[15] Even if it were, as DNA encodes the biological characteristics of human beings, its course could not be predicted, any more than an individual's biography can be predicted from their biology. It depends in principle (though each individual case differs) as much on what happens to them. The nature/nurture debate, seeking to rank their relative importance, is a sterile ideological reflection and nothing else. At the same time within their history human beings strive from time to time to take control of events and determine their course. The Modern Age was a high point for such striving.

1.6 The Configuration of the Modern Age

How we have to write a theoretical history to arrive at the specific characteristics of an epoch

Our rejection of historical determinism, social scientific or otherwise, is by no means a rejection of theory. The equation of theory with scientific determinism is another modernist error. We cannot arrive at the specific characteristics of any epoch without generalization and abstraction, or without a profound analysis of the way the age features in the lives of ordinary people and in the dominant institutions of society.

So if we explore the Modern Age we have to identify the abstract factors of modernity, but also try to specify the ways in which they are embedded in national traditions, promote dominant personality types, and carry forward the inheritance of Greek philosophy and Judaeo-Christian religion. As well as congruences they include contradictions, such as the promotion of rights and the exclusion of people from those rights. This is historical theory which is not reducible to any other discipline, even though it can draw on all in its attempt to make sense of an age. The problem is to find terminology which does not assimilate historical theory to something else.

In the modern period the terms 'system' and 'structure' have been the Trojan horses of social science, representing characteristically modern approaches to history. They carry too much theoretical baggage from the past. We need another term which does not carry the same connotations of completeness, self-sufficiency and internal regularity. I am choosing the term 'configuration' as a helpfully neutral way to refer to the ordering and connectedness of a set of features without prejudging the nature of the connections.

'Configuration' allows us openness both in respect of features of an age and also in respect of the way they relate to each other. So we can include any or all of people, ideas, places, production, institutions, feelings, nations or worldviews or any of the other elements which go to provide the basis of historical description. We can allow for both causal and logical relations. They can work through physical impact, power, influence, as a market, through direct or indirect communication, or through ideas. They can be stylistic, narrative, situational, random, intermittent, continuous, or systemic. They can be objective or subjective.[16]

A variety of different types of connection may operate for any combination of the elements. It is this which gives historical accounts their plasticity and makes it impossible to provide a formal set of rules for history writing which would guarantee their general validity. It also produces special problems in naming configurations of the elements and their connections. For it is that totality to which the 'Modern Age' refers. We have to be wary of claiming more for the name than that it is a convenient label. At the same time the character of the age has stemmed in part from the connotations of the 'modern' which over centuries have given the age a special character.[17]

In principle both the beginning and end of the modern period could be open-ended and ever moving. There has certainly been a tendency to bring the beginning of it forward, from sixteenth to eighteenth to nineteenth centuries.[18] But the obvious break occurs at the point where a previous age is labelled and the principle of novelty is acknowledged. So the identification of 'the Middle Ages' was associated with an idea of modernity which characterized the era coming after.[19]

Modernity has been associated with rationality ever since it was regarded as the task of new thought to cast out the errors of the old. The modern as the rational goes back at least to William of Ockham in the thirteenth century, and the application of rational thought to techniques and ways of living has come to be regarded as a hallmark of the modern period. But, as we noticed above, there is more to modernity than rationality.

Rationality provides structure. It has thus been the source of all those organizing conceptual oppositions which characterize modernity, for instance between romanticism and rationalism; individualism and collectivism; conformity and deviance; planning and markets; state and civil society; citizen and foreigner; elite and mass. It is indeed misleading to characterize modernity through rationality. More precisely the principle of modernity is the application of the dichotomy rationality/irrationality, where both sides require and indeed feed on the other and are equally prominent, even to the point of the advocacy of irrationality.

This dichotomy also gave the thrust to modernity. It provided the inner change dynamic, a ceaseless quest for improvement. Dedication to rationality is the generic method for the production of the new. It made modernity the production house of ideas run by intellectuals (hence their vested interest in it). In their hands, as modernism, it even transformed the transmission of culture into calculated cultural production and reproduction.

But if the production of the new had depended solely on intellectual activity it would not have had its all-pervading effect on the Modern Age. Ideas arise also out of new experience, breaking the bounds of existing knowledge and custom, and to be put into practice they need new resources. In European history the new experience was provided by wave upon wave of intensive contact with other cultures, by travel, trade and conquest. The very idea of rationality was extended to comprehend other cultures and intensified to meet their challenge. The development of modernity came to be the story of the expansion and transformation of European, subsequently Western, culture.

Territorial expansion was both the necessary fuel and the product of modernity. It supplied the momentum for the development of the European nation-state. It became the basis for the expansion of trade and the capitalistic enterprise. It stimulated the application of science and promoted the idea of the individual. These were intimately related, and often elaborated together, in a nexus of ideas of law, sovereignty, citizenship, property and the market and technical progress.

Rationality developed principally in four sites, in the individual mind and conscience, in sovereignty and law, in profit calculation and in the control of nature. The linkage of these with the expansion of Europe was epoch making, for it gave rationality a realization through power which has been fateful for the rest of the world. It became known in the twentieth century as 'modernization' itself, the conversion of the rest of the world to the standards which had become institutionalized in the Western state and in individual behaviour.

Modernity is then a nexus of ideas and power sited in institutions, in which the new, the up to date, is associated with the expansion of rationality. Ideas, power, institutions all expand in the modern period through new territory and new experience. Expansion offers shares in these goods to individuals and collectivities. The interweaving of these profiling factors through the Modern Age as a whole is complex and not reducible to a formula. The relative weight of each on the others is determined not by their intrinsic characteristics but by the salience they acquire over time as a result of their relations with what was outside them.

This is why the attempt to conceptualize developments over time through the idea of a system can never be effective as an account of historical change. Certainly we can hold on to abstract notions like rationality, the state, even capitalism, and show how they penetrate and organize daily lives and social processes at any one time. We cannot go on to derive the direction of social life from their abstract relations.[20] For they in turn are directly influenced by a variety of external factors: natural resources, population, climate, disease and the unanticipatable consequences of scientific discovery.[21] Biological engineering is made possible not only by the rational organization of science; its possibilities depend on and are intrinsically limited by the fact that DNA is constituted as it is.

The Modern Age was impelled by the quest for human control over nature, the economy and over humanity itself. Any account of the Modern Age then has to include the way it sought to theorize itself in scientific terms. In recent writing this has been called 'reflexive modernity', although by remaining within the thoughtworld of modernity this approach has not fully grasped the historical limitations of this reflexivity. We can, however, gain a full theoretical hold on the Modern Age only when we recognize those limitations.

The shaping of the configuration of the age above all depended on self-renewal through everlasting expansion. Now we are beginning to realize that this was not a permanent condition of humanity. We can see that the configuration of the Modern Age had its own central and peculiar feature. It is best summed up as 'the Modern Project' and in order to prepare the ground for a new narrative of the present we need to review that project as a historical phenomenon. Only in this way can we escape modernity's inherent tendency to assimilate the present to the past, to make each one of us into the agents of its everlasting renewal. We will do this by examining the growth of modernity's main agency, the nation-state society.

2

The Construction of Nation-State Society

2.1 The Modern Project

Showing how even the idea of the project is grounded in real conditions as much as in ideas

The tension between theory and history is at the heart of the self-misunderstanding of the Modern Age. The theorization of the age becomes confused with its essence. We have called modernity a nexus of ideas and power. When its ideas are inflated beyond the power to implement them, or when the idea itself is imagined to harbour more power than toiling populations or nuclear weapons, or carbon dioxide emissions, then it imagines itself to have an unlimited future. The idea of the Modern Age as the age led by ideas promotes this delusion of immortality.

This aggrandisement of ideas is expressed best of all in what Jürgen Habermas has called 'the project of modernity', in connection with the eighteenth-century attempt by the Enlightenment philosophers to transform the everyday world to accord with science and logic. For him it was essentially then a commitment to the unlimited extension of rationality to every aspect of life (Habermas 1983: 9).

He could almost have said modernity *as* project. The very concept of a project, a concerted, rational disposition of activities and resources to realize an idea, is intrinsically a modern notion. It was avidly pursued in the eighteenth century. The Abbé de St Pierre conceived of the 'Project for making roads passable in winter', the 'Project for making dukes and peers useful' before lighting in 1713 on 'A project for making peace perpetual in Europe', which occupied all his attention for fifteen days![1]

Habermas identifies modernity with the Modern Project, both in time and substance. To that extent he is one of the *philosophes* himself, sharing their belief that it is ideas which dictate the direction of history, that it is rationality which directs ideas and that it is philosophers who dispose of rationality. There is no doubt that the Enlightenment philosophers contributed considerably to the Modern Project, but as a historical force it was much more broadly based than in the Paris salons.

'The first known expression of the modern idea of Humanity' has been credited to Dante (by Étienne Gilson 1948: 179). His *Monarchy* (1312), written in defence of the Emperor against the Pope, makes that crucial linkage between the expansion of human rationality and the necessity for world government to serve as the legitimation of the state's pursuit of empire. It was a concept of an administered humanity, where 'nations, kingdoms and cities have different characteristics which demand different laws for their government, law being intended as a concrete rule of life' (Dante 1312/1954: 23).

The basis in ideas for the Modern Project existed before the political conditions for its realization. For this reason Stephen Toulmin (1990: 22) disagrees with Habermas and traces its origins beyond the Enlightenment and back to the literary Renaissance of the sixteenth century. But this too over-emphasizes the ideal roots of modernity. There is more to a project than ideas and imagination, just as there is more to history than the history of ideas. A project is the gathering up of energies, resources and practices into a coherent whole, endowing them with purpose, direction and sequence. Competition between the Italian city states, between emerging nation-states, the discovery of the New World, the influx of gold provide the substance of living, on which ideas can feed and flourish. Projects require a variety of elements to be bonded in numerous different ways. They use material resources. They place people in relations of authority or exchange with each other. They promote ideas and animate enthusiasm. They fashion products.

The beginnings of projects may be in the dark recesses of the imagination and the end may be dimly or not at all perceived. Projects don't even have to succeed. The concluding page of Adam Smith's *Wealth of Nations* (1776) decried the way the rulers of Great Britain had 'amused the people with the imagination that they possessed a great empire on the west side of the Atlantic. This empire, however, has existed in imagination only. It has hitherto been, not an empire, but the project of an empire . . . .' Smith was concerned that it consumed resources and made no profit: 'If the project cannot be completed, it ought to be given up' (1776/1868: 404).

Smith was seeking to bring to earth and confine within economic reasoning the project which subordinated economics to its ends. For the project is more than a production process, or even an economic system. This is why it cannot be equated with capitalism, although capitalism became an integral part of the Modern Project. This is why the giving up of the project has consequences going far beyond balancing a profit-and-loss statement.

As with capitalism, we have to imagine the project as something more than, and other than, the designs of those who fashion it or call it their own. It becomes a project without an author, even without a collective author, since its nature and design escapes the full awareness of those involved in it. Social scientists have often pointed to the authorless phenomenon. Smith's market worked to the common benefit through a hidden hand; Marx's capitalist process swept its agents unwittingly to eventual destruction. The point is that while what happens in human history cannot have taken place without human agency, that agency is not fully in control of its actions, either their intentions or their outcomes.

The Modern Project was the co-ordination of human activities around purposes, whose common element was purpose itself, which had as its outcome, though not often as the intention, the practical unification of humanity. All kinds of lesser activities found a space and their legitimation effectively by sharing in this project.

Here we must be quite clear. Let us beware of false conflations. All epochs can be conceptualized in terms of a configuration. Not every configuration of an age is to be seen as dominated by a vast project. The error of modernist historiography is to find projects in every epoch. The ancient world was not configured in this way. Nor, we will see, is the Global Age. Nor is the project simply an idea. It is organized around one, to be sure, but dependent on material and human resources, on a benign social and natural environment.

Furthermore the Modern Age amounts to more than the Modern Project. But they are intimately connected with each other, and without the project, both as abstract idea and as projects in general and particular, the unity and sequencing of this particular age as a historical period cannot be conceived. It might be said that it is the hold on the age exerted by human control which marks out the Modern Age as a distinctive period, and which itself gave rise to the idea of scientific history. But historical periodization is *sui generis*, not reducible to a particular factor or process derived from theory. In the longer, broader view, scientific history is only a passing episode in the vainglory of modernity.

The Modern Project is the movement of modernity over time, the general direction of human activities through the dominant institutional structure. Once it was even equated with society as such. We know now that it was a passing stage of history. The modern period saw the Modern Project take off, dominate other ways of organizing human life, and, like any project, finally reach its limits. It was taken for granted by its protagonists for centuries and is still familiar enough to prevent us thinking clearly about the configuration of the Global Age.

In 1902 it was still possible for one of its interpreters to say that it was the period in which 'the problems which still occupy us came into conscious recognition, and were dealt with in ways intelligible to us as resembling our own. It is this sense of familiarity which leads us to draw a line and mark out the beginnings of modern history' (Creighton 1902: 1). But by 1990 there are advocates for the case that the completion of the Modern Project is impossible and its values are no longer shared (Smart 1990: 27). Only slowly does the appreciation take hold that modernity is not the only way in which human beings can find a meaningful existence. The shift from the modern to the global arouses as much mutual incomprehension between proponents of different ways of life as did the transition from the medieval to the modern.[2]

There is an alternative to the continuation or completion of modernity. It is, and always was, inherently incomplete because it depended on limitless expansion of rationality, resources and territory. But those requirements betray equally the possibility of its termination before completion. The limits of them all, in inherent non-rationality, in depletion and in enclosure indicate why modernity could not ride triumphantly forward as pure idea. The Modern Age wound down and lost direction precisely because modernity was dependent on so much more than ideas. We can even see this in the experience of the Enlightenment philosophers who did most to bring the Modern Project into full consciousness.

2.2 Territory, Experience and Universalism

Illustrating how the open minds of philosophers depended on the opening of new worlds

Accidental features of European history were as important for philosophy as they were for the development of the Western economy. We have to look for contingent linkages. Always look for connections beyond the boundaries to make sense of what happens within. So we find that territorial exploration and material accumulation were intimately connected in the activities of Italian merchants in the thirteenth century (Burke 1987: 1). The most obvious culmination of this linkage, making it indissoluble for European minds, came later, with two voyages, the so-called 'discovery' of the New World in 1492 and the circumnavigation of the earth in 1522.

The first in itself confirmed as a vital priority what had already been a stimulus and excitement. It was after all a quest for the East and its known potential rewards which justified the voyage west. The second confirmed the circumference of a globe, identified the finite space which was shared with other peoples. The two voyages gave an urgency to the deliberate seeking out of other lands, to the development of the technology of sea travel, to cartography, and the introduction of new products. It was a pattern characterizing European history until the twentieth century.

The sustaining motives were many, but competition between the emerging national powers of Europe for new resources combined with quest for a new life on the part of individuals. Both were inspired by images of unknown territories and strange peoples. Exploration, power, wealth went with an expansion of human experience which called for a reassessment of the human condition altogether. Exploring humanity itself, a permanent reflexivity, came to be central in the Modern Project. These comments are not simply wisdom after the event, 400 years later. The most agile and powerful minds grasped them at the time. So the last book of Francis Bacon (1561–1626), *The New Atlantis* (1626), combined a story of a voyage of discovery to a lost continent with the extension of the empire of human knowledge through invention.

What began as the quest for wealth, with the aid of technical rationality, developed into the quest for principles of social order. Reason was applied in two separate respects to society. In the first it became the technique of the modern state, in the army, administration, education and later the welfare state. In the second it was used to generate principles and ideals which could comprehend the bases of interpersonal relations between any people whatsoever, principles which could govern contact between Chinese and Europeans as much as between members of one's own nation or even family. The resultant universalism became a potent legitimation for the imposition of Western ways on the rest of the world. Reason knows no territorial limits. In essence its appeal is to principles which are unbounded by time and space and its strength depends on engaging with the manifest variety of human custom.

The core ideas from which Western empire builders drew their intellectual inspiration were not naïvely and arrogantly ethnocentric. The expansion of Western thought was intimately connected with Enlightenment, often at odds with ruthless imperialism. Knowledge of other lands may have been unsystematic and lurid, but alternative wisdoms were not carelessly denied, as we saw with Montaigne (see 1.2 above). Instead the claims of the European philosophers more subtly transcended different cultures; by learning from them they claimed a route to the universal.

Western individualism was therefore generated as much by the need to comprehend otherness and to take account of cultural differences as it was by any indigenous ideology stemming from the Renaissance. The stranger in your midst, even more strangers who themselves are different from each other, demand a treatment which recognizes their similarity. The idea of the individual is generated by the notion of infinite possible differences between people. It provides a minimum point of common reference.

The Modern Project effectively sought to unite the world through a process with two linked but alternating phases. One phase was the imposition of practical rationality upon the rest of the world through the agency of the state and the mechanism of the market. The other was the generation of universal ideas to encompass the diversity of the world. Each accorded a particular position to individual rationality: the first to technical capacity, the second to values. In each case individual growth and attachment to a supreme source of meaning is guaranteed.

The generic structure of the Modern Project as it related to universal values and the world as a whole suffused the great works of European philosophy, but more in the origins and course of the writers' arguments than in their doctrines. Repeatedly they reported on a journey they had undertaken, sometimes literally, sometimes through literature. It went through three stages: finding oneself too in other people's strangeness; feeling detached from one's origins; defining oneself in relation to the universal.

It was a journey in which the traveller emerged different at the end from the beginning. It was described by René Descartes (1596–1650) in the *Discourse on Method*. He quit both his country and his books and spent seven years abroad to study 'the book of the world' (Descartes 1637/1912: 8–9). He then found that other nations made as much good use of human reason as did his own and that it was custom rather than certain knowledge which grounded human opinion (p. 14).

The result for Descartes was that he had to examine himself and use his own reason. He was thus led to logic and mathematics, which he sifted for principles of thought which might be of practical use. At the same time he formed a code of morals which involved keeping to the faith and opinions in which he had been raised, since it was better to act on doubtful grounds than not to act at all. The culture of reason occupied the mind, while in the world one acts on faith (p. 22). He then roamed from place to place for a further nine years.

Framing a different philosophical approach altogether, John Locke (1632–1704) went through a similar experience. His *Essay Concerning Human Understanding* initially lavishly illustrated his conviction that there were no innate practical principles by reference to exotic customs from Asia to Peru. He affirmed, like Descartes, that all ideas had to be discovered individually, by thought and experience, even the ones which were indisputably true (Locke 1690–1706/1961: Book I, ch. 4, paras 23–4).

He concluded by acknowledging that the greater part of mankind must then be in error (Book IV, ch. 20, paras 3–4) because the current opinion in their own country was no infallible guide and most men were too enslaved by the necessities of life and by those in power to have the opportunity to exercise their faculty of reason. But reflection on one's own thoughts could still produce new truths.

So frequently represented as deeply divided and champions of the opposed creeds of rationalism and empiricism, Descartes and Locke shared the paradigmatic experience of the Western intellectual: the discovery that other cultures are neither more rational nor more irrational than one's own and that it must be left to the individual through personal efforts to reach universal truths. Individualism and universalism joined in ever expanding experience and acquisition of knowledge. But in each case it was the experience of other lands and cultures which was the essential imaginative resource.

2.3   Rationality in the Service of Power

How the expansion of rationality has as a corollary the extension of irrationality

Modernity was not confined to a set of abstract rational principles. Its dynamism depended on the extension of experience to other territories and cultures as much as on logic and calculation. It was the combination which had such fateful consequences for the world. For many features of the Modern Age have existed elsewhere and previously. The ancient Greeks linked rationality and certain kinds of individual achievement. The Phoenicians were early capitalist merchants.

The organized social production of innovation is uniquely modern. That in itself cannot ground an age since, without an anchorage, the new is at best ephemeral, at worst destructive. Modern innovation has been based in the expansion of rationality generally. Since Max Weber this has been called the rationalization process and there has been a general acceptance of his view that it has been the specific characteristic of modern Western culture.[3]

Where the core distinction between rationality and irrationality was pushed to the margin, as it was in rival civilizations, such as India and China, which operated with different conceptual frames in totally different configurations (karma, yin/yang), this represented a challenge to the whole Western way of life. Exchange with those cultures is now a factor in the transformation which makes the Global Age. For they proved resilient and capable of resisting Western domination and their survival highlights the limits of modernity.

At its simplest the expansion of modernity rested on the belief that truth and error take their shares from a finite pool of possible knowledge. Expand truth and error declines. Increase knowledge and ignorance diminishes. Increase control and the world becomes more predictable. This view of the 'world' makes it a finite entity, coterminous with a material reality like the earth. But the world of human experience is an expanding universe of culture, without finite boundaries. Rationality has a main share in this expansion, but what is outside it remains in principle infinite. If we seek to identify the most characteristic element of the rationality which has become known as 'Western' then it probably has to be binary logic, where 'no' and 'yes' are mutually exclusive, where the world is classified into that within and that outside, where there is nothing between being and not being.

It is a common misapprehension that the expansion of rationality means the diminution of irrationality. Weber insisted on the contrary that the rationalization process was accompanied by all kinds of irrationalities which could never be overcome. It even contains within it the emergence of conflicts between rationalities.[4] If we accept his lead, we have to recognize that modernity depends not on the exclusion of irrationality, but on the perpetual attempt to extend the application of the rational/irrational dichotomy. It has given us the computer, but also the Cold War; it has given us citizenship, but also the foreigner. It has given us human rights, but also sexism, racism, ageism. For all these movements rest on giving power to exclusivism; definitions are given force. That in essence is the role of the state and capitalism in Modern Project, the forceful extension of their definitions of reality. This is in principle an endless task. The problems arise for modernity when it is no longer possible or attractive to go on doing this.

The centrality of this for understanding the end of the Modern Age is such that we need to consider more closely what is meant by the 'expansion' of rationality. It has three linked aspects, 'extension', 'intensification' and 'pluralization'. By extension we mean the application of an idea to new areas and the multiplication of instances of those applications. We can find instances in any branch of science. For instance, electronic circuitry, beginning with radio, extended to all forms of communications technology, domestic appliances, transport and machine tools. These extensions are not confined to production technology. Whole areas of everyday life have been transformed by the extension of a rational idea – the personal identification number, the address code, the international dialling codes, or more fundamentally, the banknote, the metric system, standard time, decimal numbers. These all contribute now to the new social technology of the Global Age.

The 'intensification' of rationality involves the analysis and elaboration of an idea, the search for foundations and implications, the search for internal contradictions or affiliations with other ideas. Mathematics is the pure case, but again intensification proceeds in widely different spheres. In economics simple supply/demand ideas are elaborated into models of how the economy works, with several hundred variables. In psychoanalysis an elementary notion of repression is elaborated into alternative frameworks of concepts developed by competing schools of thought.

As so often in the history of ideas, intensive elaboration leads to finer distinctions around which differing views can crystallize. This 'pluralization' can equally arise, however, out of the increase in extent to which an idea is applied. Variation rather than standardization results, as in worldwide voltage variations in domestic appliances.

Extension and intensification of rationality may proceed on occasions relatively independently of each other. Thus the metric system is now worldwide without having undergone significant change; the rules of chess have changed very little over the time the game has taken to spread to every country. On the other hand, sometimes the one requires the other. The extension of computerized information systems throughout a nation-state or the adoption of artificial methods of human reproduction stimulate the development of new regulatory principles. In administrative systems the requirements of purposiveness and feedback on outcomes which the application of modern technology imposes represent a clear case of intensified rationality (Albrow 1987). These are relevant issues to what has since become known as reflexive modernization (Beck 1986/1992, Giddens 1990, Beck et al. 1994). Yet it may also be that an individual works for years elaborating an idea, as Charles Babbage did with his plans for a computer, before the idea is taken up by others. Equally, elaborated ideas may actually lose their hold on people as alternatives oust them.

It is none the less the case that in general the intensification and extension of rationality provide important spurs to the further development of each, and normally each are integral to the expansion of rationality. Moreover the more people there are who come to be adherents of an idea, the greater the chance of the pluralization of its interpretation and application. This expansion of an idea will normally require both greater use of resources and the enlistment of others as partners in discourse, while potential uses to other people are more likely to be revealed. Finally there is always an attempt to contain the pluralization of rationality by inventing mechanisms to transcend differences.

The expansion of Western rationality has not then been the imposition of a set of fixed and immutable ideas on a completely malleable material. For a start it is 'Western' by association and not by its nature. The Renaissance involved the absorption of ideas from both past and parallel cultures, above all Greek and Arabic. Secondly, in its expansion it encountered ideas which influenced its course: Chinese bureaucracy, Indian astronomy, American Indian democracy all stimulated and helped to shape the direction of the Western response. On the other hand, the expansion of rationality and the emphasis placed on its different facets depend on the motives and resources available to its adherents. In this respect the association of rationality with the nation-state and capitalist organization provided an impetus to expand in a certain direction. A nation-state defines itself by what is under its jurisdiction, a capitalist firm by what it owns.

If the state expands, it has to convert what did not belong into what does. Equally it has to define afresh what or who is outside it. If the firm expands it has to redefine itself and its customers. What is added to one side of the equation has to be added to the other, but the meaning of one side is only established in relation to the other. The outside threat, the market, the unknown or the irrational have always to be replenished.

Expanding knowledge and expanding the state or the firm are often equally expressed in terms of pushing back frontiers. The materiality of the state's frontiers or of consumer demand simply means that limits to their expansion become more obvious and consequences are perceived earlier than is the case with knowledge.

The paradoxes which arise out of the Modern Project are, however, manifold. The expansion of the nation-state eventually confronts the finitude of world resources. The expansion of rationality increases the complexity of action. The expansion of the means of power diminishes the rationality of the world from the individual's point of view and increases perceived risks and insecurity.

In these respects the expansion of rationality is equally the expansion of irrationality. The greater the area of a territory, the longer the frontier which has to be defended. Irrationality is certainly part of the configuration of the Modern Age, but it was repressed as an element in the Modern Project. We need to examine the consequences of this in more detail in connection with violence and the state.

One of the most important consequences of the sixteenth-century Reformation was that it removed the social from the predominant tutelage of the Catholic Church. It then became a free-floating resource and prize in the political struggles which created nation-states. There were various ways in which the social was domesticated. Violence was one. Control of access to markets was another. Both, however, were associated with the rationality of state machinery.

Elias (1978, 1982) has set out at length the consequences of the centralization of state power from the sixteenth century in Europe for the codification of manners and the development of self-control. They proceeded *pari passu* with the state's monopolization of the means of violence. The correlate of that was a specific identification of the individual with the nation. The passions arising in social life could then be transferred to the aims of the state.

The idea of the nation linked the state with the people it governed and provided the legitimacy for what were often arbitrary boundaries and jurisdictions. It focused passions on foreign adventures and justified penetration into the recesses of individuals' lives. Already by the eighteenth century in France, wrote de Tocqueville in 1854, government had influence in a thousand ways, not only over the general conduct of affairs, but over the destiny of families and over the private life of every man (1854/1996: xi). The roots the nation-state planted in daily life were the intrinsic accompaniment to the Modern Project.

In the United States, Henry James, speaking at the beginning of the twentieth century, found that it was a 'pretty practical problem of national economy, as well as of individual ethics' to ensure that people lived at their maximum of energy. Where they fell below, 'a nation filled with such men is inferior to a nation run at higher pressure' (James 1907/1917: 42).

When industrialization threatened the very integrity of this union of individual and nation, the social problem which arose in its midst was dealt with by the deliberate fashioning of the welfare state. The origins of the world wars of the twentieth century and the rise of the welfare state were correlated processes, each based on the linkage of the fate of the individual with the fate of the nation-state as a whole. Total mobilization and social security went together.

Deconstructing the linkage of nation-state and citizen enables us thus to make sense of what may otherwise appear to be contradictory aspects of modernity. Rationality and irrationality, often regarded as contradictory, sometimes seen as earlier and later phases of the modern period, or in the extreme case, with irrationality regarded as the mark of the postmodern, was the specific binary code of modernity and governed the nation-state's relations with the citizen.

The nation-state, with its quest to monopolize the means of violence, legitimized violence in its own defence. Emotionality in the service of the nation-state was encouraged, even if the technical tasks of the state required equally the development of discipline, science, technology and rational administration. The willingness to risk life in the service of the state, which simultaneously called for a disciplined workforce, was thus only sustained through the promotion of contradictory thrusts in the personality.

It was a Faustian bargain, capable of generating vast collective energy and heroic individual deeds at the risk and often actual expense of lives on a massive scale. Bauman (1989) is therefore right to see the Holocaust as part of the inherent dynamics of modernity. But modernity did not collapse from its own extremes. Its central steering managed to promote and combine equal and opposite tendencies.[5]

2.4 The Expansion of the Nation-State

How the Modern Project depended on the expansion of the
nation-state

If it was in territorial expansion that the thrust of the modern nation-state was realized it was because it could offer its citizens opportunities, direct their energies and focus their activities.[6] This applied whether it took the form of military service, frontier exploration, oil prospecting or the administration of empire. And if a particular nation-state failed to expand, it had to defend itself against those that did.

It is not a new thesis. Acton advanced it when he saw the motive force behind the rise of the modern state as domination fed by dreams of expansion.[7] This was what the exploits of Magallanes and Cortez conjured up for Spain. 'This law of the modern world, that power tends to expand indefinitely, and will transcend all barriers, abroad and at home, until met by superior forces, produces the rhythmic movement of History' (Acton 1906: 51). The rhythmic forces Acton referred to resulted from the combined efforts of the weak uniting for self-government and resisting this relentless force.

One hundred years ago this was the view of modernity of a liberal Catholic, an insider with a long enough perspective to be detached, but without yet being able to imagine anything else than the internal dynamics of an all-embracing process. He hoped for the progress of liberty as a result of countervailing forces within a system. He wrote to a friend, 'All liberty consists *in radice* in the preservation of an inner sphere exempt from State power' (Mathew 1946: 170).

But that was an optimistic interpretation of the benign potential of unlimited modernity. The German historian Otto Hintze, who saw the demonics of modernity in the First World War, still agreed with Acton on the essential linkage of nation-state and expansion. He made the worldwide penetration of the capitalistic spirit dependent on the nation-state, and called on Max Weber's authority in support of his view (Hintze 1942: 120).

Through mobilization for conflicts and through their expansion, state organizations steadily acquired a dominant position over other social orders in the early modern period, in particular over feudal estates, cities, merchants, churches or intellectuals. None of the principles or interests around which such groups could crystallize – status mainten-ance, market power, belief – were as powerful as the threat of viol-ence supported by a belief in its legality. If we date modernity from the early sixteenth century, we do it in full recognition that it was not therefore at its outset associated either with industrial capitalism or with the rationalism of the Enlightenment. Moreover capitalism had an adjunct, not the leading, role.

Nevertheless the holders of state power, of aristocratic or warlord origins, or both, disposed their force in such a way as to take eco-nomic activity into its frame and sought to mould it to their advant-age. In Joseph Schumpeter's terms (1976: 136) the rise of the bourgeoisie was symbiotically related to the aristocratic powers which controlled the state, or as he put it on another occasion, the nation-state arose as 'feudalism run on a capitalist basis' (1954: 144). They needed each other, but in no sense did the one produce the other. Indeed, it was precisely because of the growing awareness that state and capital operated on the basis of distinct principles that economics arose as a science for those who held state power.

In its European origins this science was not about free market prin-ciples. Rather it was the product of state administrators rationaliz-ing the practice of monarchs, seeking to fine tune a system of colonial rights, manufacturing monopolies and trading privileges to the max-imum advantage of the holders of state power in the name of the nation as a whole. It was, then, about the allocation of advantages between different social groups and this was premised on their prior existence and their pursuit of economic activities.

If the economic activities of these social groups were taken as a whole, they certainly did not amount to anything like 'capitalism' or even the economy. If there was one word, it was more likely to be 'society' than anything else; in Adam Smith's terms, 'the general busi-ness of society' (1776/1868: 2). But he was setting his ideas against the claims of the state. His self-assigned task in a nation-state society, Great Britain, where the state had never dominated the social order in the way it had in Europe, was to show that restricting government expenditure to a necessary minimum was conducive to the aggregate growth of individual wealth and hence the nation's wealth.

Smith may have denounced his European rivals for their adherence to state intervention, but at the same time he revealed the basic terms of discourse which he shared with them, namely that the social order could be reconceptualized in terms of the pursuit of individual interests attached to a national feeling, with the state as an arbiter. This was the underlying purpose of writing a book to demonstrate that the benefit of the division of labour between professions and in manufacture was to the advantage not just of individuals, but of the whole nation. At the same time, that attachment to the nation derived from other than individual interests.

Smith's contemporary, Adam Ferguson (1723–1816), Edinburgh Professor of Moral Philosophy, identified the source of attachment to the nation in this way:

> Without the rivalship of nations, and the practice of war, civil society itself could scarcely have found an object, or a form. . . . Could we at once, in the case of any nation, extinguish the emulation which is excited from abroad, we should probably break or weaken the bands of society at home, and close the busiest scenes of national occupations and virtues. (1767/1782: 39–41)

Here we find beneath the surface an intimation of the duality of the social which emerges in different epochs of human history and troubles any administrator of social forms or theoretician of rational principles. It was the core theoretical focus for the establishment of sociology as an academic discipline.[8] For sociality may either transgress the boundaries of social forms, or alternatively social forms may intensify sociality. In any event we cannot assume, just as Ferguson could not, that the only bonds human beings would forge would be within the pre-existing frontiers of an established authority. The attempt to resolve this issue was central in the expansion of the modern nation-state.

2.5 The Modern Conflation of State and Society

Showing the contrivances modern thinkers used to demonstrate the indissoluble unity of state and society

The problem of the relation between the state and the social is an abiding one in Western thought. In the classical account of Aristotle the political community was the supreme association within which citizens could pursue the good life. It certainly was the true fulfilment of, but it also necessarily had its grounding in, common social life. On that basis he drew the lines distinguishing citizen from non-citizen, identified the behaviour appropriate to man as man, as master, as friend, as slave, and developed fine distinctions between relations of reproductive pairing, dominance, mutual interest, friendship and sharing in the good life.

From the beginning then the question of political structure was the problem of its relation to society, or the way it could regulate the social processes in which it was enmeshed and which equally often threatened its affairs and very existence. Aristotle's account made the classification of good and bad constitutions depend on the participation of citizens. The very structure of the state arose out of social process.

The argument of the present book depends on conveying to the reader a sense of being part of history. It asserts equally that all the arrangements for living which human beings have ever made are transitory. Some are, however, longer lasting than others, and as our own lives are short it is not always easy to know where we stand in the flux. If it was easy, we would not hold so strenuously to the notion of limitless modernity. Epochal change is easier to identify for the distant past than it is in our time.

It was at the beginning of the Modern Age that the use of the term 'state' became current, with a wide variety of nuances around the ideas of stability, standing and political organization. Those meanings have to this day become more elaborate, never finally crystallizing, making it vain to seek some legislative fixing of the term.[9] At whatever point one engages with an idea of the state, the characteristics of the time are inscribed in it. We can illustrate this with an example from the middle of the modern period. Adam Ferguson wrote in his *Essay on the History of Civil Society* about ancient Sparta:

> this people did not languish in the weakness of nations sunk in effeminacy . . . They fell into the stream by which other states had been carried in the torrent of violent passions . . . they ran the career of other nations . . . the last community of Greece that became a village in the empire of Rome . . . the history of this singular people . . . made virtue an object of state . . . We live in societies, where men must be rich, in order to be great. (Ferguson 1767 / 1782: 270–1)

His narrative moves easily from people to nation, state to community and back to people and state again. But they all refer to the same entity, Sparta. The terms could be used interchangeably, concluding with the interesting shift to 'We live in societies.' No theoretical weight hung on the vocabulary.

There were two reasons for this. First he was describing a form of social organization which no longer had an equivalent, the Greek city state or polis, for which in a sense each of these terms was equally anachronistic. The other was that Ferguson was living at the time of the crystallization of another form of social organization, the nation-state society, which depended on equating ideas like people, nation and state, which otherwise, if kept apart, could imply quite different forms of organization.

The dictum that the modern state has created society is a cruel transposition of historical priority.[10] The idea of society, as the association of human beings, predates the state in ancient, medieval and non-Western versions. For instance there are fourteenth-century Christian and Islamic versions in Dante (1265–1321) and Ibn Khaldun (1332–1406) respectively. Dante wrote of 'universalis civilitas humani generis' as the all-embracing human society for which ultimately a single world empire was the fitting political frame (1312/1954: 5). Ibn Khaldun wrote of 'umran', civilization identical with human social organization, and proposed a special science to study it (1958: 77–9). They both took Aristotle as their benchmark for his discussion of the polis and then drew out the consequences of recognizing different political forms depending on the type of society. In Catholic theology, Thomas Aquinas (1224–74) replaced Aristotle's dictum that it was natural for the human being to live in a 'polis', to be a 'political animal', with the declaration that it was natural to live in the society of many others, to be 'socialis', a 'social and political animal' (Aquinas 1954: 2–3).

Aquinas sought very deliberately to ground the political in the social. True he had an interest in doing this. He thus ensured there was an arbiter between secular and religious power. For the social was subject to God's laws, and ambitious claims of earthly power could be brought under the same rational scrutiny as the laws which God had inscribed in human nature. For the medieval Catholic theologian the stress on the social provided a defence against the encroachments of secular rulers.

Most of the modern theory of the state was devoted to demonstrating that its particular form of social organization was indeed the true and permanent expression of the nature of society. But the fact is that a particular version of the state, the nation-state, sought to create society in its own image. Thus from a late modern perspective the state appears as primary and the social a sphere to be controlled by it.[11]

There is no doubt that high modernity brought society into new focus by treating it as an object for scientific analysis. The conception of a positive science of society gave rise to the academic discipline of sociology. But then there was no sphere of life untouched by these conceptions. It is also the case that governments in Europe in the late nineteenth century were all preoccupied with what was known as the 'social question'. This basically centred on how the state could control the social forces which industrialization had released, in particular the rise of a mass proletariat which threatened established regimes.

But none of these undoubtedly important shifts in the relations of state and society warrants the jump to a modernist interpretation which would leave society as a product of bourgeois consciousness.[12] All such accounts can be traced back to a materialist version of the sociology of knowledge which regards the only significant previous ideas of state and society as bourgeois inventions. It equally ignores even the genealogy of Marx's own developed idea of the social, which was very close to Aristotle's.

This modernist error arises from neglecting the term which linked state and society, namely the nation (whether land, country or people). This provided the specifically modern answer to the problem which Aristotle answered with the polis. It was the state's answer to the problem posed by the division of labour when it set up rival claims for the individual's sociality.

2.6 The Crisis of Industrial Society

How the threat of the rising working class provoked the ruling class into promoting both the welfare state and a science of society

Until the mid-nineteenth century either the 'invisible hand', in the term of the political economists, or the rational spirit fashioned a wonderful concordance between individual and national ends. Any lesser groups to which individuals belonged were part of the greater social organism. To this extent the theory of the nation-state simply overlaid the older feudal order of society. But by the middle of the nineteenth century it became clear that the rise of a new class profoundly disturbed the accommodation of the early modern period between state and civil society.[13]

As the forces of industrial capitalism increasingly revealed the shaky nature of the bridge between state and civil society, Marx sought to make the divide wider and deeper by challenging the old theory and by adopting the cause of the rising working class. He proved to be largely successful in prompting the recasting of theory – but at the cost of his political aims.

In his early years of writing Marx had invoked the social nature of the human being in true Aristotelian manner. But he was impressed by two things which at a deeper level were not unrelated. The first was the alienation of the worker in an impersonal industrial system. The new structure of production relations left working people engaged in activities over which they had no control and which meant nothing to them. The second was the intellectual analysis of economic relations, which equally postulated an impersonal system of laws and forces. The association of the two meant that at least for the duration of industrial capitalism full human social nature was suspended. For Marx only with the end of capitalism would human beings resume their truly social nature.

Marx had at his disposal the increasingly impressive analytical methods of political economy. Equally, he sought to predict the future course of society. Bringing those two together had fateful consequences for social theory for a hundred years. The great intellectual prize for opponents and supporters of nation-state society alike became the invention of an analytical system which would explain the future course of society.

Marx's method was the prototype. It involved three aspects: analytical, historical and synthetic. The analytical defined key abstract concepts like capital, labour and rent and developed a model of their relations under hypothetical conditions. This revealed processes such as the necessity for the rate of profit to fall and was intellectually powerful, if flawed. Then the historical looked to the real relations of social groups and how they changed over time, to the political conflicts between parties, what was happening to the family, relations of town and country, even how intellectuals fitted into society. Finally the full social theory involved mapping the historical changes on to the analytical processes, using the latter to explain the former. So owners of industry, workers and landowners were mapped on to capital, labour and rent, and the forces of the analytical system threw the classes into a growing antagonism which would eventually, in accord with Marx's wish, result in the collapse of capitalist society. Marx sent shudders through nation-state society. It was not only the message of hope he sent to working people. His theoretical method was impressive enough to send the nation-state into overdrive to find alternative and better theories.

Marx's work revealed the deepest problem for the future of nation-state society, namely that its trajectory would be influenced by forces which crossed its boundaries. For any analysis of the economic system showed that it was intrinsically connected to the world as a whole. Mapping the social on to the analytical then gave him the international working men's movement. His method opened up the possibility of world revolution. Marx's ideas struck terror into the nation-state and simultaneously gave internationalism the reputation of subversion.

It is well known that the response of the nation-state to the social transformation which industrial production brought in its wake was to domesticate the problem. That is, the forces which were worldwide, the new threats from uncontrolled society, were converted into problems within the nation-state. The 'social problem' was a code to refer to the problem of incorporating the newly formed industrial proletariat into nation-state society. It was a big enough problem setting to generate simultaneously socialism, the welfare state and sociology as an academic discipline.

The practical solution to the social problem renewed the Modern Project. Basically welfare states represented the nationalization of the problem in the context of mobilization for war. At first the conflict was between nation-states, culminating in the two world wars, and then between capitalist and socialist state systems in the Cold War. Effectively this adopted Ferguson's suggestions in the eighteenth century for encouraging national spirit.

A hundred years later the nation-state project lost momentum and the welfare state has been challenged as a result. One challenge effectively means a reversion to the idea of civil society. It reinterprets the welfare state not as a means of social integration but as a struggle to distribute collective goods and benefits between existing interest groups. The nation-state was never wholly successful in becoming society, never completely muffled the clamour of interest groups. Welfare expenditure can be represented as incurred for 'other people'. This in turn is paradoxical, since the costs of the welfare state, including health, education and care for the aged, arise in large part because of the universality of its benefits – not for 'other people', but for you and me. But the question of legitimacy arises when the state loses its universalistic appeal and appears to serve sectional interest.

This happens as a result not of cost but of wealth. It is the increased wealth of nation-states as a whole which largely creates the problem. For two reasons welfare appears as an increasing burden. The first is the relative price effect. Welfare largely takes the form of services, where productivity does not grow in the same way as in manufacturing, and therefore costs grow relatively. The second is that as countries have become wealthier the distribution of wealth has become more polarized and, for this and other reasons, a higher proportion of people have become completely dependent on state transfers.

The legitimation crisis depends then not on fiscal issues in their own right but on a perception that the nation-state can no longer offer the same benefits as it did. But this perception represents the failure of one of the nation-state's methods of integrating individual and society. Quite apart from this, it is more difficult for the nation-state to divert groups away from distributional issues by rewarding them for participation in the Modern Project. The organization which is the nation-state has no new aims to realize, no new fields to conquer. Under these circumstances it is not surprising, and the imagery is apt, that there should be a widespread demand to 'roll back the frontiers of the state'. Its advocates should only be under no misapprehension:

this means both reducing the scope of the nation-state and freeing society from its control.

2.7 Systematizing Nation-State Society

Showing how much of the theory of society has previously been the voice of the nation-state

The welfare state was an attempt to relate individuals to national society directly and to transcend feudal and interest group politics. In parallel with it came a theoretical development to meet Marx's challenge. As was appropriate to a project, the state came to be seen as a total action system. So, in the same way as Marx conflated the social with the economic, the nation-state assimilated people into rational systems of action, managerial, market or bureaucratic.

We can use the problems of Marx's theoretical method to exemplify the problems of all such theory. The abstractions are themselves taken from life. They therefore take on different meanings depending on whether they are used in everyday life or in a theoretical system. It is not at all unambiguous whether, at what time and for whom any or all of bank deposits, money due, industrial machinery, goods in stock, orders for goods, customer goodwill, product names, technical knowledge, motor vehicles, dwellings and land represent 'capital', let alone what money value might be put on them. Marx resolved such problems by considering those things owned by capitalists to be capital. What labourers owned had to be ignored (Schumpeter 1954: 634).

The problem is compounded when real social identities are mapped on to the technically defined relations. It is a conflation of real society with abstract economic theory which effectively plays into the hands of nation-state theorists. For it gives them additional licence to remap the old identities within the nation-state on to new administrative categories.

Looking back we can recognize how much of social theory was effectively designed to reflect back to the state its own efforts to control society. In each case this meant downplaying discordant aspects of the reality which would subsequently disrupt the theoretical vision. But then this was a necessary feature of this type of theory. It seeks to derive historical change from analytical concepts, with the nation-state's control over the individual as the main premise. We can distinguish three versions which in broad terms we can call the theories of industrial society, capitalist society and modern society.

The theory of industrial society effectively challenged Marx's centring of society on economic relations and instead focused specifically on the mechanisms of authoritative control. The idea that it would be possible to read off the nature of society from an understanding of the laws of the economy, leaving the state as a cipher, could never be justified in any absolute sense. Moreover the success of governments in warding off the dangers of the industrial proletariat was already becoming evident by the end of the nineteenth century. It led to the belief that running the state involved principles, even 'iron laws', of equal power to those of the economy.

Alongside the principles of capital arose principles of organization and management, enshrined both in state bureaucracies and in the practices of the powerful emerging industrial corporations. Rationality appeared to require a single form of discipline and organization across all sectors of modern life. Whether in capitalist or aspiring socialist states the logic of large-scale industry was held to be identical. The class which was necessary to run both state and corporation, the managerial, appeared to dominate modern societies whatever ideological viewpoint it advocated (Burnham 1941). The concept of authority and the process of the institutionalization of conflict were the analytic equivalents of profit and the concentration of capital. The theory of capitalism became the theory of the large corporation, while the theory of the state became an account of bureaucracy. The distinction between socialist and capitalist states came to be little more than convenient political rhetoric for opposed blocs of nation-states as their structures appeared to converge on a single model of organization (Kerr et al. 1960).

The theory of industrial society was a theory of the concentration of power. In this way the project of the industrial organization paralleled the project of the modern state. Set against the observed trends of growth of state activity and the large corporation, the idea of liberal democracy appeared increasingly as so much ideological window-dressing. Parliaments were talking shops, trade unions mechanisms for institutionalizing conflict and in any case subject to the same bureaucratic principles as state and corporation, and the welfare state was simply a device for the domestication of the masses. Instead of liberal democracy we have mass democracy (Kornhauser 1957). At the same time the theory of industrial society posed problems of national independence. If the mechanisms which guaranteed state control were so similar worldwide, what was there to guarantee the independence of the nation-state?

Effectively this convergence revealed the inner contradiction of the theory of industrial society for the nation-state. The concentration of power appeared to work according to processes which were non-national, and the homologous nature of state and corporations of any description made it increasingly difficult to identify a future for the nation-state except in terms which were outside the theory.

The theory of modern society offered that possibility. In this case, instead of adding the political to the economic as a parallel, ultimately merged order, further analytic spheres are added, the most important of which is the cultural. It is a theory of the plural basis of society held together by a common denominator or principle. So while modernization is a transnational process, the bonding of the separate sectors occurs through a specific element of national culture.

Effectively the theory of modern society updated the eighteenth-century theory of the division of labour to reinforce national identity. It meant handling the question of relations across state boundaries with a certain brio. Émile Durkheim accepted the older view that economic exchange was also social and therefore constituted society. But since society for him was essentially nation-state society, exchange across frontiers had to be defined as only 'mutualism', not truly 'social', since it occurred even between individuals of different animal species! (Durkheim 1893/1933: 282).

Parsons's version of the theory of modern society developed an account of roles from a base in action theory which was also at the same time an effective development of the theory of the division of labour. The development of occupational diversity linked benefits for society with the pursuit of individual interests and the deployment of special skills. To that extent markets produced alternative definitions for the meaning of individual action which could compete with the state. In turn the state provided frames for the pursuit of interests through the law of property and contract.

Even the theory of capitalist society, with direct descent from Marx, could not evade the problem of the success of the nation-state solution to the social problem. By mid-twentieth century it was obvious even to dedicated communists that the nation-state managed a control over people which extended far further than Marx's original theory of capitalism allowed. Antonio Gramsci (1957) sought to account for state control over the whole way of life of a nation-state society with the idea of hegemony. Althusser (1971) developed an elaborate structuralist account around repressive and ideological state apparatuses.[14]

Common to these three theories was the assumption that the nation-state society revolved around a common basis of action, which we have called the project. The premise, rarely stated, was the sovereign power of the state. The hold of the state on action was enhanced by talking of systems and indeed finally squaring the circle of individual and the state by talking of systems of action.

Two problems beset the theories of nation-state society. The first was the setting of boundaries. The intellectual methods which fix system boundaries, across which one measures inputs and outputs, can only arbitrarily be equated with the boundaries of nation-state society. Ultimately it is facticity guaranteed by power, incommensurable with logic, because what power determines, power can change.

The second problem concerns the units of analysis. The state depends on treating individuals as devoid of ties to traditional groups. At the same time individuals are the locus or the bearers of system properties, as legal agents or rational actors, role players, citizens or whatever. The individual then is stripped of social qualities and kitted out with system properties. But this is in theory only. Individuals remain people capable of transforming system properties into something else.

This confusion of the analytical and the concrete is not inherent in theory. More modest theoreticians have kept their eyes on a wider reality. The economist Alfred Marshall, for instance, distinguished two concepts of capital, one as used regularly in business and by individuals, the other social, from the point of view of the community as a whole, by which of course he meant the nation-state society. His starting point was the broad general usage of these abstractions; thereafter the economist added technical qualifications (Marshall 1890/1920: 69).

If we take a similarly cautious line we avoid the grosser elisions of society and economic system represented by 'capitalist society'. Equally we can allow for the transformative effects of the social on economic relations as much as for the disruptions of the social by economic growth. The problems which arise when analytical rather than historical accounts take hold are the limitations they impose on recognizing people in their full social capacity.[15]

Parsons's theory of modern society required a citizen to be imbued with the values of the national culture, to become in the words of his critics a 'cultural dope'. The theory was a distortion of reality but at the same time was close enough to strengthen aspects of it. But it is not only dominant orthodoxy which both reflects and reinforces at the same time. Marx's theory required the alienated worker to fit a view of society as it might be, and then social behaviour to correspond with that counterfactual state of reality.

All these examples indicate how analytical theory can easily become ideology. But the relations between social science and social life are rarely straightforwardly ideological. The double hermeneutic between the two may just as easily involve people taking up suppressed premises in the analytical theory.[16] For instance the cultural 'dope' may employ the idea of culture in a radical rather than conservative way; the alienated worker may adopt and cherish the alien lifestyle.

There are alternative approaches to theory construction other than the reification of analytical concepts. Habermas's (1981) 'colonization of the lifeworld' depicts the extension of the state into everyday life. It has a historical base and in conveying the similarity between appropriation of territory and control of the lives of citizens there are implicit alternatives. We shall see later that those who are 'colonized' may indeed use that experience to assume control of their lives.[17]

In eliding the difference between analysis and history, theory ignores the socially formative possibilities of people's lives, the way they can take forward elements of their own and predecessors' social experience. An analytical theory of action which takes account of these non-systemic features becomes a theory of practice. But that is already to suggest alternatives to the project which the nation-state controls. In any event, whatever the theoretical underpinning of nation-state/ society, by the middle of the twentieth century it was more than theory could do to repair the damage caused by the decline of the Modern Project.

3

The Decay of the Modern Project

3.1 Modernity, Modernism and the Epoch

How the intellectuals sought to imprint their own trademark on the age and have now to give way to the people

We can now sum up the specific dynamism of the modern epoch, an important step towards understanding the transformation which the Global Age involves. The expansionary thrust of the Modern Project has lost underlying momentum. This depended on the continual possibility of drawing the non-rational, what was external to the modern, into the frame of rationality and irrationality.

In the case of the nation-state the obvious form of expansion, the acquisition of territory, has virtually vanished as a possibility. But its extension into the soul has also come up against inherent limits. And in the area of the economy, the state and the market have always to find an accommodation. The main shock to capitalism has been the discovery of the consequences of finite resources and worldwide recognition of unsustainable development.

Even the penetration of modern culture into all other cultures has lost its force. We can see that in the fate of modernism. For the thrust of those varying artistic and intellectual moments known as modernism has always depended on revitalizing the rational/irrational frame, from one side or the other. To do that it has always had to absorb what was outside, from other cultures, or from the non-rationalized recesses of modernity. When Irving Howe wrote of the modern as 'an inclusive negative', as a perpetual revolt against established style, he expressed the dilemma of the period by declaring that we were unable to see how it would end (1967: 13). We can now. Where there is no established style, rebellion loses its point.

The old-established cultural dichotomies, the rational and romantic, the scientist and the artist, even the traditional and the new, have lost their capacity to mobilize opposing camps. This is not the end of all order, but in part the resumption of older premodern and non-modern directions. For although modernity has repeatedly been linked with the expansion of rationality, its institutionalization was always embedded in the projects and *practices* of the state and capitalism. They worked together intimately through the structuring of sexuality and gender, discipline and the management of emotion, the stimulation of need, the use of anxiety, the threat and use of violence. As was argued above (p. 25), the expansion of rationality is more properly seen as the categorization of life in terms of the rational/irrational dichotomy rather than as the exclusion of irrationality. There is always a 'pre-rational', though not necessarily 'anti-rational' substantive basis to which that dichotomy is applied.

Rationality may be the dominant feature of a practice, but no practice is constituted by rationality alone. The other elements in the life of a practice are more appropriately termed non-rational. They are not specific to modernity. 'Irrationality' on the other hand gains its special place in the Modern Age precisely because of the privileging of rationality. The dynamics of its relations with rationality are best understood by appreciating the new place won by modern intellectuals. Their rise as scientists, not as craft workers but as the autonomous agents of change, was prefigured as long ago as 1620 in Francis Bacon's *Novum Organum*.

The lifting out of intellectual activity from the embedded practices of the age was a key element in the configuration of the Modern Age. The novel idea was not a mere reflection of the world around. It imagined futures and other worlds, it discovered new forces, it challenged the assumptions of its time. If the state and capitalism encouraged new thinking, at the same time they had to struggle to contain the results of the Faustian bargain they made with intellectuals.

In this way the realm of ideas was set up in permanent tension with what it was to shape. The roots of ideas, of innovation itself, were also beyond rationality, in the imagination, the unconscious and the unanticipated outcomes of experience. In each case they were defined as irrational. But that very definition was an intellectual act, the product of the professional makers of modernity.

This is the configuration which underlies the various 'modernisms' in art, architecture, music, literature which came to characterize the Modern Age. Working with the contradictions generated within modern culture, emphasizing alternately recovery of tradition or innovation, sense or sensibility, effectively current and countercurrent within modernity, intellectuals have promoted its ever recurring renewal.

The Modern Project time and again absorbed explicit opposition to modernity. Nietzsche was embraced by the Nazis, William Morris's radicalism became Liberty, the prestige store, not a campaigning organization. The prophet of erotic love, D. H. Lawrence, relayed the messages of German intellectuals.[1] Marcuse inspired a counterculture, but 'make love not war' became a consumption slogan. The ultimate paradoxical apotheosis of modernity came perhaps when Lenin saw the future of socialism in the assembly line.

This is not to deny genuine anticipations of a different era, but the new age we live in has not been the product of these visionaries. It is not primarily a cultural product, even though cultural production is a central process. Movements dominated by intellectuals were far more characteristic of the age which is past. But it remains vital for understanding the trajectory of the Modern Age to sustain intellectual skill, to develop and employ concepts which allow us to express these tensions and contradictions. We need moreover to achieve this understanding of the past if we are to appreciate the break which the new era signifies, and as a defence against some of its threats. The Modern Age has passed but some of its achievements need defending.

For our own time increasingly reabsorbs the intellectual back into life. Neither the green nor the women's movement is dominated by an intellectual elite in the way socialism was. Capitalism has lost faith in nostrums in direct proportion to the proliferation of its forms. But intellectualism has become a necessary ingredient of everyday life and the quality of that life and the ability of individuals to cope with it is enhanced by the quality of the ideas embedded in it. In this sense education in the Global Age has ceased to be the transmission of dominant ideas and much more becomes the mass opportunity to participate in the cultural production process. But then quality needs defending on all fronts in all sectors.

My conclusion from these first considerations of the passing of modernity is a modest one, but widely applicable. It is to call for the common use of conceptual distinctions which will aid orientation to the new age. In brief review I will suggest that we need to hold on to a few key distinctions which have underpinned my argument up to now and will provide reference points for later discussion of the Global Age.

If we begin with 'modern', meaning anything up to date, new, innovative, of the present, 'the modern' as the whole assembly of those things labelled in this way has no special epochal significance. On the other hand when we talk of 'modernity' we refer to a connected set of features which represent a dominant way of life and set of institutions central to the West and to the Modern Age. Together they can be characterized as a project and the Modern Project is the dynamic assemblage of modernity, or modernity in active mode.

Modernity was a nexus of features which were labelled 'modern' and which together gave the Modern Age its character as project. It included the combination of rationality, territoriality, expansion, innovation, applied science, the state, citizenship, bureaucratic organization, capitalism and many other elements. Together they provided a frame for the practical activities of the vast mass of ordinary people.

By 'modernism' is meant all those cultural movements led by intellectuals, artists and writers who sought to develop the inner logic of modernity, or take an idea of or from the modern and explore its consequences for creative activity. Modernism did not define modernity; rather it drew from it and sought to lead. The 'avant-garde' was an apt image for the proponents of modernism. It was the struggle of intellectuals for leadership of the age over and against all the other groups who contended for that position, the politicians, soldiers, capitalists, managers. But the self-image of none of these parties was ever adequate in itself to provide the historians with the definition of the age in which they lived.

Neither modernity nor modernism, separately or taken together, completed the configuration of the Modern Age. They were defining aspects of it, helped to shape it, but their coevals were the rural populations of the poor countries of the world, and the old world religions. Traditional cultures were not bypassed by modernity. They were ever present features of the Modern Age, without being modern. The Modern Project sought from its beginning to expand into them. Its dynamic depended on using their resources and often cannibalizing their ideas. From its own standpoint it summed this up as 'modernization' and 'development'.

It follows from this examination of the trajectory of the Modern Age, of the place in it of the Modern Project, of modernism and modernization, that its decay did not depend on some inherent self-contradiction. The Modern Age did not contain the seeds of its own destruction in any obvious sense. It was not subverted by enemies within, even when they announced its end. Its transformation occurred as a result in part of its on-going success.

The Modern Age entered terminal decline when the Modern Project had absorbed as much of people's lives as it could, taken in the territory of the world, and met with forces it could not control. The complex change which took place cannot be summarized as the victory of the irrational. As some of the proponents of postmodernity have recognized, the change is one where the rational/irrational frame no longer provides the axis along which daily conduct is organized. The symptoms of the change occur across all sectors of life and not in any one intellectually defined sphere. It is in the broadest sense historical.

3.2 The Counterculture

How oppositional values have played into the state's hands and reproduced modernity

As we have just seen, it is a misjudgement, hiding its true nature from analysis, to imagine that modernity requires the elimination of emotion, or more generally of irrationality. Rather modernity has operated with the rationality/irrationality distinction as its core organizing code. So the modern state required disciplined commitment for its ends, and the modern economy required unbounded exercise of irrational tastes for it to work.

The social defined as emotional and irrational was the form of opposition which reinforced the modern state's self-image. It was the attitude of the nation-state which prompted Émile Durkheim (1895/1982) to define crime as useful for society because it invigorated social control. Utopian visions of a world different from the present were characteristic expressions of modern society.

From this point of view the psychoanalytic theory of neurosis as frustrated sexuality was characteristically modern, as indeed Freud acknowledged.[2] The problem with such theories was that they always had to posit a reservoir of needs and drives which, pent up under the requirements of modern social life, broke out from time to time. They were therefore essentially theories which reinforced the state's account of the ever present danger of a loss of control. The use of the term 'subterranean', of the underworld, is a vivid reminder of the equation of crime and passion.

However plausible the accounts such theories provided, they stopped short at a crucial point, namely in identifying just how much pressure had to build up in the reservoir before it overflowed. It is always wisdom after the event which has to wait for the act of violence before it can proclaim that the pressure was too great. The two most fruitful influences on recent thought on social structure and individual personality were from Elias (1978, 1982) and Foucault (1967, 1977, 1979), who escaped the self-image of modernity by stressing that the nation-state was responsible not for the repression of emotion, feeling or drives, but importantly for their structuring and production. The discourse of repression becomes then just that, a discourse, utilized by the state and its agents to turn potential alternative forms of meaningful action into individual failure.

In the broadest sense the nation-state did not simply monopolize legitimate violence, it managed it and shaped the public expression of emotion. The extreme forms of public violence in peacetime, as in international football violence, are not accidentally linked to nationalism. Nationalism is a state project, not some primary urge out of which the state arises, and when nationalism opposes established state structures it does so on an agenda defined by the statehood to which it aspires.

But given the predominant position accorded to rationality by the state it has been a repeated aspect of its operation to stigmatize oppositional or alternative social relations and movements as irrational. Those movements have even been ready to accept and enjoy that definition of themselves. It was this tacit acceptance of state definitions, a licence for licence, which led Marcuse (1955, 1964) to warn of 'repressive desublimation'. The free expression of sexuality within the state's frame may only serve to stabilize existing social relations.

In other words the counterculture has been a standing feature of modernity and the avant-garde intellectual has always been faced with the dilemma that outright opposition to the dominant values of modernity has become itself a hallmark of the minority position of intellectuals. 'An unyielding rage against the official order' is the way Irving Howe characterizes modernism (1967: 13). This is paradoxical only for those who fail to see that the characteristic of modernity was not rationality alone, but the use of the rationality/irrationality code. The impulse to overthrow, the energy of resistance, the determination to explore beyond known territories were key characteristics of modernity.

There is no escape then from modernity through ideas alone, certainly not critical ones, since critique has long been institutionalized as a specifically modern way of thinking. In this respect the story of Friedrich Nietzsche's work and its reception is the most instructive. In part he undertook outright opposition to modernity by lauding irrationality. He sang the praises of power and violence, despised humility and charity, mocked chastity and respect for women, regarded the Christian religion as a disastrous fraud and declared that God was dead. He overturned existing values, 'transvalued' them so that it was their opposites which were to be the guiding lights. He prompted an unprecedented panic among the educated classes, not just of Germany, but of the Western world. But in part he sought also to suggest alternative ways of living which rested not on irrationality but a positive acceptance of qualities which sat transversely across Western values rather than merely opposing them.[3] But it was as an opponent of Western, and specifically Christian, rationality that his reputation was established and for which a crowd of lesser figures looked to him.[4]

The expressive countercultures of the twentieth century have no more prefigured the end of modernity than did their predecessors, even though they have on occasion achieved a temporary dominance. But Ascona did not prevent the arms race towards the First World War.[5] Flower Power in the 1960s did not prevent the nuclear confrontation of the Cold War which transformed the world. So when Theodore Roszak (1970) applauded youthful opposition to technocratic culture he was knowingly discounting the repeated experience of romantic generational rebellion.[6]

The real break, rupture with the modern, shift to a new epoch, comes not with the victory of the irrational over the rational, but when the social takes on a meaning outside the frame of reference set by the nation-state. This happens when the state is no longer able to control new forms of social organization. Only when the state has to bow to the autonomy of the social has the Modern Age run its course. On our account, that cannot happen through ideas alone, but only when the project loses its hold on the organization of everyday life and the daily practices of ordinary people. We can, however, understand how this has happened by deconstructing the theoretical integration of the project.

3.3 The Theoretical Penetration of the Project

How new theory has arisen to interpret the consequences of the decline of the old Modern Project

The extension of the state into people's lives is not a matter simply of the activity of outside agencies. That was how it could seem in the eighteenth century. The king's government was an agency invested with power, but still in competition with other foci of social organization. The separation between the state and the ruler led over time to a further distinction between official duties and private life. This in turn preceded a more general distinction between public and private in the lives of citizens. It prompted the later role theory, in which the person became the site for a set of activities which did not belong to him or her by virtue of self, but by virtue of participation in abstract systems.

Of those systems the state was more important than any other. By virtue of the twin processes of extension of its scope and the incorporation of national populations into the resulting action systems, people became themselves increasingly active participants in the state. This was not just a question of paying taxes, doing army service or seeking election. The change was much more pervasive, a transformation of the meaning of daily activities. Action in regard to the state may include acting as its agent, in employment or not; providing it with services; fulfilling obligations; enjoying privileges and benefits; suffering coercion; seeking permissions; complying with its exhortations; or seeking to influence or change it. In the modern nation-state very little daily activity did not fall within one of these categories. This was the everyday realization of Habermas's 'colonization of the lifeworld' (1981: 522). It is obvious that the theoretical equation of state and society in the era of the nation-state was not without foundation in reality.[7]

Individuals therefore in the modern period became increasingly enmeshed in and an integral part of a highly complex system of state activity. But further we should recall that they equally became the locus of other institutional spheres, defined as systems, at a minimum the economic and the cultural. Models of complex social systems have relied on treating individuals as sites with unlimited space to permit the competent performance of these system requirements. Very little attention has been paid to the individual performers by these theories of society and whether they really do have the capacities to perform as the systems require.

Two theoretical movements have partially sought to fill that gap. The first arises essentially out of a historical view of social structure, namely it accepts that people do belong to social groups which have longer or shorter histories and that the affiliations they form in their lives arise out of historically conferred identities. In the main these are not social classes, but identities of an ethnic, religious, language or gender nature. The routes into this standpoint are many and varied; some come from a Marxist route, others from a study of social interaction, others from Weberian conflict theory, but the convergence on this view is powerful and reflects a major shift in approach which corresponds with the declining hold of the nation-state – a paradox which does not negate the idea of the colonization of the lifeworld, but which will require much more explanation before the end of this book.

The other movement has an origin more in philosophy. It is not analytical but it deals with concepts and seeks to grasp reality through them. The philosophical turn known as phenomenology aims particularly to grasp the nature of the world around through examining the individual consciousness of it. In its origin it may have seemed altogether removed from the hard realities of life. But increasingly it has become a discourse to engage with the experience of the new epoch. The reason lies in the situation I have just described.

The development of the state has meant the growth of the *polyvalence* of human action even as it has enveloped it in an all-encompassing frame. The same activity can mean very different things as viewed from the standpoints of states, individuals or observers. Husserl (1937/1970) and Schutz (1932/1972) in particular have focused attention on the multiple frames of meaning which individuals have to negotiate under contemporary conditions. They have sought to identify the presuppositions for establishing personal and intersubjective meaning in the lifeworld.

At one and the same time the state official may be executing an administrative order, securing an income, adding to promotion chances, commissioning a firm to provide a service and stigmatizing a claimant for welfare. The same act can be described quite differently by a welfare official, a firm of investigators and a person applying for state welfare, and there is competition between the parties to establish their own description as the one with the most valid claim on the attention of observers.

Phenomenology has been criticized for its disregard for differential power as a variable. This criticism misses the main thrust of phenomenology. The complexity of the lifeworld arises out of the multiplicity of power relations, and phenomenological critique removes any *intellectual* claim the state might have to provide privileged descriptions of action. It is the state's *power* which privileges its descriptions of action. It has the capacity to impose a solution and possesses a seeming objectivity, impersonality and durability above and beyond the purposes of particular individuals. If the same act is described by the poor mother as providing for her children and by the state as stealing bread, there is little chance for the former's description to carry more weight.

But the state has one huge disadvantage as the generator of privileged meanings, namely that they are always conveyed and received by individual human beings, who in principle can always, and in practice frequently do, differ in their interpretations. The state has the same kind of objectivity as a text, a human construction, manifestly existing to be dissected and deconstructed, admired and reviled, elaborated and dismantled. This is the facticity of the state which has no superior intellectual foundations to those of any other human product.

Hence the individual who refuses to reify the state by accepting it as the ground, premise or means of action but instead objectifies it through critical distance asserts alternative bases for action. And such critical distance is enhanced when the state finds more and more difficulty in renewing and reinvigorating its own purposes. This is bound to be the case when the supply of new land, resources and people ceases to fuel its expansion.

Critique and phenomenological reduction do not in themselves undermine the nation-state's claims to define action. Indeed they have been the reflex of its development, since it was the development of the state and modernity as the Modern Project which designated action itself as the meaning of human existence. The other conditions are that it must lose its momentum, and real alternative bases for human conduct have to be in place. Finally something has to tip the balance in favour of the latter.

The Modern Project developed the idea of action as a premeditated choice among alternatives, in which means were chosen in relation to ends, not only in terms of those they served best but also in terms of their costs. It transferred the intellectual analysis of practice from the human and divine to the organization of the state and the business firm. In turn the terms of the analysis of their system rationality became the criteria for judging individual action. But society never can be an 'action system' in that sense. It depends on longstanding bonds and gratifications of the moment, experience of living and responses to the world which are not programmed or planned. Moreover, in reality, states can never in practice exert that kind of power over people's lives.

The state has always had other contenders for the position of prime adjudicator for meaning in people's lives – churches, associations, markets, the family, to name but a few. The scope for each of these to exert a defining influence also varies from time to time. Their relation to the state is historically variable and with the expansion of the modern state each from time to time has taken on a more sharply accentuated tension with it.

The overreach of the state in the Modern Age leaves each of these contenders ready to assert an authoritative claim to legislate for the meaning of human activity. At the same time the polyvalence of human action at the dawn of the Global Age is the basis for a widely disseminated sense of the fragmentation of discourse, multiple personae and social disintegration. The paradox is that this appears as the result of the expansion of something which had promised coherence, namely rationality.

3.4 The Decentred State

How the rationality of the state becomes a shared aspect of a world beyond the nation and correspondingly removed from the people

The nation-state has been rooted in the people like no previous state. But its roots are not immune from attack. Nation-states have had to assert themselves in an environment of other nation-states, as well as against competing associations, like the family, local community, the church or the business firm. It is engaged in power struggles and it defends territory. From the beginning the use of force has seemed inevitably bound up with its nature, not only in relations with other states but also in relation to its own people.

In the history of the theory of the nation-state, certainly since Machiavelli (1517) at the beginning of the Modern Age, violence and coercion have been seen as central to it. But in the Aristotelian tradition of defining the rational ends of human association, and later in German idealism, reason occupied an equally important place. Still later the technical rationality of the state was emphasized most famously in Max Weber's account of bureaucracy in *Economy and Society* in 1921. In these different ways theory has postulated inherent links between the state and rationality.

The nation-state's self-image is as a sphere adjudicating between the competing interests of its population, where joint purposes are conceived and co-operation engineered. Both processes are subject to rational imperatives. The rational application of explicit criteria enables parties to disputes to recognize the legitimacy of even disagreeable outcomes. Similarly collective decisions occupy a shared frame of reference where people can have rational expectations both of the state and each other.

This is why even avowedly empiricist pluralist power theory acknowledges that competing groups in society have a common interest in creating agreed institutions to guarantee freedom to pursue their interests. This unites such disparate theories as that of Robert Dahl's model of group conflict (1961) and Talcott Parsons's systems approach (1951), which views power as a resource exercised on behalf of society. For both, rationality is in effect the source of a master code for the creation of media, a resource equally accessible to all parties, in principle inexhaustible and freely generated. It requires certain predispositions on the part of the people who draw on it, most importantly at least the temporary suspension of attempts at coercion, and a free submission to its principles.

Similarly with law: even if its origins are arbitrary, and even if it is administered tryannically, it remains in the interests of the power holder for it to retain predictability. Even the tyranny of Stalin required some spheres of predictable decision making, and at least an approximation to rational bureaucracy. The idea of law, and hence rationality, are intrinsic to the state.

The rationality of the state arises out of the multiple, often conflicting requirements of its citizens, rulers and ruled alike. But at the same time it evades the nation. Rationality exists in an ideal sphere; it does not belong to a people. Thus, however far a group seeks to exclude non-members from the benefits of membership, it is in the interests of its members to ensure that when abroad they will receive equivalent treatment to that of visitors to themselves.

The idea of law then governs relations between groups as much as it does relations within them and, where national laws differ, massive ingenuity is exercised to find rational solutions.[8] The result is that large spheres of human interaction become progressively detached from purely national regulation. They begin to inhabit a sphere which requires international agreements, courts and other agencies. Even where the implementation of a decision falls within a national territory, it is governed by the international frame of law. Governments have acceded freely to the jurisdiction of bodies such as the European Court of Justice. In kind such bodies differ in no way from state agencies; but they do not belong to a nation.

But it is not simply the ever developing framework of transnational legal institutions which removes the state from purely national control and which leads to the lament of 'loss of sovereignty'. The early twentieth-century discussion of the process of bureaucratization found that the state increasingly came under the control of professional administrators. The tension between bureaucracy and democracy had as its counterpart the transformation of production organizations as the managers of large corporations gained control from sole or shareholding owners. Each process has been part of an ongoing modern dynamic. Within the business organization this has resulted in the much-noticed transnationalism of production process and corporate structure. Less noticed has been the development of transnational bureaucratic practice.

Quite apart from the development of transnational collaborative arrangements and the development of an international bureaucracy serving the United Nations and other agencies, there is now an imperative to develop the best administrative techniques as available to any nation and to share in their development. The worldwide use of computer records of individuals, coupled with the extension of the use of personal identification numbers and machine readable cards, has brought the administration of the state into the same dependency on a universal technology as the large manufacturing corporation. There is now a social technology which facilitates the international exchange of information and relies on the use of experts and the exchange of expertise worldwide. It is now impossible for any one nation-state to extricate itself from this worldwide administrative logic without damaging itself drastically.

In an earlier period the fear was that the bureaucrats were establishing themselves as an independent group, separate from both government and the people. But it was still a tacit assumption that the new power base was the nation-state administrative apparatus. The new social technology makes clear what was always inherent in the nature of administrative technique, that the state is now a nexus of transnational practices.

Once Hegel (1821) had identified the state with reason on earth he had difficulty in attaching it to a people. He could only do so by invoking the virtues of the German officialdom and locating rationality in the soul of the solid educated middle class of his time. But reason is in principle open to all people. The state, viewed as rationality, knows no boundaries.

Whether in law, or in collaborative transnational practices, or in the new social technology, the rationality of the state reveals what was always its potential, namely its objective and universalizable quality distinct from any particular nationhood. Even as the nation-state developed, state practices transcended the boundaries which Hegel erected around it. The state's roots are no longer in the nation; its extent is worldwide. It does not belong to a particular set of people at a particular time, though it may have arisen from their needs. The state in the Global Age has been uprooted. Governments find that the deracinated state they administer does not belong to themselves, or even to their own people. The origins of its rules are multilocal, polycentrically administered. From that point of view it is now possible to think of the state as a worldwide web of practices, with no one centre.

Nation-states grew within and depended upon an idea of independent sovereign political entities which transcended them. The idea of sovereignty required acceptance within a much wider discourse than the nation. Now, that discourse becomes more important than the idea it produced. Instead of treating states as separate entities, we are obliged to recognize people and governments engaging in state activities. The state has become a globally extended sphere of meaningful activities. Multiple agencies engage constantly in defining the nature and limits of their respective jurisdictions.

We have discovered the historical limits and conditions of the 'nation-state'. Even as nationalisms seek to acquire the political power which statehood once guaranteed, the state withdraws into a realm of technology, law and transnational organization. But in a world where individual activities have so long been energized by the aspirations of the nation-state, where the state has colonized so much of daily life, where social life has been framed and regulated by state, the consequences of its transformation for individuals and groups are profound.

3.5 The Fragmentation of Economy and Society

How the completion of the Modern Project weakened the capacity of nation-states to withstand the forces for the dissolution of nation-state society

With the dissolution of the Modern Project the nation-state loses control of the forces it previously contained. The ensuing fragmentation is the result, even as nation-state societies cover the earth's surface. It is this penalty of success which needs most to be understood. Individuals can understand it in terms of personal projects as the anticlimax, the let down, the feeling of nothing to look forward to, the loss of a dream. But the Modern Project did not belong to individuals, even if it required their services. The discourse of the Modern Project did not permit that kind of subjective account. It was beyond the personal, but in its own terms its winding up exhibits equivalent features: loss of control, nothing to hold different parts together, no sense of direction.

The disintegrative forces did not arise from nowhere. They had been harnessed together and their potential independence concealed in the Modern Project. Indeed they in part arose out of the growth of wealth and technical power the project generated. But in the end the project depended on the control of people and, in spite of its claims to control sociality, to be a comprehensive social organization, once it was bounded by other nation-states and all were faced by the logic of limits to expansion, the nation-state discovered the limits of its control over people too.

We may distinguish five main contributory forces for fragmentation: the corporate organization, the market, science, culture and the social. Their impact, however, only becomes truly disintegrative when the Modern Project loses its momentum. The first was the capitalist organization itself as it expanded beyond nation-state boundaries. Public concern came in the form of a panic about the place of the multinational corporation in the 1960s. For even as the activities of corporations beyond national frontiers spread modernity, at one and the same time they illustrated that economic logic dictated their relative independence from the control of any one state. This concern could take several forms, either on behalf of poor countries exploited by the rich, or by rich countries losing control to other rich countries. In either case it drew on a recognition of the relative autonomy of economic relations from state control.

The second force equally represented the autonomy of economic relations, namely the market. A state which was always extending its frontiers offered individuals expanding opportunities for gain, either in direct service of the state, or through grants of land, licences and monopolies. Moreover internal markets did not appear as a threat to the state, rather as a strength. But a static state immediately came into contradiction with the market principle, which is nothing else than exchange to mutual advantage free of outside restriction. It could only meet long-established expectations of continuous gain by dropping barriers to economic exchange with the outside world and by expanding the sphere of market relations within the state.

It is not only market rationality that has sprung the boundaries of the nation-state. As a third force the universalism of science was always perceived as a danger to state control. In human affairs universalism also seemed to hold out the prospect of world government. The model of the end-point of this process was nothing less than a replication of the nation-state worldwide and a single world government. But it has not happened in the form which was expected. Certainly the nation-state is the dominant form of the state worldwide, but instead of a single world government we have the decentred state and an expansion of social technology which is out of control.

Rationality has become detached from social order even as communicative rationality has replaced bureaucratic rationality. No particular social form now seems to follow from the adoption of rational principles. In the case of economic organization this has led to what Lash and Urry (1987) describe as disorganized capitalism, as flexible work patterns and contractual arrangements replace the old hierarchic rulebound structures. The very technology of communication itself makes the boundaries of nation-states merely factors in locational decisions rather than barriers to movement.

In this sense rationality, the very animating principle behind modernity, appears to have lost its grounding. It no longer has a base in a particular kind of social organization. We have already drawn the consequences of this in the concept of the decentred state. It certainly is not represented either in capitalist economic activity. For the abstract rational principles of the market prescribe no specific form for economic organization. It is historical accumulations of property and power which set the parameters and characterize the economic relations known as capitalism, rather than rational economic principles. In this respect the transformations of the world economy demonstrate more than anything else the relative decline, not of any particular state, but of the nation-state as a form of social organization.

Under these circumstances, with the loss of confidence in the rationality of large-scale social organization, the quest to identify rational choice in individual behaviour gains in intellectual appeal. Here, however, the contrast between two types of modern personality, the calculating advantage seeker and the ontologically insecure seeker after self, illustrates the way rationality as such provides no definitive point of departure for either analysis or action.

This disembedding of rationality equally assists the autonomy of culture, the fourth of our forces for fragmentation. Again the experience of other cultures has been central to modernity and itself a corollary of the expansion and exchange between nation-state societies. In its pure form nation-state society expressed nationhood as a distinct culture, with language and literature distinct from the rest of the world. The contradictions within this idea were revealed by the expansion of the English language and in particular by specifically American cultural products. The panics about culture in Western society expressed themselves as a concern for youth, and as such could be converted into a crisis of generational relations within the nation-state. Youthful rebellion could be represented as a domesticated phenomenon, an expression of the rebelliousness and irrational romanticism to which modern societies were prone from time to time. It was quite another thing if it represented the spread of ideas, the attraction of exotic images from another society. It meant that culture demonstrated its independence from the frame of nation-state society. Concern about the hippies in European countries was not just that they were young rebels; they were *Americanized* young rebels and as such they opted out of the national project.

The association of culture and youth evoked energization, the magnification of affect when people come together. The fifth force was the social itself. It expressed itself in different ways throughout the 150-year period of the dominance of organized industrial capitalism, as workers' combinations, socialist parties, as revolutionary movements, as communism, as new age, peace, green, women's and other movements of the 1980s. Broadly these looser or tighter associations of people with similar interests or ideals demonstrated the potential arising out of collective action which was outside the frame of nation-state society. 'Outside' meant both geographically and conceptually. The autonomy of the social crossed both the territorial boundaries and the prescribed behaviour of nation-state society, and each experience reinforced the other. Even though the nation-state sought to frame society, the creative potential of ever-renewed social contact always posed a threat. In the language of nation-state social science, the social was confined by images of 'socialization' or 'social reproduction', but the threat of altogether unpredictable outcomes of encounters and relationships was never far away.

The crisis of nation-state society has frequently been represented as the culmination of modernity, as a stage towards a new modernity. For some the expansion of rationality appears as a reflexive modernization, modernity with a rationalization of its principles. But this linkage of reflexivity and modernity conceals the indeterminacy of rationality as an organizing principle. Reflexive rationality is no more capable of providing foundations than simple rationality, indeed even less so since it draws attention only to the infinite regress involved in the quest for ultimate principles. At some point there has to be a decision by fiat or agreement which fixes or accords a value to some element in the world and ends the, in principle, endless search for reasons or for guarantees against risk. Nation-state society did that by associating rationality with its own expansion and equating society with its own structure. It became the basis for the ontological security of individuals as well as those social units between individual and the nation, like family and community. The new security for individuals arises out of elective social units and the choices are made on the basis of values, faith and trust.

The decay of the Modern Age did not arise out of its inner contradictions or some predetermined end-point. The culmination of the project happened as an accident, when the conditions for its continued progress could no longer be fulfilled. The simplest formulation is to say that this happened when one world came into being. But so many senses can be given to this that it does not convey adequately that the transformation which counts is the collision of nation-states both with the limits of their territorial environment and the finitude of the resources available to them. There is no territory outside the frame of state control, and resources cannot be increased through territorial expansion.

Clearly this epochal transformation has not happened at one moment, although the full consciousness of it has been more sudden. Perhaps the most clear-cut point of full recognition came with the oil price increase by the cartel of oil-producing countries in 1973. This fed through into public commentary in Ralf Dahrendorf's terms (1975) as the end of expansion and the beginning of a new agenda of survival with justice. At that point the forces which had been kept within the frame of the nation-state by the momentum of the Modern Project could no longer be contained. The pressures are now for new kinds of social organization. We have been living through this transition from one epoch to another in the last fifty years.

3.6 The Most Modern Nation

Recognizing the United States as the arena in which the fate of modernity is being decided

The decay of the Modern Project can be traced most precisely in the course traced by its pre-eminent historical agent, the United States of America. Modernity gained its most characteristic expression in the experience of what has turned out to be in the twentieth century the nation-state above all nation-states.[9]

Of course modernity was equally associated with European imperialism. The intertwined history of each is coeval with the beginning and end of the Modern Age. This is not to deny the rivalry and tension between these two faces of the Modern Project. Indeed in certain respects they are contradictory, the essentially non-racial nature of US citizenship contrasting with descent-based concepts in Europe, the interest-based conception of world politics of the USA contrasting with European notions of international law. But these are two sides of the same coin, namely the nation-state as the main historical agent.

Nationality in the USA had to be created on two fronts simultaneously, both of which characterize an aspect of core modernity. The first was the contest with an aboriginal, earlier culture defined as primitive and savage, which was resolved by territorial conquest. The second was the challenge to absorb the immigrant, to absorb original ethnic identities into the superior state of American nationality.

Observed from Europe these struggles continued the story of the Western encounter with irrationality and the rise of modernity.[10] Nature had to be tamed by modern rationality. The absorption of ethnic identity into a higher national identity accorded with the same model of control of an earlier, more irrational condition, and citizenship came to be regarded as the true expression of the rational state.

These connections were long visible to analytical observers of the United States. One of the most interesting must be Hugo Münsterberg, Professor of Psychology at Harvard, himself an immigrant from Germany, friend of Max Weber and like him fascinated by the constitution of nationhood.[11] He linked the special nature of the American nation with the extension of the frontier, 'an unremitting pushing forth over new domain'. It was a community of purpose built upon an individualism pervading four spheres of life, the political, economic, intellectual and social as self-direction, self-initiative, self-perfection and self-assertion.

Munsterberg's account merged the hitherto egregiously superior Kantian rationalism in which he had been raised, with a rough and peasant transatlantic culture, coloured indeed by the images of Indian savagery. His new American assumes the virtues of self-determination, the ultimate statement of Protestant means to salvation, from which Kant's ethics derive.

The 'vulgar' expression of this ('vulgar' because Munsterberg was still too much the observer to be a true believer) was a belief in

the world-wide supremacy of American ideals: and a part of this necessary paraphernalia of popular assemblages will naturally consist in a reaffirmation that the duty of America is to extend its political system to every quarter of the globe: other nations will thus be rated according to their ripeness for this system, and the history of the world appear one long and happy education of the human race up to the plane of American conception. (1904: 6)

Selfhood becomes a project associated with the experience of expansion, rather than the passive reception of laws and injunctions. So the relation of state and individual acquired an American dynamism equally admired by Max Weber. It was a counterweight to Kant's dreams of universal peace, long regarded by European exponents of *Realpolitik* as effete and subversive cosmopolitanism.

The fascination which the USA exercised for the twentieth century was not then as an escape from modernity into a past primitivism, but as a true representative of a more advanced modernity, as the site where the rationality born of complete self-reliance was free from the shackles of tradition and feudal relics. The *New* World became the new *world*, dominated by the United States and American culture.

For admirers of the United States the national assumption that 'world history is part of American history' was on balance healthy since that inclined Americans to assume world leadership (Brogan 1944: 147). After the debacle of internationalist ideals it was felt that this was the only chance of order in a world of nation-states. It followed that the final act of the drama of modernity was played out in the Cold War with two main actors, the USA and the Soviet Union, the one a melting pot, the other a multicultural empire, sharply opposed versions of the nation-state. Both socialism and capitalism were truly modern products and each side mounted an intense drive to absorb the rest of the world into their version of the modern frame. The future of the whole world appeared to depend on the ultimate nation-state contest.

In 1947, James Burnham, one of the major interpreters of the late Modern Age, and a renegade from Marxism, declared that the Third World War had already begun in April 1944 when a Soviet-inspired mutiny took place among Greek sailors serving a British command (1947: 1). He saw no alternative but a struggle for world empire between the Soviet Union and the United States, and called on the latter to establish a federation of states to dominate the world and to impose democracy.

Burnham, closely following Toynbee (1939–61, vol. 1: 150–3), distinguished the unification of the world on economic and technical bases, which was far advanced, from political and, even more, from cultural unification. A victory in the Third World War for the United States could be a bridge to the goal of a genuine 'democratic world order' and world government (Burnham 1947: 242). It was leadership of the world or nothing.

Fifty years later the most modern nation appeared conclusively to have won the supreme contest. But its drama had diverted attention from the consequences of modernity which meant the world looked very different from what Burnham had envisaged. The other forms of world unification had developed to the point that they outweighed political power as a factor in determining events. The 'New World Order' had a hollow sound as global forces undermined the efforts of the dominant nation-state to impose its will. The agents of the Modern Project had lost control.

3.7 The Passing of American Hegemony

Why globalization is a threat to a specifically American conception of world order

The 1992 American presidential election was fought very largely against the background of a global threat to American hegemony. Competing in the new 'global' economy became a cliché in the presidential campaign. Both Bill Clinton and his running mate Al Gore succeeded in promoting a message which carried a double force. They emphasized the identity of the United States as the predominant world power, a factor which cut across all the divides within the country. Simultaneously they identified insidious threats to that position arising out of the 'global' change, suggesting a common insecurity. It was a campaign theme long prepared through systematic research and brainstorming sessions.

The title of Gore's book *Earth in the Balance* neatly suggested this doubly loaded message: precariousness, hence anxiety, and at the same time earth as totality and the real basis of our lives. The message encoded in the campaign came out in sentences like this: 'The global environmental crisis is, as we say in Tennessee, real as rain, and I cannot stand the thought of leaving my children with a degraded earth and a diminished future' (Gore 1992: 16). The global becomes local, and then serves as the code for a political campaign in which the Democrats effectively gathered together the American people to face the global threat. The 'environment' served as a signifier for everything which had gone wrong in society.

Clinton maintained this theme immediately after his election success: 'We need to regain our economic strength in order to play a significant role in the new world, and to compete and win in the global economy.'[12] His acceptance speech on the same day reaffirmed the American nation's role in the world: 'I accept tonight the responsibility that you have given me to be the leader of this, the greatest country in human history.'[13] This is an authentic text of the main actor in the Modern Project. Only in one country has it been possible to utter these sentiments in all sincerity.

There is no intrinsic reason why a political campaign premised on the global threat should win the prize, any more than one based upon spiritual renewal, individual freedom or political integrity. Successful political messages have to be salient for the times in which they are issued. We therefore have to ask why the global message was an effective communication for the United States electorate in 1992. The answer to that lies first in the history of the United States, and second in the world crisis events of 1989–92, which appeared to shake basic assumptions created in that history.

Clinton's and Gore's skilful play on the insecurities created by a new global situation allowed them to transcend the issues of the 1980s. Then the Cold War meant that the Americans knew where they stood in the world: internal issues were the divisive ones. The sources of the new American unease exploited by the Democrats included:

1 The enormous budget deficit and indebtedness to the rest of the world which had been built up in the Reagan and Bush years, in part to pay for an intensification of the Cold War.
2 The increasing penetration of imports into the United States, in particular from Japan, which for the first time came to be seen as a threat to the premier economic position of the United States.
3 The relative decline of the United States as the centre of world capitalism with the rise of financial centres in Europe and the Far East.
4 The collapse of East European socialist states so that the victory of the West over communism removed the prime sense of purpose from the military and overseas posture of the United States.
5 Increasing evidence of internal divisions between black and white, Hispanics and the rest, rich and poor, men and women, young and old, all of which cast doubt upon the unity of purpose which characterized the American Dream and the possibility of fulfilling the mission to the rest of the world.

Whether one includes concern about the environment within this list is very doubtful. This is certainly a matter of concern for many Americans. But texts about the environment so often carry with them messages about control of other people and being controlled by them that it is easier to read them as expressions of unease about declining global power.

However sincerely meant, the messages Gore's book conveys about the effect on humanity of present industrial practices have less voter impact than his identification of Japan as the country which has the most advanced and profitable technology for dealing with global warming. In other words, for global warming read the Japanese threat, and this is a reading actively encouraged by Gore in placing the issue within the context of 'America's ability to compete' (1992: 335).

The passing of American hegemony is not accompanied by any obvious successor to the title of dominant world power and the United Nations is patently not a world government. This contributes to the sense of bewilderment, for world empire is so intimately associated with the Modern Project.

Instead there appear to be multiple centres from which influence radiates outwards, and these are not simply seats of government. They can be financial and cultural centres – Frankfurt or Hollywood – and sometimes they have no particular physical location at all. International finance lives at the ends of telephone and video links. It is in this context that the idea of globalization has taken on significance as the process which makes the world one, while removing it from any one nation-state's control. The culmination of the Modern Project involves the disorientation of its chief agent, the dominant nation-state.

We should be cautious before advancing any ambitious theory to account for this historical irony. Certainly there are elements of what could be called the 'logic of the situation' which place the United States in a new dilemma. What is required from the winner of a contest is quite different from what is needed for victory. The military–industrial complex no longer has the same legitimacy in making claims on the state and citizen. The international security networks are no longer bonded in a common task and no longer need to look to the United States as co-ordinator-in-chief. The competitive system which was nurtured as the source of strength has its own dynamics quite independent of the Cold War. All these factors appear to have an inherent logic to them which suggests the mighty must fall, that pride precedes destruction.

These 'logics' would however have none of their remorselessness were it not for forces which have gathered strength from sources outside the nation-state's control, even if they have been used by it. The dynamics of technology and in particular of communications and information technology have facilitated a new worldwide intensity of interaction between organizations and individuals. Both at ideal and instrumental levels the globe has become the reference point for cultural and economic activity. At the same time the frame of international relations within which nation-states establish their status and identity is not under the control of any single nation, or even of one group of nations.

In turn individuals and organizations draw their own consequences from the changed position of the nation-state. They increasingly seek solutions to their problems outside its confines and are inclined to invest less of their emotional energies in its fate. For those who do still hold their nation in sacred awe this decline of faith is an affront and globalization itself the equivalent to a world without religion.

The consequences are particularly disconcerting for the citizen of the United States, where the nation took on an overt significance as the arbiter of self-identity, given that it absorbed such a variety of ethnic identities in the course of its construction. The United States is the quintessential modern nation-state, forged out of a shared project of individual freedom, built on the notion of the future, not the past. Globalization is, then, a threat to the American idea of world order, which has to be an order of nation-states. But it is also a threat to the internal cohesion of the United States, and in two ways. The American dream bonded ethnic diversity with the hope of future economic prosperity. Globalization offers both economic competition and cosmopolitanism as an alternative to the historical construction of the American hyphenated identity. It therefore even contains within it the nightmare of a possible world without America.

4

Globalization: Theorizing the Transition

> It was the Second World War which first accorded full weight to the contribution from everywhere, to the globe as a whole. The war in the Far East was just as serious as that in Europe. It was in point of fact the first real world war. World history as a single history of the totality had begun. From now on the interim period of previous history appears as a dispersed field of unconnected ventures, as so many beginnings of human possibilities. Now it is the totality which has become the problem and the task. It ushers in a complete transformation of history. The decisive thing is that there is no more 'outside'. The world closes. It is the earth's unity. New threats and opportunities appear. All essential problems have become world problems, the situation is the situation of humanity.
>
> Karl Jaspers, *Vom Ziel und Ursprung der Geschichte*

4.1 Not the End of History

Recognizing the profound historical change we experience

With hindsight we can see that the Modern Age was bound eventually to hit its limits.[1] The territorial expansion intrinsic to the modern state has its own form of culmination. For the intellectual missionaries of modernity there was another kind of expansion, the extension of reason or rationality to comprehend the world as a whole. Linked with territorial expansion it generated ideas of universal human rights, universal order, of world government.

It was the linkage between universal reason and world empire which accounts for the persistent modern Western belief that at some point history would come to an end. If history was the progress of reason and there came a point when the whole world was under its sway, then we draw a line under history. The idea of universal reason had become real. The theoretical expression of this combination of Western imperialism and universalism is the idea of the emergence of a world-wide civilization.[2]

For some the end of the Cold War verified this rationalist interpretation of modern history. Francis Fukuyama (1992) regarded it as the vindication of Hegel's version of the development of a rational liberal state. But he treated the worldwide spread of liberal democracy as the effective 'end of history' because something had been lost, which effectively was identification with a national mission.

The unification of the world was therefore double-edged. It appeared to undermine its main agent. The nation-state promoted trade and created money, and they then freed themselves from its control.[3] For Spengler, money located itself in a few world cities and ran a world economy, while in remote places patriarchal relations still prevailed (1919–22, vol. 2: 598). The separation of the world of money from both the state and technology has remained a theme to the present, with the deregulation of the world's money markets in the early 1980s being for many the final triumph of the inherent principles of markets and monetary exchange.[4]

Oswald Spengler concluded his account of the decline of the West by declaring prophetically that the drunken soul wanted to fly over time and space, an unnamable yearning for limitless distance was taking human beings beyond the earth to circle it in space (1919–22, vol. 2: 629–30). Spengler's 'decadence' appeared to Ortega y Gasset to be a source of limitless human possibilities: 'the content of existence for the average man of today includes the whole planet . . .' (1932: 27). But Ortega also saw the rise of fascism and communism as evidence of the insatiable demands of mass-man.

These are all authentic voices of the end of the Modern Project. Spengler, Fukuyama and Ortega are all decrying the inability of the state to shape the aspirations of individuals and to gather them up into collective political aims. 'For the first time,' says Ortega, the European is 'checked in his projects, economic, political, intellectual, by the limits of his own country' (p. 109).

He looks to a new European state to measure up to the new tasks. Fukuyama resorts to a Platonic idea of *thymos*, a vital drive for recognition, as the vehicle for a new historical collective movement. For Spengler it was the race. The deep assumption for them all was that the fate of the state and individual identity and direction in life had been intrinsically interwoven in the modern era.

Spengler and Ortega wrote under the impact of the First World War and registered decline in the European context. But they each actually looked forward to the revival of Europe in new political form, Spengler celebrating the emergence of Caesarism in Germany, linked with socialism and imperialism until the year 2000. Cecil Rhodes, with his slogan 'expansion is everything', provided for him the hero image of the future. Their faith in a transcendent historical mission for Europe only matched their contempt for the masses.

Neither saw the way the United States was to take up the modernizing mission in the twentieth century, nor did they appreciate that its history gave it a quintessential modern character beyond anything Europe possessed. When Fukuyama writes, he takes it for granted that the United States had acquired the leadership of the 'modern liberal project' (1992: 333), equating it with the liberal democratic state, which has homogenized its own people to love its system (pp. 214–15), fights only non-democratic states and drags mankind behind it like a 'long wagon train strung out along a road' (p. 338). The question he then finds unresolved is what possible worthwhile struggle can people find when the world is 'filled-up, so to speak, with liberal democracies' (p. 330).

But these are all modernist problem settings, imbued with the assumption that state, society and the individual need to exist in an indissoluble purposive bond and that anything less denotes a crisis. There is a sense today of a deep transition taking place, but the diagnoses are products of the older period, either modernity or nothing. For the making of one world has arisen neither out of the progress of reason nor from a single world empire. It is not the triumph of universalism. It has come about when the Modern Project has found limits in the globe. The result is a fragmentation of modernity and a shape to the world which few anticipated, but it is not the end of history.

4.2 Beyond Postmodernity

*Why the theory we need for the new age will both grasp
ephemerality and reach across ages and cultures*

Theorizing the new age means grasping the nature of the novelty by developing concepts. Theory is the reflexive discursive construction of reality, finding potential in the past and imagining alternative futures (cf. Lobkowicz 1967). Notwithstanding current emphasis on 'reflexive modernization' (Beck et al. 1994), it is not peculiarly modern. The major impetus came from the Greeks, but many cultures have contributed to a collective product which spans humanity.

Even if the vast bulk of theory stems from the just-in-time production process of the late modern academy, the end of the Modern Age will not stifle a growth with its roots so far in the past and in so many cultures. In any case, the coming of the Global Age only deprives modernity of its defining function within the Modern Age.[5] Modernity, and even modernization and modernism, find a subordinate place within the configuration of the new epoch, which derives its defining features from the global. So we can expect the linkage of theory with modernity to continue for some time yet.

None the less we certainly have to detach the idea of theory from modernity if we are to gain an appreciation of the epochal shift involved with the advent of the Global Age. We need to refresh awareness of theory's full scope, and challenge attenuated notions of theory which special projects of the Modern Age promoted. For instance, we need to contextualize and hence recognize the strict limitations of such hypertrophic theories of rationality as psychoanalysis, scientific management, rational choice theory and the socialist state.

The theory of the Global Age will redefine the human condition in the light of all time past as well as all present cultural experience. The technical reason of modernity will no longer occupy the prime place in the moral ordering of social relations. Indeed the problem with the prevalent late modernity idea is that it cannot escape from the modern sense that the social is determined by the technical.[6] Conversely, theorists such as Franco Ferrarotti who reject technological determinism appreciate the novelty of the current social transformation.[7]

The theorists of late modernity seek to stabilize a sense of direction in the flux of the present by holding on to the master narrative of technical advance. But this centring of the age on technology equally gives rise to the postmodern imagination. The postmoderns betray their modernity in their emphasis on technology but simultaneously deny the possibility of finding a human sense in the narrative of modernity.

From this point of view the postmodern imagination is indeed the hypertrophy of modern innovation rather than the expression of the new age. Human interaction and communication become mere adjuncts to the latest technical device, celebrated for its own meaning as a device among devices, just as Baudrillard's *America* (1988) grasps the meaning of artefacts without ever leaving the confines of the car. The American people cease to exist. It is a warning of tendencies which *are* immanent in modernity, rather than portents of a new age.

The strongest point for the postmodern imagination is that it penetrates the narrative of periodicity. But it betrays its modernity by being unable to envisage any other alternative except chaos. The postmoderns are the Red Guards of modernity. By virtue of theory, an idea which spans times and places, it is possible to reject the threat of the postmodern which the modern implicitly holds out against the claims of any rival.

At the same time we have to concede to the postmoderns that the greatest danger is the assimilation of the new to an older discourse, thus misrecognizing its novelty and indulging in a reassuring normalizing account. The postmoderns always make us acutely aware of the danger of dissolution, of being on the brink. To that extent we must accept their warnings and not ignore the sheer complexity and unintelligibility of much that passes in the present time.[8]

On the other hand we are not obliged to make the choice between modern, even late modern, and postmodern. The opposing representations of the present time are so contradictory, while their recognition of fundamental change is common to them, that we have to entertain another alternative altogether, namely that we have entered a new historical period.

But on our account of epochal shift this will generate a discourse which is in some respects discontinuous with the past, will produce self-descriptions which are incommensurable with those of the earlier period. In some respects the two ages will not speak to each other, and incomprehension between generations is one indicator of this.

We must fulfil two requirements if we are to grasp the nature of this change. First, the new age demands phenomenological description, a severely empirical register of what is happening to the frames of meaning in people's lives as globality, globalism and globalization take hold. Just as important as the negative aspects of modernity are the positive aspects of the new age, and the task which makes most sense is to register the sense they make to most. Effectively this means finding ways to record the way the experiences of people under globalized conditions operate through recognizable social forms and relate to cultural objects.[9]

Second, it equally requires us to hold on to the transhistorical and cross-cultural potential of theory. Theory will seek to grasp the nature of the new age, try to make sense of new experience, link individual fates with historical change. It will do it differently from the past, but not in such a way that continuity is lost, that peoples will lose the possibility of talking to peoples. Indeed, as global forces impel change at unprecedented rates, there will be ever increasing demand for new discourses on individual and collective ways of living. Yet, however dramatic the transformation through which we live, the theory of the new age will still be an account of what it is to be human.

These requirements were prefigured in Husserl's assertions about the unavoidable everyday response to the lifeworld. Our interest in its present reality and enquiring into past historical periods were similar activities (1937/1970: 143–8). He then proposed, not as a replacement for them but as an intellectual pursuit in its own right, to escape this natural attitude with his transcendental *epoche*. Husserl's ambition is on a par with the prophet's.[10]

The thrust of my account is essentially mundane. It tends to identify the way new experience recasts our understanding of old concepts and encourages us to develop new ones. It is a pragmatic universalism which remains sceptical about the possibilities of ever discovering timeless truth in human or natural affairs, while recognizing the necessity to affirm truths on the best understanding available to us in our own time.

4.3 The Conceptual Shift

How the prominence of 'global' in public discourse compels us to acknowledge a change in the social construction of reality

The grand narrative of the theorists of modernity can never permit us to enter a new age. For them the future has to be a continuation of past trends. Yet if we accept the strictures of the postmodernists, who are prepared at least to contemplate the end of an epoch, we cannot find a foundation for the new narrative. These are the intellectual obstacles placed in the way of the conceptualization of a new age. They represent the grip which modern/postmodern theory has on our imagination. We shall have to evade it.

Our best strategy, before we engage in theorizing the new age, is to seek a pre-theoretical intimation of it. Indeed, if the belief that a new epoch has emerged is based in reality, the evidence for it will be in people's experience and it will surface in an obvious everyday way rather than in philosophical or sociological treatises. Just as Berger's phenomenology of modernization found the directions of the time inscribed in everyday consciousness (Berger et al. 1973), in the same way, in the 1990s, we can listen to the new age in the street. Equally, just as the name for the Modern Age arose from the discourse of the period, so the name for the new epoch is already equally in the public mind. Can it be anything other than the 'Global Age'?

The end of the 1980s and beginning of the 1990s has seen an explosion in the use of 'global' and its associated terms. Its use is ubiquitous in advertising, job descriptions, mission statements, journalism and book titles.[11] This itself suggests a conceptual shift. Malcolm Waters has said that globalization is to the 1990s what postmodernism was to the 1980s (1995: 1). The fashionable terminology has changed. Even before we attend to the question of whether this reflects deeper change, we should explore both the new usage and what it has displaced.

For a start we can attend to the derivations from 'global'. Ever since McLuhan's 'global village' (1962), 'global' has undergone a progressive amplification through the suffixes '-ism', '-ity' and '-ization'.[12] These are conventional linguistic markers which confer both theoretical character and objective quality on an idea. They suggest the constitution of processes, ideologies and objects in their own right. 'The global' is no longer the accidental quality of something else; it becomes something in itself.

To make this clearer let us look at the example of the elaboration of 'nation'. It expands into 'national', 'nationalism', 'nationality', 'nationalization'. Of course each term is embedded in a particular historical, political discourse. The connotations of 'nationality', an imputed property of individuals in the first instance, and 'nationalization', a process of increasing state control, betray the contested and not purely logical character of the relations between state, nation and individual in Western thought.

It is the same with global. It refers back to globe, but the subtleties of the expansion of the idea depend on the different place given to human agency in a global as opposed to a national context. The nation occupies a contested natural/ideal status; the globe has an undisputed materiality, however far removed it is from the daily behaviour of those who refer to it in their thoughts and deeds.

The elaboration of modern is different again, but in this case because there is no material referent at all, nothing to equate with nation or globe. Modern is a quality without abiding substance. Modernization relates to modern as globalization does to global, but if global relates to globe, what does modern relate to? The answer is nothing material, because the modern is the abstract quality of a historical period, in which the rational and the new form a dynamic alliance, subordinating nature, human or otherwise.

There is no material object or social entity from which modern derives, which is why, if we want to understand the social agency underlying modernity, we have to turn to the nation-state and capitalist organization. We can thus see why the nation and the modern are conjoint concepts, and equally how the global is a challenge to both simultaneously.

The global, or the abstract quality, globality, both transcends and intrudes on the national in territorial terms; it replaces the time aspect of the modern with a spatial reference, which however is indeterminate. Globalism operates to temper the particularism of nationalism, while decentring values from human to material referents. It counters the abstract nature of modernism. For both rationalism and the value placed on novelty it substitutes open and pragmatic communication between people and peoples and interaction with nature.

These are preliminary remarks only on the linguistic frame which concepts like the national, the modern and the global occupy, not an elaborated comparison between them. But they are sufficient to show that the global has purchase on social and cultural reality broadly equivalent to those other concepts, while sufficiently contradictory to them to indicate that they do not coexist easily at any one time and place. On the contrary, in so far as they represent dominant features of a historical period, the global and the modern or national already appear more as alternatives than complementary.

If we attend to the linguistic markers of the Modern Age and the Global Age, the parallelism between their uses alerts us equally to the way those epochs have a complex unity which far outdistances the qualities of modernity or globality. Just as we have to acknowledge that the forces of the anti-modern and non-rational are equally characteristics of the Modern Age, so we find in the Global Age that its shape is as much determined by the anti-global as by the global. Indeed it is the tension between them which defines its character.

For this reason, when we consider configurations of the Global Age we will not be able to see them as simply an extension of globalization. It is the assumption that they are which causes so many misreadings of the coming age. It is a mistake equivalent to seeing the Modern Age as a period of rational progress without recognizing the social contradictions of capitalism. At the same time, unless we acknowledge the dynamics unleashed by globalization we will not appreciate how the counterforces arise, just as capitalism's development is not understood without taking into account underlying technical advances.

4.4 Globality, Global Forces and Globalism

The glossary of the global provides an entry into the descriptive and analytical concepts for the new age

The term we employ to refer to the total set of inscriptions of, or references to the global is *globality*. Globality is to the global, the Global Age and globalism as modernity is to the modern, the Modern Age and modernism – at least grammatically. Indeed, one of the reasons it is so easy to identify the 'Global Age' is that it simply completes the series which begins with global and proceeds through globalization.

The parallelism, however, breaks down at a semantic level; and if it did not, the claims to a transformation would be weak. It is not possible, for instance, to talk of individuals being global in the same way as we can talk of them being modern, although the aspiration to individual globality can be recognized as a peculiar distorted consciousness which seeks to assimilate the global to the modern by making the global into the latest fad or fashion. But there is not going to be a dominant global personality in the way social scientists have conceived of a pure type of modern personality. And that is one of the reasons the Global Age presents challenges to the individual. We will come to that later.

'Global' references inhabit different planes of meaning from 'modern'. Modern is above all a time reference, highlights innovation and obsolescence, sifts and rejects the useless old, applauds purpose and control and thence expansion. Its space reference is an outcome of its production and consumption of time. 'Global' is above all a space reference, the product of the location of the earth in space, a material celebration of the natural environment on which human beings depend, the evocation of the concrete wholeness or completeness of existence, embracing humanity rather than dividing it.

Entrepreneurs draw on a common stock of meanings arising out of lived experience. Even if the product comes to symbolize it, globality was not invented by Coca-Cola assembling a multi-ethnic choir on a hillside. It was a pre-existing ideal resource of which free use was made. It is a hallmark of successful capitalism that it exploits for profit what was hitherto common property but, because it was held in common, was not even recognized as a resource.[13] But the commercialization of ideal meanings, such as those in love and sexuality, can be as damaging to them as the appropriation of natural resources can be to the environment. 'Global' itself now carries connotations of the commercialization of humanity.

'Globality' leaves open the question of human agency; indeed, like modernity, it is the objectification of the outcomes of human interaction with the world and therefore takes on an independence, not only in respect of individuals but even with respect to humanity as a whole. Science and rationality in modernity take on an inhuman, juggernaut quality, as Giddens (1990) has suggested. Similarly, globality brings humanity under the thrall of natural forces. Whether human beings individually or collectively can make a difference is left unresolved in the idea of globality. We need to define *globalism* and *global forces* if we want to highlight these further distinctions.

Where human beings assume obligations towards the world as a whole, where they espouse values which take the globe as their frame or reference point, there we can speak of globalism. It has its most obvious expression in the green movement, in the emphasis on global ecology, the finitude of natural resources and the need for sustainable development.

Globalism has penetrated other areas too, health, the struggles for women's rights and human rights generally. In this way it has merged with older modern movements which relied on universalistic principles and notions of international harmony and peace. Universalism, the belief in principles true for all times and places, especially vital in the area of human rights, and internationalism, the belief in the community of humanity, were key ingredients in the expansion of modernity. But both contained an optimistic progressiveness as well as abstract idealism which have often appeared pious and unrealistic compared with the later material concerns of globalism.

When confronted with the finitude of the globe and the realities of global forces, power and markets especially, the older movements have been absorbed in more pragmatic and direct involvement in struggles for redistribution, for aid, to redress biases in international institutions and more generally to pursue special interests on a global scale. The globe has become the real frame and field of operations for movements of all kinds; in relation to this arise regional and local definitions of values and approaches. In this respect the global movements have become the counterpart of, and seek to influence, institutions which operate at the global level.

The international institutions which developed after the Second World War settlement arose partly out of these older ideals and partly from accommodations between great powers. But today the managers of these institutions abide by the practical necessity of taking the globe as the frame of reference and find its material reality the inevitable check on universalistic principles, as well as on national ambitions. In that sense globalism is always a response to realities, a bringing down to earth of universalistic principles in the face of global forces. It becomes equally a categorical imperative: wherever there are deeds to be done, do them in the light of the needs of the world as a whole.

Globalism itself brings to the forefront of attention what is meant by the idea of 'forces'. These were a key concept in early Marxist thought, but lost their centrality in its later idealist versions. But they are equally important in market ideologies and in all thought which recognizes that human projects are subject to pressures and constraints which are unavoidable and only partially controllable.

Forces may arise in the natural environment, in the human organism, or as undirected outcomes of collective action or of aggregated individual acts. Crucially they do not respect human boundaries, whether territorial, moral or aesthetic. Boundary setting is one of the main ways in which human beings seek to control forces, whether it is a barrage across an estuary, an age for sexual consent, capital/lending ratios for banks, or a limit on alcohol consumption.

But because forces breach human boundaries, the quest for their limits encompasses the globe as a whole. Markets work on the principle of potential supply and demand from anonymous third parties. The supply of any one commodity locally is ultimately affected by the total demand for that commodity anywhere, whether you know the persons buying or selling or not.

The erosion of soil on any one part of the world's surface correspondingly increases the pressure on other parts. The emission of CFC gases from aerosols and refrigerators has long contributed to putting the world's atmosphere at risk. Only when there is an immediate prospect of the Asian economies following the course of the West is the problem seen as a global one. But the globality of the forces at work has always been present.

This is where globalization has effectively altered the framework of human action. The global interconnectedness of human relations brings awareness of the globe in its train and makes it possible to conceptualize global risks. Globality becomes an ever present aspect of human calculations once the limits of action are the globe itself. Ulrich Beck's coinage of the 'risk society' (1986/1992) seeks to reflect the importance of the translation of risk from being purely a local matter for individual response to a global concern of profound political significance.

A transformation has taken place and the word which captures that is globalization, conveying as it does a change from one state to another. It is now the most used marker for a profound social and cultural transition. But time and again it is used as explanation, rather than as something to be analysed, explored and explained. The appeal to globalization as the explanation of almost any contemporary change in any sector of life pervades academic accounts and journalistic commentary. As such it takes on an almost magical quality, an intellectual alchemist's stone to provide universal enlightenment. But this indiscriminate use reflects the limits of current understanding rather than its extent. We need critical conceptual analysis of the idea of globalization to appreciate how and why it has this appeal and to allow us to extend our thinking beyond ritual invocations of some new and mysterious force.

4.5 Defining Globalization

Finding that when general usage is confused and variable we are forced to make difficult conceptual choices

All '-ization' verbal nouns imply change. The decades-long debate over 'urbanization' provides us with a prototype discussion of '-ization' in the mode of social change. It has variously been used to refer to the increasing population of cities, to the growth in the number of cities, to the impact of cities on the surrounding environment, to the effects of cities on people's lives. Yet these changes are not independent of each other and urbanization has come to be used to cover the sum total. Instead of remaining a technical term it is often used as a label for a broad process of change.[14]

The problem which then arises, as with all the other '-ization' terms associated with modernity, is that this brings a heavy theoretical loading. A 'process' is a sequence of change governed by scientific laws with a determinate end-point. Using the term 'process' for historical change elides the difference between open-ended transformations and repeatable, predictable sequences. The fate of modernity has long left 'scientific' theories of urbanization, democratization, industrialization where they belong, as relics of the self-understanding of a bygone age, with their validity limited to the extent that they conveyed useful accounts of trends in their time.

We should be just as wary of the idea of globalization having some inherent direction, even though we have to note that it is often used in that way. Just as urbanization was recognized as a fundamental change by a wide variety of people in public life, as well as by scholars in different disciplines, so globalization has become a focus of concern for groups as diverse as politicians, historians, geographers, businessmen, management consultants, economists and literary critics. The sheer extent of this concern requires exploration. But to impute any scientifically determinable direction in a process called globalization is quite a different matter.

The term 'globalization' binds the syntax of the global and its derivations into a ramifying set of meanings. They are thus effectively entwined in an unfolding story over time. It conveys a widespread sense of transformation of the world. But this tendency to blanket coverage should in itself indicate how unlikely it is to have a precise analytic set of reference points.

The social sciences have responded to the demand for control of nature and society through providing clarity of concepts, precise data and testable propositions. But that clarity and precision is often highly context and time bound. 'Globalization' appears to revive modernity's flagging hold on reality. It carries with it the favoured 'process' connotations and expands the frontiers of relevance beyond the narrow time and spatial boundaries of modernity. To that extent it has become the equivalent to the Marxist lodestar, the scientific theory of historical change.

In part this is an old dilemma: the tension between science and history which has generated fundamental discussion of method in the social sciences. One of the great appeals of Marxism was its claim to have solved the problem of rendering historical transformation intelligible and controllable. Historical materialism provided accounts of the past which appeared to make it amenable to logic and scientific accumulation of data. As for the present, it suggested that history could be controlled by being made. Either way social science appeared to fulfil the promise of control. The end of the Modern Project has left both Marxist and modernization theories without purchase on contemporary history.

For the bulk of the social sciences a chasm has opened up between historical explanation, faithful to the flux of the past, and the models of mathematical social sciences, serving the management and administration of state and capital. Only the past is real, while the present becomes counterfactual. 'Globalization' appears to fill a gap. It reintroduces grand narrative by evoking older, not simply Marxist, attempts to provide an account of underlying processes in historical change. At the same time it brings history into the present. It relativizes models of invariant relations between defined variables. What price statistical tables for GNP, migration, balance of payments when national boundaries come and go? The present now becomes reality in flux.

At the same time the real changes in the world provide the most direct challenge to established paradigms in the social sciences since the upsurge in Marxist theory in the West in the 1960s. At that time much of the response to Marxism was dictated by investments in the Cold War. That made it possible for dominant Western paradigms to reject the demands for intelligible, meaningful accounts of contemporary social life as leftist, even Soviet-inspired, propaganda. Sociology above all suffered from this imputation of guilt by association.

We should, however, be very wary of claiming for 'globalization' the quality of being a 'process' which explains the social transformation around. If we do, we repeat the modernist errors and produce a dated modern theory for the Global Age. We should rely on more sober forms of conceptual analysis which go back long before modernity in order to get our thinking straight. In the first place it will be useful to attend to a formal definition of globalization. We will then be able to turn to the complex issues of interpreting historical change today which are our main concern.

With these points in mind we need to take up the challenge of the idea which appears to transcend the specific and local and to bring it down to earth with a definition:

GLOBALIZATION

1 Making or being made global:
   (a) in individual instances
      (i) by the active dissemination of practices, values, technology and other human products throughout the globe
      (ii) when global practices and so on exercise an increasing influence over people's lives
      (iii) when the globe serves as a focus for, or a premise in shaping, human activities
      (iv) in the incremental change occasioned by the interaction of any such instances;
   (b) seen as the generality of such instances;
   (c) such instances being viewed abstractly.
2 A process of making or being made global in any or all of the senses in (1).
3 The historical transformation constituted by the sum of particular forms and instances of (1).

These formulations are nuanced to do justice both to the ambiguities and complexities bound up in the daily use of the term and to the scholarly issues I have already mentioned. They are more than a preliminary orientation. They are more than purely technical terms, arbitrarily defined for clarity's sake. So they are not an ideal type in Max Weber's sense. They seek to grasp the essential features of globalization as expressed in an informed general usage and set them out in an ordered and coherent way. They do not affirm the scientific validity of the ideas. Indeed it ought to be clear from my account that I think that meaning (2) is both widely current and misguided. It is further not identical with meaning (3).

This is by no means the only way in which we could approach a definition. At the same time it is important at this juncture not to be deflected into a discussion of social scientific methodology. While such discussions have important uses, the position this author takes is that methodology is not prior to method; rather it is the *ex post facto* justification of what proves to be good practice. In consequence it is the demonstration of the fruits of this approach in the text which will convince anybody of the worth of this definition, not an abstract account of the logic behind it.

For the moment let us note that our formulations have antecedents stretching back centuries. They employ distinctions between three kinds of definition with quite different functions. The first is *analytical*, attaching to specific facets of social life, which are replicated in innumerable different ways under contemporary conditions. It is capable of generalization and being referred to as an abstraction. The second we can call *realist,* and that I apply to the process notion in so far as it contains the sense that there is an underlying, subsisting sequence of change which forms the real basis of the variety of forms of globalization. The third is concrete and *historical,* referring to a once-and-for-all transformation which takes place in a definite period of world history, as with, say, the Renaissance or the Industrial Revolution.

'Globalization' is used in all ways, sometimes to refer to abstract conceptual elements which enter into concrete social relations, sometimes to refer to a complex set of social changes which have taken place over historical time. The former properly may be subject to social scientific treatment; the latter belongs to the language of contemporary history and political commentary. When they are conflated in realist definitions, modernist confusions arise.

Indeed it was the conflation of the two types of definition and the methods which underlay them which led to the errors of Marxism. They arose out of the conviction that an analysis of the abstract laws of capitalism would provide adequate projections of the future of capitalist society. At the same time it was precisely the recognition that both types of account were necessary for an understanding of the world which provided Marxists with huge advantages in terms of the perceived general public relevance of their work compared with the confined specialisms of their opponents.

The major test for post-Marxist social theory and historiography is to explore the manifold ways in which analytical and historical accounts enter into any worthwhile narrative for our times without ever conflating them into realist ones. That is easier said than done. Accounts of 'capitalism' confused the abstract elements of a theoretical framework with the complex reality of a real economy and way of life.

It is hardly surprising that opponents of globalization, both of the concept and the reality, should level the same charge that was made against Marxist accounts of capitalism, that accounts of globalization function only within an ideological outlook. But opponents of Marxism time and again missed the centrality of the theme of capitalism to people's lives because they could not get beyond its ideological confusion to matters of substance.

Globalization is the most significant development and theme in contemporary life and social theory to emerge since the collapse of Marxist systems. It would be ironic if its critics again missed the substance of the issues of post-Marxist theory because they think their ideology critique guarantees them a superior social theory. The challenge which globalization poses to contemporary history and theory is as fundamental as the continuing effort to understand capitalism, as theory and social system. Moreover the two tasks are not unrelated.

4.6 Indeterminacy and Ambiguity in the Analytic Concept of Globalization

Why we have to be careful both not to expect too much of a good concept and not to discard one because it falls short of perfection

The analytic concept of the global can never be as precise as that of capital. This is where the comparison we have just drawn highlights the ultimate and unavoidable indeterminacy of any analytic theory of globalization. But if we were to end our concern for the meaning of globalization because of these limitations we would be perpetrating an error and attitude akin to terminating interest in art or religion because they are imprecise. We need to pursue analysis to its furthest useful point, not going beyond that, but not falling short either.

We can at an early stage indicate the outer limits of the usefulness of the globalization concept. They concern talk of the globe as part of discourse on society and culture. As a natural object the globe can find a determinate place within astronomy, geology or the biological sciences. In geography and environmental science its qualities become less determinate. But as soon as we speak of the field of human action and ideas, which is where the idea of globalization has found its place, then there are inherent limits to being able to talk of the globe in any literal sense.

Globalization discussions rarely focus on a literal sense of the globe. What would they amount to, anyway? If they were to concern the qualities of the earth as globe and their significance for human activities, they might include the following: the importance of circumnavigation, round-the-world flights or orbiting the earth. Certainly the image of the globe has been potent for the artistic imagination since Copernicus and Shakespeare. The Globe Theatre didn't get its name for nothing. Similarly the image of the orbiting satellite is as important a marker for the Global Age as was Magallanes' voyage for the Modern.

Even so, in globalization discussion the fact that the surface of the earth is shaped as a globe is of less significance than the finitude of that space. If we talk of the globe entering into the assumptions of human activities, we are not appealing to some 'spherical turn', but to the way that all that lives and moves and has its being on the surface of the earth has become the conscious frame of reference for many of the decisions both of international bureaucrats and of the ordinary citizen and consumer.

We have to be clear then that 'thinking globally', 'going global', were, are and always will be metaphors for a range of related meanings. No matter how important those meanings are, because they are referenced in this metaphorical way there will be an irreducible indeterminacy and ambiguity to the discussion of globalization which our definition cannot convey.[15]

This is not to diminish their importance. The Renaissance was a great metaphor holding together a disparate range of phenomena, whose connections were best understood this way. The globe metaphor has a vital significance for indicating in the broadest sense both the full and actual amplitude of human activities as they are distributed on earth and at the same time a disregard for any of the divisions which human beings might establish between themselves on that surface. From that point of view the transcendence of nation-state boundaries is the most potent of the meanings of globalization.[16]

But our recognition of the metaphorical nature of the reference to the globe brings us also close to the root indeterminacy of the idea of globalization. For 'finitude', 'completeness', 'transcendence' are clearly abstract and ideal points, never achieved in actuality. The future global despot intent on completing the globalization of the world could set its whole population to work to traverse every metre of its surface without ever achieving it, or, more importantly in the case of crazy dreams, ever knowing whether it had been achieved. The anxious consumer, scanning the ingredients on the packaged food, can never know that each individual item and the morsel in that package was produced entirely without cruelty to animals somewhere, harm to the world's environment or injustice to human beings.

The lack of both a determinate end-point to globalization and the impossibility of arriving at a complete enumeration of its impact has a consequence which is equally important for analysis. It is not possible to indicate a single route when the goal is ill-defined in both time and space. We don't know when we will reach it or where it is.

In practice then globalization is always relative to some past state of affairs, say to nineteenth-century colonialism, or to a standard which aspires to something less than world relevance, say the rules of the Academie Française, or German social insurance. A European common currency clearly transcends national boundaries. It might be a step towards a world currency, which could appear to be the ultimate in globalization, the transcendence of all national boundaries. But even as the idea is realized so alternative futures can be conceived – local money currencies, alternative media for exchange, competing world currencies. Is a world with more than one world currency more or less globalized?

There is no inherent logic to globalization which suggests that a particular outcome necessarily will prevail. Since we are in a world of more or less rather than all or nothing, for the foreseeable future, rather than always or never, there is in the concept of globalization nothing which ensures its perpetual advance. Both the motives and technology for developing private and localized worlds, as separate as possible from the teeming billions, are easily conceivable.

In addition to this inherent indeterminacy there is a problem of ambiguity. It will always be open to question whether globalization brings the possibility closer of anyone broadcasting anything to any part of the globe, or the possibility of everyone in the world receiving the same programme at any one moment of time. The debates surrounding homogenization versus diversification or hybridization reflect precisely this ambiguity. They concern the issue of whether culture and all forms of social activity are becoming more standardized, or whether multiple cultural contacts lead to an ever increasing variety of new forms.

It is an ever-recurring debate.[17] One attempt to resolve it is to use a semiotic argument on the nature of communication and to say that both are necessarily happening simultaneously but at different levels: for instance there is a standardization of channels of communication, but diversification of contents. Another is to argue from a perspectivist standpoint, as Don Gifford did in his account of the paradoxes of quantity and scale which arose out of the 1851 Great Exhibition at the Crystal Palace. The quantity and variety of exhibits was so great that the total effect was one of sameness (Gifford 1990: 129).

Each argument supplies insight and understanding. But they do not remove the paradox. Indeed they are important precisely because they enable us to live with the realization that ambiguity may be a necessary and inherent aspect when we reference some concepts. And this enables us equally to recognize the necessity to use metaphor for grasping some realities. The fault lies not in our imaginations but in the texture of the human condition that a metaphor may be the best way to convey its open-ended quality. This is particularly the case when we seek to grasp transformation over time.

If we turn to our analytic definition of globalization we can see how this is the case. For we could easily present the variants we identified in definition 1.a.i–iii as phases in a process, with the global entering in at different points. Very easily then we can move from this point to seeing an inner coherence in definition 1.b and from there to assuming the reality of a process as in definition 2. But these are huge leaps, because to begin with we don't even know, just from a reference to globalization, which one of aspects (i), (ii) or (iii) apply, let alone whether they are part of a process.

Whether any or all of them hang together at any one time will depend on factors which are extraneous to globalization, like the concentration of capital, the strength of democratic forces or the development of technology. Globalization as such is as much a dependent as a driving force and can hardly provide the answer to which of these prevails at any one time.

This effectively is the same kind of message Roland Robertson provides when he stresses that globalization also involves a kind of localization. The global by virtue of its scope can be located anywhere. He has therefore advocated the merits of a term originating in Japanese marketing, 'glocalization', for the localization of the global.[18] But what kind of globalization does not have local impact?

This ambiguity is inherent and necessary. To seek to remove it rather than work with it is the fault of both positivist and idealist versions of social science. The former seeks to divorce ideas from reality, the latter tries to deduce reality from ideas. The working historian or social scientist employs ideas pragmatically, accepting their necessary place in accounts and their inherent limits in the face of changing reality. We may thus overcome the inherent ambiguity of static analytic concepts in sciences of social life. But does this mean we should move from globalization as analytic concept to the account of a historical transformation? We turn to this question now.

4.7 Globalization as Historical Transformation

Why we should reject the idea of the 'Globalization Process' as a law-governed change but recognize globalization in sum as an overall historical transformation

Our analytic concept of globalization serves many uses. We use it to label the spread of the religious ecstasy of the 'Toronto Blessing', or the information technology concentration of Silicon Valley, or the development of London's Canary Wharf, or buying a Big Mac in Beijing, all as instances of globalization (definitions 1.a.i–iii). We can consider the transformations of the pharmaceutical industry or the international capital markets, or the development of the Internet as interactive outcomes of incremental change (definition 1.a.iv).

These are all particular changes in historical time. Now let us consider them generically, treating them as representative instances of the same phenomenon (definition 1.b). This is how the leading proponents of the idea of globalization illustrate their theories of it. We may, as Robertson (1992) and Giddens (1991) have done, find that in general globalization involves a relativization and destabilization of old identities, whether of nation-states, communities or individuals, or, like Hall (1992), we may stress the creation of new hybrid entities, transnational phenomena like diasporic communities. We may find, as the OECD studies (1993) have done, that it is flexible transnational sourcing, production and marketing which mark the globalized firm.

In this way, in spite of what I have called the indeterminacy and ambiguity of the concept, a new narrative for our times has been established, breaking away from the frame provided by time-honoured modern concepts like nation-state, organization and community and enabling us to highlight processes which previously were either embryonic or unnoticed (the difference obviously being both important and contested).

But that narrative is not the result of an inductive gathering of instances. For our theorists it normally emerges from an already formed theoretical account of modernity, or of the development of world society, or of late capitalism. In other words there is an abstract concept there related to a more general theoretical field (definition 1.c). Very often this merges with definition 2. Even the empirically based studies like those of the OECD sketch a developmental process from low to high international integration and see it as a transformation of the world economy.

The embeddedness of these narratives in past theory leads them to see a generalized 'Globalization Process', a generic transformation of the contemporary world. But by this intellectual decision we are in danger of moving from science to myth.[19] Moreover, paradoxically, by assimilating globalization to a past discourse on modernization, the profundity of the shift is minimized.[20]

We have already seen how the analytical concept of globalization is fraught with indeterminacy and ambiguity. There is no warrant therefore for assuming that diasporic communities, just-in-time production and negotiated gender identity are necessarily linked in the same comprehensive and relentless process. They may well be related to different aspects of globalization which even run counter to each other. We will have assumed the existence of a new entity dependent on the metaphorical use of the term 'global'. Those different senses of globalization may relate to relatively independent processes such as technological development, concentration of capital, modernization and rationalization. The complexity of their linkages and the difficulty in determining the direction of causation between them are such that we have to be ultra-cautious before we interpret them as belonging to some underlying unidirectional process.

Should we therefore, as some have suggested, discard all talk of globalization because of the danger of fabricating a myth, a new grand narrative making sense of history, serving ideological ends? Some would see it as a new version of the belief in progress of the unity of humanity serving the end of the expansion of capital.

But this is an intellectual strategy equivalent to the one we have already criticized, namely ignoring accounts of changes of great substantive significance because they are associated with a misguided methodology. There is an alternative strategy for dealing with instances of globalization and their mutually determining and determined factors. We see them as part of a non-directional period of historical change, characterized by globality but with an open future. Globalization then is the term which becomes prevalent in a transitional period in history, not a single overall process of change. It characterizes the beginning of the Global Age simply because the weight of reference to globality displaces modernity from prior position in characterizing the configuration, but it has no inherent direction or necessary end-point. In this respect it is unlike modernity. As we have argued, the end-point of modernity is when it arrives at the exhaustion of the Modern Project; but globality is not a project.

The difference in emphasis is profound. Not only is globalization not just a continuation of modernization: it isn't a lawlike process either. The contrast we are drawing is as great as that between alternative explanations of the experience of, say, elderly people today, either in terms of a new process of ageing, or in terms of their altered place in social structure and culture. In the former case we appeal to a scientific law-governed sequence of change. In the latter case we are concerned with aggregate effects, with individual responses to contingent changes in environment and milieu, and with the communication of these responses in social interaction. In these we can see the configuration of a unique historical period.

If we use 'globalization' to refer to the aggregate of historical changes over a determinate period of history, this is quite different from referring to some developmental logic. In this sense we address a phenomenon equivalent to the Renaissance, Reformation, Enlightenment or the Age of Imperialism. All those countless instances in which the global is taken into everyday life, where national economies merge with a global economy, where satellites provide news on the world worldwide, where protests erupt in one part of the world about conditions in another – putting them all together and recognizing the way in which the one reinforces the other we can see a transformation which is of our time and unique. It may not penetrate absolutely every aspect of social life, but its scope and pervasiveness is sufficient for us to say that it both represents the specificity and dominates our experience of our time.

Writing about the present in this way is what Karl Jaspers was doing in speaking of the epochal events of 1945 (see the epigraph to this chapter). He was writing in the context of an account of universal history, the story of humanity. There is no reason, to my mind, to change our view on that event in the light of later experience, only to recognize the equal significance of the events of 1989 and to modify his view of the nature of the new age into which we have entered. It is a mark of that whole period of time as the culmination of modernity that he felt the future of humanity depended on the way human beings treated each other. The revelations of the Holocaust and the engagement with socialism were sufficient to confirm him in that late modern view.

The story of the transition out of the Modern and into the Global Age between 1945 and 1989 is precisely the shift in recognition that the future does not depend just on humanity's relations to itself, but also on its relations with nature. By 1975 one of the period's most perceptive commentators was summing up the change in those terms. Ralf Dahrendorf, who had made his initial mark on the times by theorizing the old modern conflict, that between social classes (1959), declared that expansion was at an end as a means to solve social problems and that the new problem was survival with justice. To meet this challenge required a break with the past, a change in the 'theme or subject of history' (Dahrendorf 1975: 70). Since then the new subject has imposed itself beyond any one person's or group's initiative. It is 'the globe'. But its thematization has not yet recognized the profundity of the break. For that to happen we need to look critically at the narrative habits behind which modernity has sought to conceal the demise of the Modern Age.

5

Historical Narrative for the New Age

5.1 Historicism Revisited

Why the new writing on globalization has to take us back to old debates on how history should be written

One of the decisive intellectual interventions in the middle of the twentieth century was Karl Popper's attack on historicism (1957), by which he meant any doctrine which sought to identify laws of history or some inherent direction from which it was possible both to identify the future and to establish a basis for action in the present. His target was mainly Marxism but also versions of the idea of progress which associated the growth of rationality with the actions of an enlightened state.

Paradoxically, Popper's own views about the impossibility of predicting the future were based on the paramount position he gave to human knowledge and the centrality of human beings in historical narrative. According to him there was no way to prevent knowledge of a predicted future being used to defeat or promote it. Indeterminacy was an inbuilt principle in so far as history was genuinely an account of human affairs.

Unfortunately it was a position which led Popper to devalue historical narrative altogether.[1] Just because we cannot fit the whole course of history to laws, there is no reason why we should not point to an enduring pattern of life lasting centuries, or point to the world historical significance of events like the Russian Revolution.[2]

Popper was a rationalist and it is bound to be provocative to hold him to be in part the initiator of the series of intellectual interventions in the latter half of the century which minimized the place of reason in human life. But effectively Popper circumscribed the potentialities of reason for tracing the course of history. He rightly emphasized human motives and situational contingencies, but offered no guidelines for establishing historical continuities. When Kuhn (1962) followed by emphasizing sociological factors leading to the rise and fall of scientific paradigms, and then Rorty (1980) asserted the impossibility of finding universal principles on which to ground science, it appeared to follow that the idea of finding a pattern or thread which made sense of history was equally nugatory, a consequence drawn famously by Lyotard's (1979) announcement of the end of the Grand Narrative. All went towards shaping the postmodern mood, the dissolution of the certitudes of the modern period.

Against this background the new globalization theory may well appear as an incongruous throwback to an earlier time, an attempt to breathe life into an extinct way of thought. Some of its leading exponents have tended to see globalization as a continuation of a master narrative with its beginnings in modernity or even earlier.

For the postmodernists these accounts appear as a crass misrecognition of their message. It was not the purpose of those who announced the end of modernity to usher in a new age. It was rather even to suggest that accounts of the past in terms of an inner logic of modernity were as misleading as projections of it into the future. The message was one of the dissolution of a sense of the direction of history.

There is no doubt that the new globalization theory makes assertions which are vulnerable to postmodern critique. The Cambridge social theorist Anthony Giddens sees globalization as the inherent thrust of modernity towards greater interconnectedness worldwide. He writes, 'Globalization can thus be defined as the intensification of worldwide social relations which link distant localities in such a way that local happenings are shaped by events occurring many miles away and vice versa' (1990: 64). His account becomes part of his general theory of the transformation of social relationships in the late stage of modernity.

Roland Robertson, Professor of Sociology in Pittsburgh, who has sought to theorize globalization for over a decade, takes issue with Giddens. He calls his account 'an updated and overly abstract version of the convergence thesis – homogenized modern man injected with a special dose of phenomenological reflexivity' (Robertson 1992: 145). For Robertson globalization is above all a cultural process in which the unity of the world is driven by global consciousness. Effectively it is a process which has been continuing for centuries. Giddens concentrates on the effects of technology on relationships, Robertson on achievement of human aspiration, but for both globalization is a social transformation which is the outcome of a long preliminary process.

It is the language of process applied to historical change which makes the accounts of both Giddens and Robertson historicist in Popper's sense. The notion 'modernity is inherently globalizing' treats an outcome as a necessary product of a process, as if it had inner laws of development. It suggests an end-state as the point to which the earlier episodes are all directed. The analysis is then teleological.

We need to disentangle the issues involved with some clear distinctions. In the first place there are forces for expansion associated with modernity which are thwarted when all the territory of the world is effectively enclosed. But it is the finitude of the globe and not the logic of a process which brings this turning point. It would, however, be pedantic to deny Ortega's or Toynbee's or Robertson's usage of 'unification of the world' as a description of the events which led up to this state of affairs. We can additionally acknowledge that to some degree it has been a humanly willed outcome.

But we should distinguish what leads up to this world unification from the globalization which effectively happens *at the point of* unification, when the globe as a whole becomes the material reference point for individual and collective actors. The consequences which flow from this are so different from the change sequences involved in modernization that we could just as well say that 'globality is inherently demodernizing'.

Globalization evidently depends on past accumulations of capital and knowledge, on vastly enhanced communications technology, on international political and financial institutions. The aspiration for world order has numerous anticipations. But at the moment when the globe as an entity is realized, a whole range of new factors comes into play.[3]

Among those factors we may mention the loosening hold of the nation-state on individuals, the end of the superpower divisions of the Cold War, the speculative crises of world capital markets, the world energy crisis and global warming. Each one of these has its analysts and prophets who have signalled to the rest of the world its spectacular significance. Fukuyama (1992) has asserted that history ended with the triumph of Western liberal capitalism; the Club of Rome brought to consciousness the world's resources as an inherent limit on growth (Meadows et al. 1972). Wallerstein (1974–89) followed Marx in drawing the consequences of world social transformation as a result of the expansion of capital.

We can only construe these outcomes as an inevitable culmination of past trends if we forget the contingent fact of the globe's materiality and forget that each has been dependent on the other.[4] Take these into account and the inevitability collapses. Without the ozone layer, no global warming or perhaps no life on earth anyway; no oil, or abundant oil, no oil crisis; no nuclear weapons, perhaps no Cold War;[5] no computer chips, no world capital markets; perhaps without Christianity there would have been no secular ideology of progress.[6]

Human beings make their history but not under circumstances of their own choosing, and the finitude of the earth is one of those circumstances which has become a central concern at the juncture where it appears as a limit to human activities. The sheer accident in human terms that the world is a globe, with a certain surface of land and sea, with a definite distribution of natural resources, is not the culmination of a process; rather it arrests anything that might have been a process. Globalization, far from being the end to which human beings have aspired, is the termination of modern ways of organizing life which they took for granted. The global shift is a transformation, not a culmination.

This is the deeper implication of the globe as reference point. Factors resistant to human aspiration, natural limits to the realization of projects, arise out of the globe as preconditions for any human endeavour. It is therefore those who appreciate the ecological limits on human action who are the least inclined to see globalization as the outcome of human inventiveness or values.

Jeremy Rifkin (1992), who proclaims a new biospheric politics to replace geopolitics, has characterized the modern drive to enclose the natural world as a vain quest for freedom from environmental dangers. The conquest of nature and the expansion of territory have each come to a shuddering halt, the former by generating consequences such as global warming which could mean a premature end to humanity, the latter by exhausting the earth's surface. Both projects have been essential aspects of modernity. To that extent the global represents an endpoint, a culmination only in the sense of a day of reckoning when the costs of reckless expansion have to be met.

Others in the ecological movement also see globalization, the appeal to the global, as carrying with it the demand to organize the world as a whole, the ultimate requirement and self-defeating nature of the expansion of Western imperialism. Wolfgang Sachs, too, sees the aspiration for planetary management as the final reversal of the process begun by Columbus; it is now the expansion of the Western nations which has become the problem to be solved (1993: 20).

There are two reasons why the ecologists write better history than the sociologists. The first is that they contextualize the human achievement, put it into a natural context and allow for contingencies outside human control. The second is that their direct interest in the impact of human beings on nature encourages them to imagine hypothetical outcomes to different courses of action to deal with potential threats and thus to treat human action as open-ended. The course of historical events ceases to be a matter of the inner logic of action. It is no accident that the only successful attempt to marry historical accounts of the course of cultures and civilizations with a theory of their rise and fall, Arnold Toynbee's *Study of History* (1939–61), focuses on the collective human response to challenges from outside. The point is that those challenges refuse to obey the laws of the culture. That is why they can alternately stimulate the new and destroy the established.

The problem with sociological accounts of globalization is not their appeal to history, but their historicism, history as 'Grand Narrative', globalization as the culmination of modernity. But the problem with Grand Narrative is that it has rarely been grand enough; it has reduced history to the banality of the growth of progress, or rationality, or the achievement of a classless society. If we consider the present as unfolding history we have to consider the possibility of new phenomena emerging, of new constellations of circumstances which change established ways.[7]

We need to entertain the idea that globalization, far from being the latest stage of a long process of development, is the arrest of what was taken for granted, a transformation arising out of a combination of different forces which unexpectedly changes the direction of history. It could be the transition to a new era rather than the apogee of the old. Such a contingent possibility can become part of the grandest narrative of all, nothing less than the story of the vicissitudes of humanity in its encounters with nature.

5.2 Axial Principles and Epochal Shift

How Daniel Bell's work illustrates that it is safer to trace history through intangible experience than through rationality

Depicting and accounting for epochal shift has become an unacknowledged central problem for the social sciences. It should have equal status with the problems of understanding and comparing different cultures as a core concern for our students and attract even higher regard from our teachers. The older problem setting has received overwhelmingly more attention for several decades even as globalization has undermined some of its central assumptions.

Cultural and epochal divides are not dissimilar states. Indeed, because the discussion of cultural boundaries has advanced so much further there is a case for treating epochal shift as a special case of the former. It may then help us to set out first, briefly, the relevant points of arguments about understanding other cultures.

If we define a culture as the generation of common meaning in collective experience, the world is divided into those who have taken part in that experience and those who have not. If we add another premise, that shared experience is unrepeatable, we erect an impenetrable barrier to mutual understanding across cultures.

The purity of those definitions is at the same time their strength and weakness; strength in that they assert ideas of the primordial, irreducible, unique and exclusive, so that culture seems to have an indestructible core; weakness in that they omit the experience of common meaning which is not collective (such as that of lovers) or of repeatable experience which is not shared (awe on a deserted coastline). In other words, the idea of separate and closed cultures denies the possibility of human beings as a species having experiences which cross cultural divides.

Indeed it is similarities in the human condition which make the idea of boundaries between cultures artificial, for they provide a basis for forming relationships across divides and hence potentially creating a new culture. In other words, for this definition to have force, culture has to be sustained over time by erecting political boundaries, against strangers and against innovation. We can also see incidentally why globalization is fraught with dangers for old concepts of culture. Equally it sharpens the appreciation of what it threatens.

Boundaries between cultures are pragmatic creations, and the assertion of primordial incommensurability becomes true by fiat. That means that a social organization, say a nation-state, which sets up barriers against the outside world does indeed create barriers to mutual understanding. So the task of understanding other cultures seems to elude the kind of universalistic procedures of classification and measurement which social science has borrowed from the natural sciences. Goethe has more to tell us about national differences than the Eurobarometer surveys of values carried out by the European Community. De Tocqueville still talks across the decades about the United States of today.

Suppose we, for instance – as indeed commentators have sought to do for the last 200 years – seek to discover the secrets of the relative economic success of nation-states, we might, for example, compare them on variables like size of population, legal system, type of legislature, state expenditure as proportion of GDP, educational attainment and many others. But no matter how many times we run correlations for these variables, or any others, the answer is never so satisfying as resorting to more intangible and circumstantial cultural factors such as the 'American Dream', the Japanese 'ai' or the British imperial experience.

These intangibles always fall outside the system of pre-set cross-cultural variables. The 'American Dream', the idea that it is within the capabilities of anyone to aspire to fortune and fame, breaks the boundaries of 'value', 'attitude', 'personality type' or any other category.

It relates to qualities which have been acquired exclusively in the context of American history and sets the United States apart as a special place for its citizens.

It is this unique cultural experience, rather than general theory, which time and again serves to explain the overall profile of scores on preset variables, as well as relations between those scores. So the close association of high valuation of personal independence, low tolerance of failure and the prevalence of anxiety is specific to the United States because these factors issue from a unique collective experience transmitted over generations.

No one has wrestled longer with these intractable problems of finding appropriate analysis for cultural uniqueness and social change than Daniel Bell. In an essay of 1968 exploring the elusive idea of national character, he identifies five facets – creed, 'imagoes', style, consciousness and modal personalities – to convey the irreducible contribution of concrete historical context (1968/1980b: 182). His imagoes, Daniel Boone, Huckleberry Finn, Horatio Alger, Charles Lindbergh, Frank Sinatra, Elvis Presley, provide styles, models of response. It is the particular personality, real or imagined, which conveys the shared meaning of belonging to a nation, rather than a conceptual formula.

Now Bell's solution here is very similar to the one we proposed earlier in connection with characterizing the Modern Age. We began with profiling characteristics and then identified a core nexus in their configuration, which, following Habermas, we called the Modern Project. We were careful to stress however that the link between the Modern Project and the configuration of the Modern Age was a historical, contingent one, not a necessary link between project and configuration. It is all too easy to be led astray by the centrality of the rational project and to impute this as central to any configuration. When Bell comes to address the question of modernity, this is essentially what happens with his famous later conceptual device, the 'axial principle'.

Axial principles for Bell have a prime place in underpinning the structuring of a configuration. The choice of the term 'axial' is tantalizingly allusive. It alludes to 'axis', the central point around which a body revolves. It suggests the 'Axial Age' of Jaspers (1955), the period between 800 BC and 200 BC when all the world's great civilizations put down their roots. It also evokes 'axiology', the branch of philosophy concerned with value. One of Bell's earliest interests in sociology had been to identify the moral bonds of Greek society (1980: 325).

But Bell is not sure what kind of configuration his axial principle underpins. At one time he considered it to be society, later he preferred to talk of 'diverse realms each obedient to a different "axial" principle which becomes the regulative or normative standard, the legitimating principle, of action in each realm' (1980: xiv).

What has happened is that the idea of a principle has come not to characterize the core of his configuration but to shape each profiling factor. Because the modern has become a collection of principles (for the economy 'functional rationality', for the polity 'equality', for culture the 'realization of the self'), they display obvious potential contradictions and disturb the idea of integrated society (Bell 1976). But then differing temporal orders become apparent too. As a result he disavows his earlier formula of 'post-industrial society' (Bell 1973) and declares that he should have been talking about post-industrialism because he was discussing only an aspect of society (1980: xv). But because each has a different rhythm of change, the degree of integration between them will vary from period to period. There is then no easy historical periodization or any single principle of order for society.

It is no minor difficulty which leads a scholar as profound and productive as Bell to shift his position on one of his basic intellectual concerns at such an advanced stage in his work. At the same time we can see how his concern with the unique features of a configuration leads easily from the cultural unit like the nation to the temporal division of a historical period.

It was a core problem for Max Weber too. He equally sought to identify the fundamental sectors of modern life with his idea of value spheres and he too talked of their basic logic, appearing to anchor them in transcendental principles. But he had two further emphases which allowed him to escape the bounds of principles as core features. First he explicitly recognized that they were based in and activated by people who were committed to them by irrational faith and from the depths of their being. Second he appreciated that such commitments are events in experience, historical moments (such as the Protestant Reformation), constitutive of bonds between people and over time.

Effectively we have the basic antinomy: the logic of axial principles around which realms crystallize, as against the experience which creates the realm in which the principle is based. At the same time, experience is of much more than principles, and this is where Bell's formulation (while it goes on to talk of postmodernity), in focusing on the centrality of principle, is quintessentially modern, and in danger of distorting the analysis both of other cultures and new periods of history.[8]

If we wish to display the irreducible differences between cultures or periods, we would be on safer ground in returning to Bell's earlier treatment of national differences, which employed concrete images of a nation's past. There we find no resort to principles. It is a historical fact that the Frontier shaped a whole series of responses which can be traced in American life even to this day; intellectualism and power have constituted a unique relationship in Parisian life for centuries; the religiously qualified man has had a guiding influence in daily life in Islam from its beginning; even Mao and the Red Guards could not expunge the influence of Confucius to this day in Chinese culture.

If we then recognize the formative aspect of historical experience in shaping a distinctive culture, we are in a position to begin to understand the nature of epochal shift. It is the transformation of culture for whatever reason. For if we allow that historical experience is all-important in accounting for the differences between cultures, we have to allow equally that it may also explain ruptures, breaks, shifts over time; and the breaks between periods become equivalent to boundaries between cultures.

Of course there is a crucial difference. As we pointed out, the boundaries of cultures are based in pragmatics and reinforced by power. The divisions between periods are based in facticity, in an even more powerful force than politics, namely mortality. It is an open question whether the nation or the generation is a more potent structural division between human beings. In the globalized world the younger generation may be readier to embrace foreigners than their parents. That in itself may signal the new age.

5.3 Facticity before Pessimism

The challenge now is to escape the pessimism of the intellectual and to depict an age for all the people

The announcement of the end of the Modern Age is not in itself new. It has been made often enough in differing ways (Nietzsche, Spengler, Toynbee, Bell, Lyotard, Vattimo).[9] But the approaching end has most frequently been seen in terms of a decline, negation or chaos. 'After us, the deluge,' but nothing clear, a sense of destruction and hopelessness.

Given the way the Modern Age has been conceived, this is not too surprising. If something is represented as the essence of the new, the expanding, the rational and the forward looking and then is given no future, it is scarcely surprising if the alternatives are looked on as at best a let-down, at worst a catastrophe. For Lyotard in *The Postmodern Condition* (1979) the philosophical basis for writing the grand narrative even of the Modern Age, let alone of an age after it, does not exist.

The reasons for this end-of-epoch pessimism are complex. But they arise in large part because the message is being carried by some of its prime representatives, intellectuals highly identified with modernity, even as they portray its decay.[10] They construct the age in their own image of rationality rather than in the experience of all the people.

The beginning-of-epoch, as opposed to end-of-epoch, narrative is most likely to come from the least intellectual academic disciplines, empirical sociology and history, both original anti-foundationalist intellectual activities. The best writing of history seeks no basis outside the story it tells except that that is the way it happened. If the resulting narrative is 'grand', it is only because it reflects the sweep, the depth, the human resonance of the times it depicts. An epoch is the landscape of a culture over a period of time in which fundamental features are formed, persist and decay. The best descriptive sociology equally grasps the sense of people's lives.[11]

The influences for change in the personal milieu of an individual anywhere in the world today may be traced to the operation of processes which are worldwide in their scope. Such is the centrality of the global reference in these that we tend to sum them up as globalization, and the recognition of their interconnection is the final step in the passage to the Global Age.

The reason globalization ushers in a new age is not that it challenges the axial ideas of modernity. Rather it signifies the disruption of all those conditions which made axial ideas central. Globalization undermines the assumption that the nation-state can provide the dominant frame of meaning for the lives of its citizens, that advancing rationality means advancing control of nature, that Western rationality is inherently superior. It emphasizes the material finitude of the globe and its resources and at the same time multiplies social relationships. It replaces universal ideas with a material globality. In other words the global shift is the arrival of a new configuration of both human activities and conditions of existence.

An account of the transition to the Global Age is based in reality, socially constructed, to be sure, but the collective outcome of innumerable social transactions is no more unreal or wishable away than the bodies in Hiroshima in 1945. Globalization is an empirical process. As such it is a transformation which cannot be escaped simply by dismissing it as yet another narrative. It is the facticity of the social which provides the basis for the narrative history of the Global Age.

5.4 Beyond Globalization

How a sense of history makes us realize that the global shift is not the end of the story

Clearing the meaning of our terminology, 'global', 'globality', 'globalism', 'globalization', is only routine intellectual hygiene. But it helps us to avoid the historicist fallacy of seeing the present as the culmination of the past, always germinating in it. Instead we need to treat each successive present as the open outcome of an encounter with a world which human beings have only partially made themselves, on the basis of a collective experience we only dimly understand. This modest and limited, some might even say negative, awareness is necessary for writing about both the past and the present. For it allows us to write about ruptures and shifts as much as continuities, beginnings as much as repetitions.

It has an important positive consequence: we are prepared for, but do not presuppose, the possibility of a shift from one age to another, and even in our own time. This is the attitude which leads me to declare that the Global Age has arrived.

We cannot yet catalogue just how comprehensive a shift this represents. We would need to review each life sphere, every institution, all cultures. The best we can do is to address particular instances where 'modern' could be displaced by 'global' as the dominant characteristic of the time.

We get a preliminary idea by making 'global' replace 'modern': 'global science' for 'modern science', evoking the way chaos theory opens an indeterminate universe, or the human genome project involves global mobilization to deconstruct human biology; 'global economics' for 'modern economics', where global measures of living standards in real terms replace national GDP or national balances of payments for assessing economic growth; 'global art' for 'modern art', where attempts to evoke diversified responses to archetypes or the quest for universally received images replace explorations of the technical limits of artistic expression.

In each of these cases we know well that 'modern' no longer conveys anything other than what is happening now and therefore paradoxically fails completely to grasp the substance of the change that is happening in any of these spheres. At the same time, centring our narrative on the 'global' fills that void which has long existed in our accounts and experience of modernity. A materiality replaces abstraction. There is an end to the sense of an abstract society. Moreover it is not just any materiality; it is a particular kind of materiality.

When we invoke the Global Age we jettison three centuries of assumptions about the direction of history. We move from seeing globalization as yet another stage of modernity, an '-ization' which is a culmination of changes arising out of modernity, to seeing it as the preparation for the global becoming part of life and globality becoming a constitutive factor in potentially any sector, sphere or institution.

Paradoxically, then, in the Global Age 'globalization' already begins to lose its meaning as a comprehensive historical process. The globe has become a normal reference point. The transformations which have taken

place lodge globality in everyday life without determining future directions. There is room for any number of quite disparate trends to gain
hold which can in no way be deduced from globalization. There is
even the open possibility of deglobalization.

Much previous recourse to the language of globalization has arisen
from the need to bring contemporary changes into the familiar frame
of modern concepts. The postmoderns have a rightful suspicion of
this. But they cannot trust themselves to depict a new epoch except in
modern terms. In other words, the intimation of the coming new age is
already there, without the conviction that anything can replace the old.
A leap is required and it is not too much to liken it to a leap of faith.

When visionaries and prophets speak of a New Age they summon
up something outside ordinary experience, and allude to non-terrestrial
and subterranean forces. Historians and social scientists talking of
a new age are equally speaking of a break from the mundane and
everyday.

The difference between the prophet and the scientist is therefore not
a matter of what they see or even what they experience. They belong
to the same time and share the same intuitions. They treat them in
radically different ways: the prophet becomes an agent of the time,
seeking to be a voice for the forces which control it; the scientist looks
for a point outside in order to exercise control over, or at least to
separate the human from, the fateful forces around.

But the new age represents a challenge to all the old modern
assumptions. Even the boundary of prophet and scientist is blurred.
In that sense the revival of interest in Nietzsche is symptomatic. He
recognized the crisis of the modern and foretold what has become the
postmodern. But neither he nor anyone else could foresee the shape of
the Global Age before it was happening.

Even as it happens we find it difficult to see. An all-enveloping
canopy escapes our attention. When we do see it, our older methods
of analysis, arising as they do out of the modern period, reassimil-
ate the new experience to the old. The confines of this kind of text,
a well understood and conventional mode of presentation, already
detract from the possibility of bringing radical novelty to the reader's
attention.

The most original thinkers have chosen to break such boundaries.
McLuhan effectively bridged the scientist/prophet divide while seeking
a divinatory/scientific genre, thus breaking normal scholarly conventions. He aimed to convey how the new age relativizes both media and
genre.[12] We cannot therefore preclude the possibility that writing about
the new age in a style reminiscent of an older one is backward looking
and doomed to lose touch with the changes which are taking place.

Two points arise in this connection. The first relates to premises which appear to hold beyond the epoch from which we are emerging. This book explores the possibilities of a narrative for the new age drawing on ideas as much premodern and non-Western as modern. It is not so much that they are universal – they change too much for that – but pragmatically their claim to harbour universality means that every age engages with them. This underlies the return to ideas of state and society in the penultimate chapter.

The second is that a sensitive, concrete but deep depiction of the new age can convey an intuitive grasp of its nature both prior to and beyond theoretical formulations. It is a pretheoretical grasp of time and place which speaks to us across epochs in the work of a Montaigne or an Ibn Khaldun. They engaged with the basics of the human condition, the life course, biography, meaning, life and death. We can hold them before us as guiding lights even if we can't hope to emulate them.

So we are not about to dip the epoch into an acid bath of modern theory, of functionalism, systems, rational expectations or even social action theory, and expect its features to emerge in clear and sharp relief. Rather the epoch will take shape as an array of items and interpretations accumulates, when finally, in the light of the widest experience we can draw on, it dawns on us that we have something new in history.

5.5 The End of Totalizing Discourse

Noting how the arrival of globality demonstrates the necessary incompleteness of accounts of the world

We are aiming to depict the character of an epoch without deriving it from any single principle, or indeed from any set of principles. We want to show what connections there are between its features without assuming connectedness in advance.

Sometimes the discussion of globalization asserts a closer connectedness in the world without, however, specifying its nature. And there are many kinds of connectedness:

- the biological relatedness of the human race
- the universally found ability of human beings to communicate through symbols
- the waterways of the world which have always existed as potential transport routes
- the worldwide network of economic exchange which has existed for several hundred years

– the network of networks of contacts between people which envelops humanity.

These factors have always made it possible to speak of humanity and human society. It has never been difficult to find connections, but globality is something more. It involves a new kind of connectedness, where events can have simultaneous effects anywhere on the globe, in which immediate response to a message can be given and obtained irrespective of distance, in which products and services are the outcome of a global division of labour, where identical products and services may be obtained anywhere in the world, or where images and icons receive recognition worldwide.

The field for these connections is the globe as a whole, which thus becomes the intentional focus equally for international civil servants, multinational corporation managers, analysts and forecasters, gurus and grass-roots activists, but also for the multitude of ordinary people seeking to make sense of their changing world, many with globalist values, with an aspiration to use and control the forces released by globality.

At the same time, what used to be connected is often disconnected. People are separated by highways where once there were fields and village streets. Neighbours no longer come from the same class or even country. One generation fails to appreciate another's music. Night is divided from day by danger on the street. This is daily experience of living in a locality.

Nevertheless, a net increase in globality does not necessarily mean an equivalent decline of locality, for two main reasons. One is that globality itself may be localized, and in many different ways, as in communities with globalist values, or production plants for trans-national corporations, or in specialist centres in the global division of labour. The other is that resistance to globality may equally become a focus for local action. It becomes hazardous to identify trends like 'decline of community' or even to impute existence to entities like communities. Globality raises questions about units of analysis which have long assumed a central place in scientific social research.

One of the main characteristics of old modern theory was the aim to develop comprehensive conceptual schemes, grasping the total phenomenon and not permitting areas of ambiguity or incongruity. Total theory was the counterpart of the assertion of the need for strong social control, and this was true for both functionalist and Marxist versions.

Totalizing discourse subjected nation, community, state, culture, family and above all society to this discipline. Nation-state society be-came the frame within which the human agent was expected to grow up, find identity, purpose and meaning in life. The separate institutional sectors, like the economy, polity and religion, were expected to preserve the overall continuity of society and shape and fulfil individual needs.

The most obvious way in which totalizing discourse operated was through the notion of system, drawing analogies and often equating nation-state society with other systems. Parsons's version (1951) was only the most famous, and corresponded well with the all-inclusive aspirations of the state. Later, when Habermas (1981) took the idea of system beyond nation-state and contrasted lifeworld and system, he was employing the idea of any system outside human control. He thus narrowed the gap between the idea of an economic system operating by impersonal forces and an eco- or biosystem. But he also restored some of the autonomy of the social even if he unduly limited its scope.

The most inappropriate way to grasp the reality of the Global Age is to seek now to refit human society back into the systems mould. Systems theory requires a firm position on what constitutes the system and what its environment is. In order to preserve the nation-state society as the unit of analysis, Parsons had to allocate other state societies, as well as the material world, to the category of environment. This was artificial even in the 1950s. Nation-state societies exist within a field of other societies, in persistent exchange and interaction. This has been part of the self-evident premises of the theory of international politics, but it applies equally to those institutions which elude state control, including money, information, science, transport, technology and law. The collapse of the Soviet system is only the most blatant example of what happens if the control attempt is carried through regardless of the risks involved. In other words, totalizing discourse was a symptom of the overreach of the nation-state.

5.6 Opening Accounts with Sociality

Why globality breaches the frame of closed social systems and releases free-floating sociality in world society

There was a more fundamental flaw to systems theory than the neglect of the transnational. Despite all efforts to locate the system outside people, in roles and institutions, the social *per se* had its basis in people. It was their qualities as social beings which transcended and transgressed boundaries, both external and internal to the state, both physical and moral.

Even if the systems concept is saved by conceiving the nation-state as a subsystem linked to the wider global system of institutions, the labile and creative nature of human sociality renders it unstable. This is true for any subsystem or global system in which human beings participate. They can always invalidate boundary assumptions and the system/environment distinction, especially if the environment is defined to include other social units.

If we simplify analysis to take any pair of societies or bounded groups in a world of such units, we can see how open the outcome of their interaction may be, viz.:

1 Boundary maintaining exchange
2 Specialization of each in relation to all
3 Debilitating conflict
4 Absorption of one by the other
5 Fusion
6 Growing similarity
7 Epigenesis of new groups.

The list is not exhaustive, and could hardly be because we generate these possibilities not out of a systems logic, but from the known qualities of human beings and their ability to form and reform social relationships. The global shift only provides new freedom and scope to exercise these qualities.

Certainly the interactions involved in our time involve globally extended media, like money, transportation and distance communications, science and information technology, law, all of which take on transnational reality. It is therefore tempting to see them as all part of the global system. But it is not accidental that the classic account of the overall development of these institutions remains Max Weber's rationalization process and that he was broadly hostile both to reifying the idea of society and to functionalist explanation. His institutional spheres are not systemically integrated with each other and their rationality develops through the accretion of practices, punctuated by historical crises. Moreover the rationalization process is attended by equally extensive irrationalization, something critics rarely recall.

In the same way we can see that Wallerstein's account of the historical development of capitalism (1974–89), involving the constant interchanges between core, periphery and semiperiphery until it becomes a world-system, absorbing the world, can adequately trace historical developments with the aid of the systems concept only up to the point, paradoxically, where the world is absorbed. From then on the system loses its coherence. It can no longer replicate itself by absorbing new lands and peasantries, and instead fractures into a whole variety of

differing strategies for production, capital accumulation and the creation of new needs. It becomes what Lash and Urry (1987) call 'disorganized capitalism'.

When we now speak of 'world' or 'global society' it is not because
they are equivalent to a world or global system.[13] Society and system
have never been so antithetical as they are now.[14] There are clearly
institutional frames and systems which now have a global operation
(Sklair 1991).[15] We may treat transnational corporations, global financial
institutions and the United Nations as aspects of a global system; but
they have emerged as the outcome of a long process of cross-national
and international transactions where the advent of globality has often
crystallized what might otherwise have been a very temporary constellation of forces or has precipitated a crisis in an otherwise unchecked
development. Thus the membership of the United Nations Security
Council reflects historical accumulations of military power. The end of
the Cold War disturbs its historic basis, the distribution of world power
in 1945.

Again, the point at which capitalism finally became global and
outside the control of any one nation found the world's main banking centre in Tokyo, the world's main equity market in New York
and its main foreign exchange centre in London. The position of those
three centres as global cities (Sassen 1991) is the product of a unique
historical trajectory, and their fates depend not even mainly on the
logic of the capitalist system but on a whole series of forces, including
nationalism.

Writing on the Global Age we must take account of institutions
which are global in their scope and operation but which in shape and
direction are by no means integrated with each other. They depend
on configurations of people, practices and forces which flex and flux
in relation to each other in a global field. Neither have the histories
of these people and their practices prepared them for globality, for
their experience is of the inherently expansive project of the modern
nation-state.

Even as they detach themselves from national definitions, institutions
lose the animating and centralizing thrust of the nation-state. Delinkage
becomes the watchword for relations between state and religion, state
and business, and business and politics as they transform themselves.
At the same time a denationalized sociality confronts these free-floating
institutional colossi.

The discourse for the Global Age can no longer rely on an idea of
society which provides an all-embracing frame in theory and practice.
World society, the sum total of human interactions, is now of a shape
where its history leaves it with uncertain and unclear organization,
and its theory has yet to escape the confines of the Modern Age. It is

not clear how far it is shaped by an incipient global society or how far such a society could extend its sway over the world. That does not mean that we jettison the ideas of state and society; rather that our research into them must become even more extensive empirically and more profound theoretically.

World society is now both less and more than nation-state societies. It has neither the direction nor control of the nation-state society in its prime. But it has the dynamism of an untrammelled sociality. It is this which has made globalization the spectre which haunts the offices of national leaders.[16]

5.7   Intellectual Work for the Global Age

Why we have to put theory to the 'test of time' and recognize alike the dated nature of the modern and the relevance of the non-modern

Western intellectuals have more problems in grasping the nature of the Global Age than anyone else, if only because they defined both the Modern Age and its dissolution as being the product of their ideas. But historical epochs are no more the product of thought than war is the product of weapons. They no more follow logic than the seasons or the life course.

But the logic of intellectual ideas holds its adherents in a cold grip, even after they have lost purchase on the world around. The usual consequence is to seek to assimilate the new age to the old and to project the features of the old order forward. This is not entirely a fruitless task either, since survivals of the older period will outlast human generations. Max Weber saw double-entry bookkeeping as essential to the rise of modern capitalism. It is equally essential in the Global Age.

But the Global Age sets the old elements of modernity in new relations with each other and introduces new elements which have transformed the total configuration. This is early in the new epoch and it is hazardous to identify its main features. None the less, four factors stand out for their pervasiveness. They have different kinds of relations with the past. Only one is a straightforward outcome of modernity.

The first is premodern, even prehistoric, and this is the ever dynamic process of forming new relationships across boundaries, having at its core the struggle to find common meaning in human encounters. This age-old process has a new prominence as it escapes the temporary and peculiar territoriality of the nation-state, but we should be in no doubt that the problem of interculturality is to all intents and purposes primordial and intimately related to the most general features of human sociality.

The second process is the expansion of the technology of communication, dependent especially on the computer chip and the new information technology. This was the prime accelerator of the disembedding of social relations in the Modern Age and continues to promote deterritorialization in the Global Age. It becomes the medium for the new globality, though providing few determinants and no guarantees for the shape of social relations.

The third is the commodification of culture. Dependent on earlier stages in the development of capitalism, it involves the refinement of tastes and the competitive display of the outcomes of discretionary expenditure, the exploration of identity through tourism and lifestyle searches, and the purchase of privileged education. It is the arena in which the postmodern most obviously appears as the culmination of the modern.

The fourth is globality itself, which brings human endeavours into relation with the extent and materiality of the globe as a whole. Political and economic activity calculate on global scope and consequence, while the global forces released by the aggregate impact of human activity on the environment react back on that very activity. Globalism becomes a main aspect of the meaning of human life.

The solutions to personal and state problems in the Global Age arise in the context of, and often as a response to, these forces. This applies as much to scholars and scientists as to anyone else. The advent of this state of affairs has come as a shock to humanity as a whole. It was hardly prefigured by previous generations. Nietzsche had intimations of it in speaking of an 'age of comparison' where various views of the world, customs and cultures can be compared and experienced simultaneously (1878/1910: 38). He suggested moreover that there would be no need for everyone to think alike in the manner of Kant's universal morality. He seemed to intimate that both the nation-state and universal order, point counterpoint of modernity, would be surpassed.

Delinked from modernity, spheres such as art, morality, the state, even science, each face reconstitution unconfined by boundaries in time or space. None of them has guarantees. Science outside modernity finds that faith encroaches on old preserves. The state becomes a medium for individual expression, art a collective enterprise.

The whole of the past and current experiences of humanity become co-present elements in the human condition without providing any fixed solution to its problems. Individuals finding their own fate in this global world have to trust without certainty, finding intimations of the universal in their transitory experience of particular others.

One of the most recent intellectual anticipations of the character of such a transformation is Thomas Kuhn's notion (1962) of a paradigm shift, where a transformation in science occurs which pervades not only theories but also practice and social organization. This is familiar to philosophers of science and historians of ideas. It has the merit too of locating science in the non-scientific. But the shift is still within science. Now imagine the shift being of the world itself.

The immediate response is the flight to safety. Intellectuals have interests like anyone else. In their case it is in preserving the continued relevance of ideas in which they have invested much of their lives. If the world is changing they may seek to find security in persisting with old ideas. But there is a wider and general need for a second-order shift, shifting science for a shifting world.[17]

Detaching ourselves from modern ideas, we may be in a better position to appreciate the Global Age. At the same time this does not involve an interminable quest for novelty. We may also retrieve what is relevant from the premodern and proceed from the non-Western as much as from the Western. And if we become modest about our modern heritage, we have to become even more modest about intellectual work in general.

Changing theory accompanies epochal shift but is not its fuel. One of the key themes of this book is that the movement of history is much more than the history of ideas, and this is especially true of theoretical ideas which seek to direct the times in which they are written.[18] It was the engagement between historical materialism and idealism, accompanying the great internal struggle of the Modern Age between capitalism and socialism, which made the ideas/interests dichotomy a central theoretical issue. It gave rise to comments like Max Weber's that 'Not ideas, but material and ideal interests, directly govern men's conduct' (1948: 280). It was a formula which scarcely began to accommodate even his own theory.

Minimally we might add two other elements in any narrative of a changing world, namely human feeling and environmental and social forces. We recognize the importance of these elements in historical accounts which allude to 'climate of the time', 'heritage', 'force of circumstances', 'collective experience', 'population pressure', and which thus avoid the intellectualist error of treating events as the outcomes of cognitive processes. For the appeal of the ideas/interests dichotomy to theoreticians is the potential it offers them for rational analysis.

There is a different kind of theory relevant to practice. It is historically grounded. It clarifies concepts in the light of the contingencies in which they were conceived and to which they relate. This applies as much to business as to politics, to counselling as to consultancy. It expands rather than curtails the horizons of decision making. For much of what purports to be theory today ignores the past to invent new technical concepts out of thin air. They have no real purchase on the present because they ignore the way the past lives on in the prevalent concepts and practices of our time.

When in our discourse we refer to 'state', 'society', 'government', 'nation', 'technology', even 'the people', we allude to complex skeins of meaning which develop under specific circumstances and become more involved and intricate as times change, or alternatively are attenuated and abridged over time.[19] We cannot assume the one or the other, and the time-spans will differ from 25 to 250 to 2,500 years (cf. Foucault 1974).[20] They may be modern, premodern or even, so far as we can judge, universal. They can, of course, also be very recent, as with the idea of globalization.

'Standing the test of time' is more than a cliché. Addressing ideas in their historical context and following them through changing times clarifies their scope and applicability. For instance, when I wrote on the concept of bureaucracy (Albrow 1970), it was still common to view it as the necessary shape of any rational organization. My own 'test of time' was to show its rootedness in eighteenth- and nineteenth-century discourse, and thus I in effect helped towards what is now a common recognition, that it was, along with much else in modernity, a passing phenomenon.

Such a test does not need to be radically relativist in the manner of Michel Foucault, who has without doubt been the most magnetic exponent of the relevance of history to theory. In his hands 'discourse analysis' demonstrates that ideas, language and social reality are interwoven in historical contexts through power and sexuality. In discourse we arrive at no more than temporary constellations of conditioned propositions, rather than timeless truths.

Foucault shares a problem with radical relativists generally, namely that if all propositions are equally historically conditioned, we are left only with the option of disposing of all of them. Each generation has paradoxically to sweep the past away even as it discovers its power, and we can see the affinity between this and modern iconoclasts who start from ideas of pure rationality.

The approach I am advocating lies somewhere between universalism and relativism, and if some would say that that is not a very principled position, I would say so be it. It rests on experience. Some ideas stand the test of time better than others, some are more timebound than others.[21] What we cannot do on the account in this book is to accept or deny an idea simply on the grounds that it is premodern or modern, or allow an epoch to claim automatically an idea as its own, or to privilege its own account beyond others (cf. Lyon 1994).[22]

The time test must always be applied and the relevant scope of an idea judged according to the circumstances: an exercise of historical doubt which parallels the pragmatic engagement with foreign cultures. We try out our ideas about other human beings in strange contexts on the assumption that with some people at least we will find ourselves on common ground.

It is this test which deconstructs the modern theory of state and society. We discover that it is in fact the theory of nation-state society which conflates ideas of state, people, society, government, nation, culture, since each one of these carries a different genealogy. The connections asserted to hold between them in the late modern period, and especially their linkage to territory, are accidental, the product of the passing dominance of the Modern Project.

6

Configurations of the Global Age: Systems

6.1 From Transnational to Global Institutions

How the decentred and delinked institutions of the old nation-state meet in the discourse of globality

The disorientation which affects much practical and intellectual activity at the end of the twentieth century results from a failure to recognize that globality belongs to a new age which has its own shape and key characteristics. Seeking to fit global phenomena into the frame of modernity only compounds the sense of dissonance and fragmentation. Globality is developing its own kinds of organization and its own kinds of personal responses and attitudes.

At the same time the world is now spanned by technical and social systems which have arisen in the modern era. Money and credit, telecommunications, transport, diplomacy, competitive sport have both worldwide scope and identifiable systemic features, namely predictable processes and sequences of transactions which are replicable anywhere. There are then systems everywhere, but the sum of those systems is not a system. The assumption of a sum is the error which has vitiated social science in its attempts to find a preordained course in the movement from modernity to a globalized world. We have to register the impact of globality on earlier systems, not the increasing systematization of what went before.

In other words, we have to leave the modernist paradigm of social science. In this chapter we will examine some of the characteristic kinds of impacts of globality on systems and the adaptations which result. In the next we shift the focus to the people on whom the animation and activation of these systems depend.

The shift from the transnational to the global in international affairs is one of the characteristic sequences in which globality crystallizes as a new level of explanation. This does not happen gradually. It requires a shock, or at least a series of shocks, since the global is more than the sum of transnational relations. It is possible to imagine an ever increasing density of bi- and multilateral relations between governments and other bodies which never attains globality, that is it never confronts the premises of the system as a whole. There have been such shocks: the impact of nuclear weapons, oil price rises, the recognition of global warming and the end of the Cold War are major instances. They have shaken the world out of the dream that its future was a managed world of transnational relations.

The concept of the transnational has long been a standard resource for students of world politics. Keohane and Nye (1971), following among others Aron (1967) and Rosenau (1969), provided impressive demonstration of its worth in a volume covering international non-governmental organization, multinational enterprises, international finance, revolutionary organizations, and more. This was at a time when global had yet to establish itself firmly in the vocabulary of politics and they spoke of 'global interactions' as 'movements of information, money, physical objects, people, or other tangible or intangible items across state boundaries' (Keohane and Nye 1971: xii). They used it as a generic term to cover two subcategories distinguished as 'interstate interactions' and 'transnational interactions', the latter of which had to involve non-governmental actors.

Already in the 1970s such distinctions were assessed for their worth in analysing the problem of the future of the nation-state, and here a cleavage appeared between those who saw transnationalism circumscribing its power and those who saw it being enhanced through regional alliances (Gilpin 1971). It was a substantive disagreement concealed by the use of 'global' to mean either of 'interstate' or 'transnational'. 'Global' on this basis might mean anything from relations between any two states or actors across borders to the sum total of all such relations. But these two extremes were at opposite ends of a huge spectrum. As yet, 'global' had not attained the strong sense which globalization was to promote and which we examined earlier as referring to the world as a whole.

A related difficulty arose in discussing the multinational enterprise, which, while it operated in more than one country, might none the less essentially have its headquarters in and most of its managers from one country, typically the United States. Keohane and Nye thus used the term 'geocentric' to identify a corporation which had freed itself from special ties to particular states. So was the extension of geocentric transnational relations the equivalent of the later use of globalization?

It is very close indeed, but a further ambiguity opens up if we stay with the idea of the transnational. For there is a freedom from the national which is not yet geocentric, nor indeed tied to territoriality at all. Groups which claim or aspire to universalism might well regard attempts to see their activities in territorial terms as entirely inappropriate. This would be true for the intellectual ideals of scientists and of religious believers.

This is where we are now in a position to move on from the theory of the transnational to the theory of the global, for the global is not simply a culmination of transnational relations, but the intrusion of a new level of organization. Notwithstanding the fact that every group relates to it differently, the globe is a material reference point and not a universal ideal. We have to distinguish globalism, the globe negating national boundaries, from either transnationalism or universalism. Globality is a new level of organization, to which any agent can relate, but which has no organizing agent. This is why we have to characterize the Global Age as an age of globality rather than globalization, which has connotations of direction.[1] At the same time we can understand why the idea of postmodernity has such attractions. Yet the lack of central organization is not disintegration.

Virtually no institutional area intrinsically belongs to the nation-state. Historically and analytically most institutions are essentially transnational, whether we think of the economy, science or religion. But by linking the theory of institutions to the nation-state and its organizations, it was possible to claim that their social hierarchies were necessary and to postulate higher and lower needs paralleling the stratification of society. It was also possible to see institutions not as the historical development of human transactions, but as the crafted plan of a sovereign body. Moreover they were indeed shaped to meet the needs of national governments and ruling elites.

There is, by contrast, no single sovereign power to claim legitimate authority over the institutions of transnationality. Even the United Nations is only one agency among many: it has no standing army and military power rests with bodies like NATO. Economic institutions similarly are supervised by separate bodies like the IMF and GATT, now WTO (World Trade Organization). Equally there is no single legislative body for international law.

The organizations which span the globe arise out of and seek to administer institutional practices which are free from the control of any one nation-state. But that means they are also delinked. For it was the activity of the sovereign power which insisted that economy had to serve state, that education had to serve economy, that media had to serve education. In so far as these are the outcome of transactions between people, there is no necessary hierarchy or priority between them, and there is nothing intrinsic to institutional areas which prevents their respective agencies from seeking to dominate others, or altern-atively trying to free themselves from them.[2]

Decentred and delinked, the institutions which arise out of inter-state and transnational relations then relate to the global in very spe-cific but as yet ill-documented ways:

- First, interstate relations have become effectively comprehensive, and thus global, with the end of the Cold War and with the inclu-sion of China.
- Second, the globe occupies the vacant discursive space which the sovereign state occupied in national discourse. The origins of the new discourse in the old nation-state mean there is a language gap to be filled. In transnational discourse people refer to the globe as once they referred to the nation, hence globalism.
- Third, the loss of an authoritative centre opens institutions to people at all levels without distinction. The aggregate of human beings on the globe has regular even if unequal access to information, opinion formation, entertainment, means of exchange, commodities, trans-portation, and technology organized on a global scale.
- Fourth, the globe itself becomes the furthest practical extent, limit and reference point for the activities of agencies and individuals when national boundaries become merely conditional rather than absolute hindrances.

The old institutional theory looked down from the state to the indi-vidual. Via institutions, the state shaped and moulded individual needs and created the people for its own ends. The state washed over and encroached on every aspect of everyday life. Decentred and delinked institutions with global outreach are vulnerable to the backwash. The citizen, colonized by the modern state, acting within the frame of the new globality, exploits the openness of global institutions, expresses the new-found globalism and draws strength from a community and commonality of feeling which the nation-state can neither control nor even define. In this way globality is associated with a recovery of free sociality, with the expression of a global public opinion and the mobil-ization of global movements. At the same time, assisting, colluding and finding a resource in globality, a new managerial or professional class emerges.

6.2 Managing Global Indeterminacy

Why globalism in the absence of global organization promotes the rise of a global managerial class

The world is spanned by institutions with global concern even if there is no world government. Those institutions have grown in various ways out of international or transnational collaboration. They may be governmental or non-governmental. Equally there are organizations, profit and non-profit making, which focus on a global market or need and seek to operate globally. It would not be surprising if those who worked for these bodies developed sufficient shared outlooks and experience to mark them off from other people. If they found the means to confer the advantages of their position on their children, we would be able to identify a global managerial class in the making.[3]

We immediately feel some resistance to this idea. The Modern Project experience is of a class system effectively circumscribed by the nation-state. We saw how the challenge for the welfare state was precisely to domesticate class structure within nation-states. But historically classes like peasantries or merchants arose out of common life conditions. The development of a global managerial class fits a much older pattern. It certainly does not depend on the existence of central control, or even on the triumph of global organizations. Indeed we can be confident that its strength will grow, even, and in part because of, their absence.

Shared experience and power arise on many different bases. Of the many antecedents for class formation there is one which is of particular relevance here, namely the growth of the professional class. Here the modern experience is well documented and one key element which marks out the professionals is their successful claim to exercise judgement in indeterminate situations. Whether it be medical treatment, legal pleading or risk assessment, at critical junctures the lay person relies on professional judgement, even when told that outcomes are uncertain. Once an area of life is governed by the exercise of knowledge beyond a rule book, which requires both training and experience, then those who command that knowledge have a privileged position both in the market and in terms of social status.

We can identify three main areas where indeterminacy is specifically linked to the new globality. The first is in international organizations. If we take as an instance the ones which are concerned with the operations of the world economy, we have a cluster of agencies including the IMF, the World Bank, WTO, OECD. Senior officials in one agency will know those in others and regularly move between agencies.

They also interact with the staff of national agencies, from whom they will probably have been drawn in the first place, and the tasks of those national officials will involve regular interaction with the global agencies.

The iterative processes operating at these levels, involving the constant exchange of reports for scrutiny, revision and updating between national and international agencies, ensure the development of a common code of communication, a shared set of concepts and a common field of discourse which, for all the differing national and regional nuances, represents the global field of economic management. This is replicated for all global institutional areas, whether it is population, agriculture, maritime law or nuclear weaponry.

As compared with modernity, however, globality introduces a new range of problems for the institutional specialists, which means that the ideal image of closely collaborating professionals working to the common needs of humanity is only one part of the reality. Professionals working with nation-states are bound to assume a state interest in the regulation of their work, and consequent political direction. This may well bring with it the familiar inner conflicts, between professional conscience and bureaucratic rules, for instance. But in the nation-state, basically the functional definition of work prevails over professionalism. The direction comes from government.

Under the conditions of globality the experts effectively enter a continuous dialogue between differing cultural definitions of their work. The strictly technical aspects are subsumed in a discourse where the focus becomes the development of common professional values across boundaries. So when representatives of the American, European and Japanese legal professions met for the first time collectively in October 1993 they agreed that a worldwide disciplinary code would be helpful to both them and their clients (Toulmin 1994: 49).[4] In the politics of globality it is the professionals themselves who pragmatically and in constant dialogue work out the collective goals which inform their work and determine whether what they do is in the interests of humanity.

The managers of global institutions are able to pay as much regard to the values at the core of their speciality as to globalist values. Each global institutional sector seeks to see the world in its own image and to organize the globe around itself, which effectively means that each produces a hierarchy of needs, values and practical requirements which extends far beyond its area of expertise. Population planners produce plans for agriculture, economists regulate working conditions, health professionals develop programmes of personal ethics, lawyers dismantle trade barriers.

The management of globality becomes a multicultural field of discourse about values, an on-going debate between sectors, each of which will assert its primacy with no authoritative resolution of the argument. There is then no axial principle underlying global institutions any more than globalism provides them with a determinate structure. Their pluralism reflects no theory of the greater good, simply the historic accumulation and interplay of national experiences and expertise coming to terms with each other.

In nation-states relations between functional areas such as education, health, employment and law and order tend to reflect long-standing and deep-seated priorities within the culture which officials have little scope to alter. For the world as a whole the functional areas are in constant competition with each other and their boundaries are in flux. Globality serves not to resolve problems of value, but to encourage a debate about values where once there was only concern for technique. This operates for the highest echelons of the institutional agencies and is yet another reason why values have become a free-floating cultural resource in the Global Age. For the officials themselves, the discourse of globality becomes an additional professional resource.

The second area where the indeterminacy of globality rules is in corporate management. The business corporation has long progressed beyond the hierarchical monolith which scientific management set up as its model of rational organization. The development towards knowledge-based, service-delivering organizations has enhanced flat, delayered organization relying more on co-operative exchange of information and teamwork.

At the same time the dismantling of exchange controls and the freeing of capital movements worldwide has opened up new possibilities for cross-national business collaboration. Joint ventures, franchising, licensing, servicing agreements and collaborative networks between firms become part of the repertoire for business development along with the older forms of vertical integration, creating subsidiaries or merging. The net effect is a bewildering increase in the strategic options for management.

In this context globalization has sometimes seemed to offer the high road out of chaos. Probably the most influential statement for business was a paper by Theodore Levitt (1983) on the globalization of markets; it highlighted the homogenization of consumers' needs and wants worldwide and suggested that successful marketing would have to follow the trend. Kenichi Ohmae (1985) estimated that 600 million consumers in the triad of the United States, Europe and Japan exhibited the same preferences. Even if options for organizational structure and financing appeared increasingly open-ended, at least a global strategy promised a clear direction.

Yet it didn't take long for it to become clear that the globe is not a destination at the end of a route. If, with a product as global as the motor vehicle, it was possible to have Toyota at one extreme, with centralized control and production in Toyota City, and Fiat at the other extreme, with licensing arrangements and joint ventures for a country-customized product, it was obvious there was no one solution to going global (Bartlett 1986: 371).

Michael Porter effectively shows how changing historical conditions reveal new conceptual alternatives for international business activity. In the 1960s American and European multinational corporations still operated on a national subsidiary basis, developed between the two world wars, allowing considerable local autonomy. The Japanese, on the other hand, favoured tight central control and close global co-ordination, which fitted 'the strategic imperative of the time' (Porter 1986a: 45). But 'going global' for a firm is not a single strategy; it means looking at local activities in the context of an overall global configuration of the industry and the firm's place in it. Porter distinguishes initially four broad alternatives depending on how segmented and how country-based a market is. The global reference point is a key shift, but it has no determinate solution.

Under the circumstances it is not surprising if globalization can mean something different for every executive and commentator. In a conference for business leaders and professors on 'Global Research and Teaching in the 1990s', held at the University of Michigan's Business School, there were as many definitions of globalization as contributors. Moreover the differences were not merely verbal. 'Integration across boundaries' and 'treating the world as one market' are quite different concepts. The first may stay at a purely transnational level, confined to a region, the latter is entirely open-ended, depending on the kind of market (Barnett 1992).

None of this means that the idea of 'going global' has lost its appeal. It was not accidental that it was associated with the upsurge in the 1980s of concern for business strategy. For strategy involves taking the whole picture into account and increasingly this meant a global reference point. At the same time it is a concern which enhances the felt importance of executive judgement. The resonance of the global with high status and responsibility holds out a 'tomorrow the world' lure for the aspiring executive and has its own rapidly growing in-group jargon.[5]

The third area of indeterminacy results from the worldwide spread of new information and communication technology, which opens options up for organizational structure and work styles quite apart from the lowering of obstacles to trade and new products. The dominant image for human organization is now the network and not the hierarchy, even if this causes problems for status. It permits twenty-four-hour dealing in an integrated global financial market where the time-zone locations of Tokyo, New York and London allow work easily to follow the sun. The executive of the global firm can be in touch with colleagues anywhere at any time – who shall be in touch with whom becomes the fraught issue. In the networked office, status barriers to communication tumble when anyone can gain access to anyone else's video screen.[6]

In the cause of clear thinking it is useful to distinguish the impact of new information technology from globalization. Their relations are complex and not in one direction. The new technology is worldwide in reach and availability. It is also a medium for all those who take the globe as reference point. It is both an outcome of modernity and at the same time contributes to the undermining of the organizational structures which have been associated most closely with modernity.

The parallel and interwoven hierarchies of state and corporation in high and late modernity shaped information channels and linked them closely with power and status. Now the structural options open. It may be as sensible to operate in several countries simultaneously with interfirm agreements as to how to operate as a single corporation. Downsizing may be as relevant a strategy as merger. It may be sensible to operate in partnership, or through licensing, rather than as employer and employee. The enhanced technical possibilities of dismantling massive state-owned corporations make privatization an easier political option.

The lack of central political control of global institutions, the open nature of global strategies for business and the new flexibility of organizational structure between them constitute a new and rarefied sphere of indeterminacy in work relations for those who manage. The managing of this indeterminacy defines their expertise. There is no one path to going global, nor indeed is it obvious that a business should go in that direction. At the same time, the global still appears to be immensely attractive for contemporary organizations. So, as part of an overall global strategy, they support human resource programmes to create the global manager.

The implication behind such programmes seems to be that success in global markets requires the model global executive just as success in national markets requires the model national executive. The logic is faulty. True there are well-established national styles in business culture, but no one has shown that success or failure depends on being more or less national. Both the good and the bad American firm may be typically American. They distinguish themselves on other grounds. Further, the frequent success of management brought in from other countries may have nothing to do with their specific national culture but be attributable to the fact that, first, they adopt different methods from the locals, and second, that it is the more enterprising who go abroad.

The impetus for globalizing the firm comes as much from the dynamics of class formation and culture and from non-pecuniary aspirations as it does from the narrow requirements of business profits. But since this impetus is powerful enough, and may indeed have corporate spin-off, we should not expect it to be checked. The new indeterminate global world of management creates the need to find reassurance with like-minded people and sustain a supportive social network. The same processes which sustained William H. Whyte's (1956) organization man in the corporate culture of the United States in the 1950s now operate worldwide. And as corporate structures are more fluid than ever, there is an even greater premium on acquiring the personal human capital and social support to cope with an unknown future (Pucik et al. 1992). Going global is the manager's password for entering the global managerial class.

There are many signs of the emergence of a global managerial class and a global elite.[7] Moreover it looks to an appropriate kind of education for itself and its children. This is as much a result of the requirements of class culture as it is of the requirements of business or the nation-state. We should not underestimate this. The mark of the professional is to be able to handle indeterminacy where the rules do not provide solutions. The ability to move easily through the maze of corporate and institutional globality will not be easily, quickly or cheaply acquired. We may even simplify to the point of paradox and say that the development of the global managerial class will come not because there is global organization, but because there isn't.[8]

6.3 The Denationalization of the Economy

How globality undermines the assumptions of nation-state economies and why governments now seek to influence economic culture

The advent of globality in the world economy provides the clearest example of the new challenge to the nation-state. For a century in modern economics there was a consensus on taking the national economy as the focus of analysis in the context of a world of national economies. Within its framework one could work on the basis of an averaging out of costs and returns on labour and capital in different parts of the nation, and assume that there would be a national currency and a centrally controlled bank. International trade was assessed through a balance sheet of transactions crossing national boundaries.

Because there were boundaries between states, the analytical assumption of free movement of labour and capital within countries did not hold between them. It was therefore important to maintain a balance of trade, because an excess of imports over exports would reduce returns on capital and labour at home; but in a world of nation-states it was unnecessary for the trading balance to be with any particular nation, only in aggregate. As Alfred Marshall said, there was a 'firmly unified and highly specialized' world money market because 'the trade of each with the world is a coherent whole' (1923/1965: 151).

In a world of nation-states the relations between the national and international economy were therefore two sides of the same coin. So neither the growth of international trade nor indeed of foreign investment threatened the frame of nation-state economies. Similarly the internationalism Keynes advocated which resulted in the Bretton Woods agreement and the establishment of the post-Second World War international financial institutions reinforced the integrity of national economies in the context of the world as a whole. The IMF exists precisely to ensure that nation-states keep to minimally effective standards to allow them to play an independent part and make an effective contribution to a world economy.

Free trade, with the dismantling of state control over activities, the reduction of trade barriers, the free export and import of capital and foreign exchange, is something different. It is denationalization rather than internationalization. Fully implemented it would turn a national economy into a geographical region, with all that that implies. Its introduction is a matter of arduous multilateral bargaining. Its attractions have been more obvious to dominant powers, and then not always for long periods because of the internal dissent it raises. In Keynes's view, British economists advocated free trade since 'they attributed the actual success of [Britain's] laissez-faire policy, not to the transitory peculiarities of her position, but to the sovereign virtues of laissez faire as such' (1930: 307). In other words the successful imperial power *would* see advantages in free trade, which makes Britain's continued adherence to free market doctrines, from Keynes's viewpoint, a self-defeating matter of nostalgia for empire.[9]

Yet it is not from free trade that globalization has received its main impetus. A single worldwide market and a single world currency are certainly pure conditions in which a global economy could indeed develop freely. But it has not been a precondition for globalization in the world economy, which is not the same thing as free trade, and not the same as the growth of international trade. There is a sceptical vein of commentary about globalization which says that if there is no global, borderless market there is no globalization (see Hirst 1993, Hutton 1995). The converse position is that the deregulation of the money markets in the 1980s ended national autonomy (see Marr 1995). But these views accord unwarranted precedence to the market notion in the shaping of economies.[10]

We should be looking at the concept of organization rather than market if we want to understand contemporary economic transformation. In this we can take a lead from Peter Dicken (1992: 1), who has emphasized the difference between internationalization and a much more recent globalization, the latter involving a functional integration of dispersed activities. We can go further still if we factor in explicitly the concern the contemporary transnational corporation has for globality as such. It cannot afford to ignore any potential source of advantage or threat anywhere in the globe.

Economic globalization involves the growth of economic activity which functions beyond national economies and is organized with reference to the world as a whole. It treats governments in the plural as factors in its decisions, but challenges the assumptions of governments and employs an alternative global frame both for economic activity and theory. The challenge it poses to national governments is a loss of control, a control which governments hitherto thought the international system guaranteed. It is this about globalization, rather than its dominance, which is not yet assured, which has made it into the central point of issue for governments and journalists.

Markets without boundaries are not intrinsic to, or a necessary precondition for, globalization. If we try to rank economic organization and processes in terms of their importance for globalization, the transnational corporation would have to come first, then production technology, consumption patterns and lifestyles, mobility of capital, international financial institutions, followed by mobility of labour and finally dismantling of trade barriers. Leslie Sklair's (1991) account of transnational capitalist practices effectively conveys the way global markets are created and dominated by players for whom national boundaries are simply negotiable conditions.

Intensive empirical evidence for economic globalization in this sense comes from a series of studies of particular industries by the OECD (1993). They develop a path for firms of five stages from domestic to global operations, which culminates in the highly globalized, where international operations include integrated management, financial control, research and development, production and marketing. They highlight the way firms both locate operations in areas which have concentrations of personnel and advanced technology, which provide global competitiveness, and at the same time seek to bring final products closer to customers. The variety of strategies which firms adopt to secure these advantages includes mergers across borders, forming new foreign subsidiaries, joint ventures, right up to fully integrated operations across borders including management, financial control, production and marketing.

It is the ever growing complexity of cross-border relations which defies national categorizations of economic activities. We can take an example from typewriter manufacturers. The company Brother, manufacturing typewriters in the US, accused a company, Smith Corona, manufacturing in Singapore, of dumping its products in the United States; Brother was controlled in Japan, Smith Corona in the United States, and the US International Trade Commission found in favour of the latter. But as Robert Brainard (1993) has shown, the idea of the nationality of a company has come under increasing strain. There are three main criteria commonly used: place of incorporation, headquarters and nationality of controllers. But countries differ in the relative importance they give to each of these and the strategies of multinational enterprises with diffuse ownership and location often make clearcut attribution of nationality impossible. If one accepts this complexity and goes on to disaggregate ownership, foreigners' holdings of shares quoted on the world's exchange markets rose from 7.1 per cent of the total in 1979–80 to 19 per cent in 1991 (Brainard 1993: 171). In this context, traditional national economic accounting becomes increasingly removed from underlying realities.

The same applies to products. Robert Reich (1991) illustrated the way that 10,000 US dollars received by General Motors for an 'American' car resulted in only 4,000 dollars going to the company, with the other 6,000 going to six other countries for a variety of inputs, including assembly in Korea, marketing in the United Kingdom, and Ireland and Barbados for data processing. It gave rise to Reich's question 'Who is us?', which he answered not in terms of ownership but in terms of personnel, as does Michael Porter (1990), who sees the home nation as important as the source of skills and technology.

The very rapidity with which capital can flow from one country to another apparently contrasts with the localization of centres of production, particularly where there is a high skills component. But this is a function of globalization, namely the possibility of production for a global market, which means that in some sectors, computing or high finance for example, a few centres can service the world. This, coupled with the living demands of people with similar tastes, makes for a new kind of local community, based not on traditional ties binding classes and occupations together in one place, but on lifestyle, similar life chances and information exchange.

This does not amount to a resurgence of national factors in the economy. For these localized areas of economic activity for global markets, with Silicon Valley or the City of London as prime examples, recruit their workforces from the world as a whole and make a virtue of cosmopolitanism. To that extent the localization of global economic activity demonstrates the new limits on national control, even as the host national government prides itself on the presence of this global centre. In this respect the historical example of the relations between the Vatican and Italy is closer to the emergent economic and social reality than that of a resurgent national economy with a 1930s Berlin/Ruhr type integration of politics and industry.

Although the mobility of workforces lags far behind the mobility of capital, none the less the new global mobile workers are significant for the nation-state because they occupy the highly paid end of the labour market and they and their firms exercise influence on the taxation policies of governments.[11] This illustrates precisely why globalization cannot be equated with free trade. The capacities multinational firms developed to cross borders were stimulated by those very borders. Then, to attract those firms, nation-states have very often lowered those borders. To this extent globalization of production and consumption has advanced free trade rather than vice versa. But, as barriers come down, if particular regions of the world are significant in terms of the location of economic activities the reasons are less and less the economic management of governments and much more the comparative advantage in the market and intangibles such as culture and lifestyle.

In this respect, national culture rather than government policy has come to be recognized as a factor in economic growth, very obviously in the countries of the Far East rim. In so far as Western governments have drawn a lesson from this, it has been to turn the direction of policy away from macroeconomic management and towards supply-side measures to improve training, skills and human resources generally. Here, to be sure, economic nationalism has returned by another route, not through the ownership or control of heavy industry, but in an emphasis on human capital. Training has become the nationalist nostrum in the late twentieth century much as health was in the early part. The shift by national governments to identify culture as a resource parallels and draws on the way firms have sought to identify the dynamic 'factor x' elements in their own growth which may be attributable to culture. The confluence of these parallel trends results in the marketing of national images, in the effort to identify national cultural factors in brand images and in the recognition of national factors in consumption patterns.[12]

The move by governments away from macroeconomic management reflects the interdependence of national economies and the ever growing constraints on government economic policy. At the same time, relative to governments, the power of both firms and consumers has risen. This is in part due to the decline of old-style industrial capitalism, dominated by the relations of government and producer groups, with war preparation as the ultimate logic. In part it is due to improvements in technology.

Either way, as the world economy has ceased to have national ends at its heart, individual consumers and their lifestyles have become the target for production. Culture is the collective form in which those consumption choices are expressed. Contemporary capitalism is culture-led rather than government-directed, and to that extent the nation, rather than the government, has entered into a direct relation with the economy. The problem for nation-state governments is that culture is effectively never as bounded as they have sought to make it. Compared with nation-state demands on economic activity, culture is far more fluid, uncontrollable and unpredictable. The new nationalism in economic life is then predicated on the weakness of governments rather than on their strength, on their need to cajole and encourage, research and propagandize rather than on their ability to control and direct resources. Furthermore, governments find that national culture is itself more elusive than it has ever been and does not coincide with state boundaries.

Even as globalization increases, there are ample indications that it cannot ever dominate aggregate economic activity in the world. But that will not save the national economy. Rather the diminution of the salience of the nation-state generates the possibility of subnational forms of activity which owe something to the boundary-dismantling effects of globalization but little to organization at a global level. For the nation-state the problem is that its role in economic management seems to be ebbing away, while there is no equivalent level of control at the global level. There is no Ministry for the Global Economy.

6.4 Environments, Reflexivity and Late Modernity

Why globality is a rupture with modernity and humanity resumes a relationship with nature from an earlier period

Modern social theory has long had an aversion to serious engagement with the interrelations of society and the natural environment. Indeed that was one of its hallmarks compared with premodern and non-European thought. Its major concern in the early modern period was anthropocentric, substituting man for God in the social order. In the period of industrial capitalism the 'social problem' was essentially the problem of class conflict, to which was added later the problem of ethnic assimilation and social integration. Famously Émile Durkheim's insistence on explaining the social by the social exhorted sociologists to

ignore both human biology and geography in their search for explanation (Durkheim 1895/1982).

In so far as 'environment' was important, it was largely conceived
in terms of spatial distributions of population and activities, as with
the Chicago sociologists in the early twentieth century, or else broadly
as the environment of other social units, as in theories of international
relations or more recently in contingency theory approaches to organizations. Only in the idea of the milieu, the familiar natural and social
frame of personal life, did social theory retain a tenuous hold on a
more profound sense of humanity as part of nature.

But a shift to bring the natural environment back into social theory
has taken place in the last two decades. One of the most prominent
examples has been Ulrich Beck's account of 'risk society'. Citing the
potential catastrophic consequences of nuclear explosions and environmental degradation through chemical use, he asserts that a community of risk has emerged on a global scale which makes boundaries
irrelevant and world society a necessary Utopia. In the risks of modernization there is 'an inherent tendency to globalization' (Beck 1986/1992:
36–7).

This enhancement of risk to a global scale is for Beck the outcome
of reflexive modernization, by which he means a development beyond
standard modernity, with its feature of a society organized around
wealth-producing industry, to a stage when those principles on which
it was based themselves come under critical scrutiny. In particular, the
consequences of industry for the environment come within the reflexive
aspect of the risk society.

Beck's account had a major impact in Germany when it was published there in 1986; it captured a sense of epochal shift in a way
which the rationalistic theories of Habermas and Niklas Luhmann still
dominating German social thought failed to do. The linkage he identified between the expansion of risk and new forms of social mobilization was important in addressing global forces which older theory was
failing to recognize. At the same time his association of globalization
with reflexive modernization is more problematical, if only because
it gives insufficient weight to the shift in theory and practice which
globality brings.

For it was modernity which transformed nature into environment. Globality has retrieved nature from the environment and redis-
covered its links with humanity. Previous and other civilizations have
treated the relations between human beings and the natural world as
continuous and interwoven. Modernity treated nature alternately as a
threat, a resource to be appropriated, an inexhaustible source of energy,
a field for manoeuvre, and a playing field. It was an instrumental-
ism which neutralized emotional and religious responses to nature and

converted it into a mere assemblage of things surrounding people, an environment.

'Environment' then is a concept born out of the Modern Project, for it signals a barrier between humanity and the natural world, and equally separates human biology from the rest of nature. As we have explored earlier, modernity is inherently expansionary. Therefore at some point it was likely to confront globality in different ways: through the world coverage of the interstate system; through the unification of world markets; through the interest of science in global forces. What Beck rightly stresses is the globality of the human impact on nature. But he underestimates the rupture which globality brings with it. For he could just as easily have spoken of demodernization. The reason he didn't was because of his linkage between reflexivity and modernity and his assumption that the new reflexivity involved in globalization must therefore be an outcome of enhanced modernity.

That there has been a vastly enhanced reflexivity at the disposal of individual and collective agents in the twentieth century is undeniable. Moreover this is in large part the outcome of the process which Max Weber called rationalization. But globalization and rationalization are not the same thing; indeed in many respects they are counterposed. Reflexivity is no more a uniform, homogeneous attribute than is consciousness. The reflexivity arising at the global level is quite different from that arising out of, say, the use of performance indicators, just as the consciousness of the Yoga practitioner is quite different from that of the modern doctor. In other words, all reflexivity is bonded to a social order and it is the way it is grounded in the social which gives it its specific character.

Globality is more an end-point of modernity than its culmination. But there is a real difficulty in appreciating this because many of the forces of modernity, especially scientific activity and technology, continue to expand, even if at uneven rates. This is effectively the main justification for the proponents of late modernity to see globalization as one further phase in its relentless advance, modifying Max Weber's iron cage of rationalization, however, to the extent that in Giddens's version rationalization acquires locomotion as the juggernaut.

Significantly, the iron cage enclosed people, the juggernaut crushed them under its wheels. The images are vivid and convey an important shift in the place of science and technology in the new configuration. The iron cage was a structure of thoroughly rationalized institutions and practices, represented in the factory and bureaucracy. The late modern juggernaut is a complex of computerized systems which threaten to be outside human control, with, at its control centre, the system which can unleash the nuclear holocaust (Giddens 1990: 131–9).

The juggernaut image emphasizes the development of rationality beyond human control, and therefore simultaneously highlights one way in which reflexivity may be a property of systems as well as of people. In that sense it extends also the notion of environment, as Giddens does explicitly, to human constructions.

This in itself signals the break which the theory of reflexive modernization reflects without fully interpreting. For modernity was above all a project of human control, and now the project mutates as it confronts an unpredictable constructed environment. The reflexivity which matters is no longer that of the project but of globality, an awareness of global connectedness rather than goal directedness. In the new configuration, globality recovers nature from the environment and in doing so displaces not only projects but principles, as such, as the ordering device for the epoch. Whether it is the use of water or the production of waste, the aggregate of human activity is such that global forces are released in nature which impact on humanity as a whole.[13]

These arguments involve subtle distinctions, but much hangs on them, just as for the left the importance of feudal survivals in capitalist society gave material for interminable wrangling on political strategy and tactics. In global society the rationalization process has its own momentum, but its outcome increasingly becomes an environment for social life rather than its structuring principle. At the moment when nature is re-embraced and humanity takes back the natural world into its self-definition, it is rationality which is externalized and becomes a resource, a danger, a playing field.

In other words the key change is not reflexive modernization, but globalization, where globality has replaced rationality as the dominant characteristic of the age. But since rationality is a set of principles and globality a material frame of reference, the change is to the total configuration of human activities. It is not like changing the destination of a journey, one day flying to Rome, another day to Mecca, and everything else such as means of transport unchanged. It is more like one day being a Catholic and the next a Muslim, without even being able to find a common concept of religion. Rationality and globality are then incommensurable.

6.5 From Abstract to Material Systems

Why the abstract society may have passed its peak

The global shift both links human beings more securely to nature and at the same time emphasizes the materiality of the world they have created. Far from globalism being an extension of the universalism of modernity, it represents the recognition of the way universal ideas have to be tempered by the realities of global conditions.

The earth as global nature represents the generalization of principles well understood by the peasant producer in premodern times. A plot of land owned and tended by one household requires constant husbanding for long-term survival. The expansionism of modernity cast that care aside, with the prospects of continual accession of new land and natural resources. Now the effective complete enclosure of the world has reproduced the individual plot on a global scale. Global environmental issues, then, arise from the impact of the collective practices of human beings on the earth as a whole.

This in itself should be sufficient to dispel the illusion that globalization has meant the triumph of abstract universal ideas. It is a misapprehension which has arisen simply because the scale of change is confused with abstractness. Globality has emerged, however, as an end-point of the dissemination of productive practices, their collective nature and their aggregate effects. There is nothing particularly abstract about these, even if their scale and scope are vast. Globality indeed makes apparent the implications of their materiality.

So the sum of externalities of economic activity on a global scale can be calculated in terms of the depletion of a common resource, such as the rain forests, or damage to a general condition of welfare, such as the ozone layer, when at the level of the individual firm these effects are invisible. It is as a total effect on the world as a whole that the greenhouse effect will work, not simply in areas where hydrocarbon gases are released. Once the scope of the institution is global, the definition of the field of forces within which it operates must also be global.

Much the same transformation from abstract to concrete takes place with world markets. Abstract market ideas have always rejected monopolies as an alien intrusion into rationality, hence national legislation against them. At a global level it is possible to see an approximation to the ultimate monopoly, control on a world scale of a scarce and valued resource. It was the material and strategic significance of oil on a global scale and its place in the real economy, coupled with the control of the Organization of Petroleum Exporting Countries (OPEC), which dictated the crisis of 1973, and not impersonal operations of the world market.

We can see all the notable contributions to debate about the world's resources, from the Club of Rome (Meadows et al. 1972) through the Global 2000 Report to the US President (Council on Environmental Quality and the Department of State 1982) to the Brundtland Report (1987), as direct challenges to the sufficiency of free-market ideas for either desirable or even possible futures for the world. They each invoke material realities against the ideal operation of abstractions, a great irony seeing that it is the environmentalists who are so often accused of being removed from the real world.

This prominence of materiality in the Global Age runs counter to a standard critique of modernity, shared by such different figures as Popper (1945/1962), Berger et al. (1973) and Giddens (1990, 1991). They all hold that abstractness is a feature of modern life and associate this with a widespread sense of the remoteness and meaninglessness of modern institutions. Popper explicitly links this to the loss of a time when people were linked by 'concrete physical relationships such as touch, smell and sight' (1945/1962, vol. 1: 173).

Even prior to any consideration of globality there are objections to this thesis. Abstractness is a quality of ideas rather than of life or living, and not all ideas are abstract. Even if it is the case that modernity saw the expansion of the scope of abstract ideas, it also saw their application in very concrete ways. Understanding electricity involves some very abstract ideas of physics, an electricity grid involves a high level of abstraction and control, but the everyday use of electricity is a very concrete and practical experience.

The idea of abstract society is tied to the notion that relationships at a distance are in some way less meaningful than those based on co-presence, even though absence as well as presence must constitute any relationship for it to be called a relationship rather than a mere encounter. Indeed if co-presence amounts to concreteness then we can equally say that modern society is concrete in that so much of daily contact is of a face-to-face kind between people who will never meet again.

At the heart of the abstract society thesis is the feeling that abstractness is equivalent to remoteness and hence a sense of loss. Even if we accept that possibility for modernity, we can detect a retrieval of proximity with globality. That was already the message of McLuhan's (1962) metaphor of the 'global village', and his concern was mainly broadcasting media. The scope for concrete contact with others worldwide through telephone and air travel has increased vastly since.

Giddens's account of abstractness concerns systems and his juggernaut effect rather than social relationships. No one can deny that nuclear defence systems involve the ultimate in centralized control and remoteness from individuals, but their abstractness may be rendered horrifyingly concrete. Equally, abstract systems such as air traffic systems and international banking require specialized expertise and high levels of co-ordination and central control. Other 'abstract' systems have become increasingly concrete and accessible to individuals with the advance of information technology. Credit cards with a worldwide validity make credit less rather than more abstract; airline seat booking systems can relay concrete information worldwide rather than work with notional allocations.

There is now a global institutional framework based on systems which function for everyday life very much as the old natural environment did, conceived as an endless resource, without boundaries, potentially threatening but also a play area. This artefactual environment, just like the natural, is also a field of communication media and has been devised as such. Local cultural requirements are limited to variations which will not impair the standard worldwide operating base.

Telephone, fax, personal computer, cash dispensing machine, all are part of a worldwide interactive system of communication. Together with global broadcasting and intercontinental transportation, they constitute the media of globalization. At the same time, experience and competence in their use, including concern for other users, become a necessary feature of the individual's general ability to engage in effective social participation. They therefore also provide an infrastructure for personalized and group innovative responses to the Global Age. The tension between standardized media and individual styles becomes a main theme for cultural critics of globalization. For political critics the new opportunities for networking global movements are a potential counterweight to the control exercised by system managers.

In all these respects globality has not made systems more remote from people. On the contrary, the end of the Modern Age may well represent a high point of abstract society from which we are now descending. The next chapter explores that possibility by examining the ways people construct, make use of and respond to globality.

7

Configurations of the Global Age: People

> For whom is there still an absolute compulsion to bind himself and his descendants to one place? For whom is there still anything strictly compulsory? As all styles of arts are imitated simultaneously, so also are all grades and kinds of morality, of customs, of cultures. Such an age obtains its importance because in it the various views of the world, customs, and cultures can be compared and experienced simultaneously – which was formerly not possible with the always localised sway of every culture, corresponding to the rooting of all artistic styles in place and time.
> Friedrich Nietzsche, *Human, All Too Human: a Book for Free Spirits*

7.1 Global Movements

How globalism and consumer capitalism collude in appealing to values beyond nation-state definitions

The characteristic politics of the new age is not nationalism, the features of which we will discuss later, but globalism, the commitment to values which reference globality, mobilizing opinion and identifying with like-minded people on a worldwide scale. Global movements do not have to be globalist, but the pressures of globality tend to push them in that direction.

If we consider the women's movement, the appeal to women to mobilize as women by its nature crosses nation-state boundaries, even as it may focus on national issues and result in national organization. The resulting internationalism then comes face to face with the globe. Robin Morgan's account of compiling anthologies for the women's movement illustrates this very well. She compiled one for the women's movement in the United States first. At that time, in 1968, she says that a cross-national network did not yet exist. An internationalist perspective surfaced, however, while she was working. Her reflections in turn on her second anthology led her to see women as the majority force in a species which has 'the capacity to eradicate all life on the planet'. She follows this comment by affirming the goal of 'redefining all existing social structures' (Morgan 1984: 3). This sequence is not a necessary one, either for a personal biography, or for a movement. It reflects epochal shift from modern to global.

The modern thrust in the universalism of the appeal to women as women binds them together within nation-states, and equally results in two broad levels of linkage: networks of national organizations, and transnational interpersonal networks. These can expand until they are global in extent, even if globality does not inform their outlook. But at the point where each recognizes what is equally the scope and potential limit of their activity, namely the condition of women world-wide – that is, takes globality into account and adopts a strategy where any feature of that condition anywhere becomes in principle a salient aspect of their work – they become globalist.

We must distinguish, then, several distinct moments in the shaping of worldwide movements in the Global Age. One is the abstract universalism of the modern period, which develops into a characteristic internationalism. Historically it was represented most obviously in the international working-class movement, to the extent that the term 'international' acquired suspect connotations for nineteenth-century governments. A second element is a sociality which crosses boundaries, inherent in the notion of a social movement where people and ideas both travel and change. This is not even particularly modern, though there was a specifically modern response to it. Norman Cohn's account (1957) of the movement of people and shared longings in the millenarianism of the later Middle Ages in Europe is not simply a precursor of modernity but an example of the interweaving of religious experience and social flux which has occurred so often in other civilizations.

The emotionalism of ecstatic religious experience has always involved the possibility of creating new bonds and social forms across existing boundaries. In the global movement the intoxication of the experience works in the same direction as what is ostensibly its opposite, the cool rationalism of belief in a universal order. But they are reinforced by a third element, new global communication possibilities. So older twentieth-century Pentecostalism acquires a new form with the 'Toronto Blessing'. Outbreaks of uncontrollable laughing and crying in religious gatherings are nothing new, but when they happen in a church at the end of a runway, the Airport Vineyard in Toronto, within nine months it is possible for over 4,000 clergy and others from abroad to visit, share the experience and take it back with them to countries around the world. It is a testimony backed up by faxes, e-mail and international telephoning (Richter 1996).[1]

The Toronto Blessing is then an obvious example of globalization in the sense of the global dissemination of a local practice, or at least of a place name which came to be associated with a practice, for the Airport Vineyard had already been evangelized by an internationally known preacher, Rodney Howard-Browne. But the movement most characteristic of the Global Age has a fourth element, namely a response to globality, the espousal of globalist values. In this respect the Unification Church of Sun Myung Moon is a typical product of the Global Age, global millenarianism. Born, in their own terms, out of the confrontation with godless world communism, they concentrate on forming a new sociality focused on saving the world, and organize and communicate worldwide accordingly.

Globalism as a general orientation belongs to the human rights, peace, green and women's movements primarily. In the slogan of René Dubos, 'think globally, act locally,' it has become synonymous with a style of political action which relies on making political statements outside the established political channels of the nation-state, by legitimating local actions with reference to global requirements. The state is effectively occluded. For this reason Alain Touraine (1981) has long campaigned to recognize the movement rather than the nation-state as the basic category for contemporary sociological analysis.

Globalist movements operate through symbolic acts of protest, networking rather than creating authority structures, demonstrating the political dimension of everyday life, opposing dominant power structures whether in the clothes worn, the food eaten, or in sexual relationships. Membership of a global movement is a matter of demonstrating to like-minded people significant commitment through a range of symbolic acts, from wearing badges and insignia at the simplest level, through to the choice of a completely alternative lifestyle.

Elements of globalist thought go back to resistance to modernity as such, to countercultural movements of the nineteenth century, romantic and anarchistic attempts to establish alternative communities. In their opposition to state-engendered rationalized living, they inherently crossed boundaries and invited support across them. But it was only in the second half of the twentieth century that these movements responded to globality.

The threat to humanity as such from a potential nuclear holocaust became the paradigmatic global condition to which all opponents of the nation-state system could rally. The activities of global institutions in promoting knowledge of world environmental and population issues supplied constant concrete reference points for oppositional cross-national political work.

Finally globality itself became the resource and medium through which the movements could operate. Communication at a distance serves the needs of opposition as much as it does of dominant institutions. It became realistic to mobilize support elsewhere in the world to bring pressure to bear on one case in one country, even on a whole system, as was the case with the anti-apartheid movement. The assumption of the presidency of the new South Africa by Nelson Mandela in 1994 represents the most important triumph ever of alternative political action.

Globalist movements derive their strength from the freely given commitment and surplus energy of ordinary people worldwide. They have no significant stock of capital in the form of equipment or money. What they have is human or, more precisely, cultural, capital. They gain from value commitments, knowledge and information which are commanded neither by the state nor by employers nor by coercive religion, and which do not have to be devoted by individuals to domestic consumption.

To this extent global movements depend on a range of features of production, consumption and employment in the contemporary capitalist system which foster the dissemination of new cultural practices, relativize group membership and encourage new identity formation. In sum, capitalism is a major factor in generalizing the idea of culture and promoting a notion of it which is oppositional to state definition and control. It is another of the contradictions of capitalism that while it operates in and through the state and relies on it for support at key points, at the same time it resists state regulation of its products and seeks always to expand its markets. This applies to cultural products as much as any others.

This is not say that capitalism has a direct interest in promoting global movements, simply that the processes which ensure that there is a receptiveness to new styles and images, which provide for discriminating tastes and require educated workforces, in other words, which relate to the consumers and producers of cultural capitalism, cannot control the discretionary use of those qualities. The discipline of the workplace is insufficient to control a workforce at those times when it exercises its consumer choices, and capitalism has to bow before, or at least pay due regard to, opinions on factory farming, carbon emissions and other widely condemned production practices – on grounds of consumer values.

Global movements, then, develop at a confluence between consumption-led capitalism and political participation. They break any easy assumption of the identity of interests between state and capital because they begin to represent an incipient global citizenship which national governments cannot ignore. The role of the environmental pressure group Greenpeace during the Brent Spar incident in June 1995 and the French nuclear tests in autumn 1995 was that of an equal interlocutor with governments and multinationals.[2]

7.2 Culture and Multiple Worlds

Globality restores the boundlessness of culture and promotes the endless renewability and diversification of cultural expression rather than homogenization or hybridization

The exercise of resistance through affirming globalist values against the interests of global capitalism appears as the most obvious example of the simple projection of nation-state society conflicts to a world level. It looks like a rather straightforward demonstration of the relevance of the old-established conceptual frame of reference. Global capitalism meets global culture.

But this is the point where such a simple interpretation misses the complexities of the Global Age. Globalization has not operated in a single dimension, nor is it a process which has altered every pre-existing tendency in culture and society. We should distinguish a series of quite distinct phenomena, broadly grouped under the heading of culture, but exhibiting quite different traits according to the economic, technical and power fields in which they are embedded.

We begin to talk about ideas, values, themes, images, imagined worlds, styles, projects, ideologies, discourses, logics, not as a lexicon of elements within some system called culture, but as diverse properties, causes and effects of the phenomena of a world constituted in ways which are open to endless exploration. The coherences we find are pockets of meaning, rather than an envelope in which all is contained.

The most significant sense in which the Global Age has brought new meaning to the idea of culture is effectively the way boundaries have been dismantled and the cluster of elements has been freed from limits placed on it in earlier discourse. But this only means that we have a better notion of the inherent indeterminacy of culture, which certainly precedes the Global Age.

Previous attempts to define culture and to bring it into a strict conceptual frame linked to social structure now appear as an inherently doomed kind of academic bureaucratic reason. The totality of a group's ideas cannot be gathered in an inventory or stocktake. Nor are they inherited by one generation from another as possessions. This is a stunted notion of the acquisition of knowledge and the creative results of the encounter between every new-born generation and the reality it experiences.

Moreover the idea that there are discrete cultures, existing on the same plane, possessed by different groups of people, so that they can be classified through a universally applicable grid of concepts ignores firstly the commonality, even universality of some elements, and alternatively the complete absence of others in some groups, so that effectively phenomena are incommensurable. Chinese script and calligraphy sit transversely across Western planes of meaning, bringing together people who do not speak the same languages. In the West the notations of music and mathematics cross the barriers of spoken language but native speech is entrenched in writing.

The universal cultural lexicon which enables us to compare and contrast discrete cultures does not exist; moreover every new development in technology brings out the possiblity of creating new planes of reality which travel across the world with astonishing rapidity. Computer technology is a complex of ideas, practices, logics and images which makes it possible for its exponents to share a potentially endless number of non-spatial worlds, interpenetrating other worlds in barely documented ways. But technology is culture too!

We are, then, dealing with an immensely complex configuration when we speak of culture in the Global Age, and we need to distinguish a range of different phenomena which relate to globality in a variety of different, sometimes contradictory, ways, and which may even on occasion be directly anti-global. The configurations differ, depending on whether we are dealing with science or sport, fashion or literature. But there are many themes which recur in these differing domains.

Margaret Archer (1988) has been scathing about accounts of culture which seek to reduce it to or conflate it with something else, usually to parallel something called social structure. Her plea is to retain the irreducible universals, and I would agree that we should seek always to find them. But the Pandora's box of what used to be called the human mind contains an infinite amount more than the universal, and it reproduces and diversifies at an exponential rate.

We may indeed also seek to combine these divergent tendencies. This was the thrust of the Inter-Cultural Performing Arts Project carried out at Goldsmiths College, London, in the late 1980s, impelled by a dialectical anthropology which sought both to identify underlying principles and to engage in the creation of new integrated theatre which would be interdisciplinary and intercultural. But as one of the participants, Andrée Grau, has pointed out, 'it would be naïve to see interculturalism as an overriding global phenomenon that transcends the differences of class race and/or history' (1992: 17). Thus, if we take as a historical example of popular interculturalism the development of the Trinidadian form of Carnival, in which a variety of arts combine with a mix of cultural traditions and are then transplanted and transformed wherever Trinidadians have moved, then we can see metamorphosis, both in art and the performer, as a dominant aesthetic (see Alleyne-Dettmers 1996). Globality in this case becomes a factor for the acceleration of metamorphosis.

The culture/society equation of nation-state discourse is a major casualty of the Global Age, but we should stress that this is not as a result of globalization *per se*. The boundary crossing of ideas, the pragmatic accommodation between peoples, the spread of new discourses and modes of thought long pre-dated the globality of the second half of the twentieth century. But so long as the nation-state imagined it could confine these through policies of pluralism or multiculturalism, they were regarded as staging points on the way to some fuller integration. With globality arrives the recognition that they are endlessly renewable irrespective of nation-state boundaries. Global culture is not a managed system.

If we take the world of performing arts, European music, dance and drama have been performed worldwide throughout the modern period without dominating or excluding other forms. At the same time, a variety of other genres have been generated, such as jazz, rock, reggae, which have arisen out of contact between cultures and from changes in technology and audiences. The proliferation of the different media – TV, cable and satellite, compact discs, radio, both studio and live performance – have in one way simply extended these possibilities of worldwide performance and this is open to performers from any culture.

But there is a new turn. The media which carry these global possibilities themselves become the focus of the celebration. The possibility of performing live simultaneously to a world audience prompts the staging of spectacles which seek to accomplish ecstasy and, simultaneously, awe at the idea of the world viewing itself. This was the intended global village effect of the Live Aid concerts overtly designed for the celebration of globalist values. These staged global spectacles are unwilling to detach the musical performance from a celebration of the worldwide audience which the technology makes possible. They have for that reason been deliberately used to raise responses to global images, of poverty and starvation, where worldwide news manufacture equally relies on finding universal symbols of the human condition.

It seems also to be the case that the fame needed to justify occupying the global stage, and which in turn is aided by it, requires music to be subordinated entirely to the performer. The audience response becomes as important a part of the event as the performer, who seeks an exposure in which art is subordinated to the celebration of his or her own uniqueness. This is necessary for the entertainer to stage an ecstatic communion of the senses with the audience and for the audience to feel equally freed and to celebrate a global unity beyond the formal requirements of aesthetic appreciation. The performer sets up a direct relation with the audience at every opportunity in the act, encouraging the breaking of barriers up to but not including the loss of the privileged position as performer. For this reason, rock has become the global performing art, although there is no reason to think it will retain this exclusive position. This is, then, the transcultural experience, especially redolent, however, of hi-tech American/British entertainment.

There could be no more striking contrast with the way technology disseminates diverse and rare cultural experience. Opera or classical Indian music may be heard anywhere in the world by the dedicated enthusiast using specialist suppliers and a well-developed knowledge of points of supply and access. Globality permits and requires this, with local centres, travelling groups or other forms of organization which will vary according to the requirements of the genre. The technical infrastructure makes all possible.

The consequence is the parallel coexistence of diverse style, genre and cultural origin in the arts replicating social diversity in any one locality. It is a challenge to those globalist values which seek to reconcile opposing groups. For example, the deliberate juxtaposition of diverse styles from anywhere in the world, presented in a way which encourages the multiple experience, is the explicit programme of the WOMAD Foundation. It was set up in 1983 'to promote, maintain and advance education in world cultures and multicultural education' and has organized music festivals in dozens of countries (WOMAD Festival 1994). Sounds from the Cameroon rainforests produced with Western instruments, Celtic styles with the didgeridoo, Arabic chants and Bali rhythms compete with each other for attention, while paralleling the music are exhibitions on Third World social conditions, opportunities to learn dance styles, join in with music and wear Carnival costumes.

Multicultural diversity was a theme of the world fairs and exhibitions from the London 1851 Great Exhibition onwards. Globality has intensified the deliberate exploration of relationships between different cultural expressions, sounds, styles and instruments swinging between juxtaposition, fusion and the celebration of difference. They are metaphors for living in a multicultural world, exploring how far the boundaries of experience can be extended within a frame which seeks always to represent the necessity of and reproduce the conditions for peace.

However, it is precisely that frame which becomes problematical under global conditions. The world of Western imperialism provided hierarchies and ideas of civilization harbouring aesthetic codes. But in the Global Age the new technical transformation of experience is as important as globalist values in conveying the impact of globality. Interactions between audiences and exponents, interpenetrating art forms, crossing cultures, inversions of medium and meaning become essential parts of a postmodern imagination. The issue which is open is whether these are freed from a specifically epochal significance. Has culture finally freed itself from time, place and social experience? The answer so far is no, if we take Deena Weinstein's account of the Amnesty International concert tour of 1988 as 'a paradigmatic postmodern event' (1989: 61). It may have escaped both the Anglo-American centricity of the Live Aid concert and the international competitiveness of the Olympic Games, and the twenty-concert Amnesty tour offered a transnational experience of world community. But the concerts were customized for different countries and the tour was equally a celebration of liberal capitalism, offering as many meanings as customers could consume.

This is a salutary reminder of how globality works on culture through consumer capitalism as much as through globalist values, and that global communication technology is bound up with both. Fredric Jameson (1991) in particular has stressed the consequences of late capitalism for culture, but it is also more open to other influences than his use of 'cultural logic' would suggest.[3] The global competition is the other side of global competitiveness. It seeks to identify the individual or group which attains excellence according to pre-set standards. Here the emphasis is on global standardization as a frame within which national training can work and which permits comparisons between nations. This is a straightforward extrapolation from the modern period, deriving its strength from the commitment of nations to transnational organization. But the signs here are that globality will result in both a proliferation and weakening of these frameworks, since their strength depends precisely on exclusive control. We cannot derive either globality or culture from capitalism. They each have their own autonomy in influencing the other.

Simultaneously, standardization of both product and consumer taste with technical advance produces a karaoke effect. The possibility of simultaneously providing and separating soundtrack, backing music, screened lyric, voice amplification and any volunteer singer to make a unique performance of a song which has become familiar worldwide makes the individual performance a global act. Anyone, anywhere in the world, might find the conditions reproduced in which they can simulate a world star. Ordinary person becomes icon, if only in the staged, ephemeral shared illusions of the club audience.

Briefly reviewing these cultural shifts we have noticed the celebration of the technology of globality and the global manufacture of fame; the worldwide dissemination and maintenance of specialist, refined tastes; the promotion of globalism through multicultural experience; the alliance of capitalism and transnationalism; competitive standardization; and global self-performance.

The variety of this list is sufficient in itself to indicate why it is impossible to think of globalization as a one-dimensional, unidirectional process, indeed why the term is often used in a way which distorts and curtails the diversity of orientations to and consequences of globality. The argument about globalization is often conducted in either/or terms, either homogenization or hybridization. The terms are unfortunate, and each betrays their origin in particular critiques of modernity. The first sees globalization largely in the light of standardization, and therefore as an extension of the mass production methods of high industrialism, with mass consumer tastes and the levelling of differences in taste between groups. The latter stems from the theory of ethnic relations early in the twentieth century and has been transferred to other sectors, referring to the results of mingling between two groups. But the origin of the term in biology, with all the connotations of the stability of root stocks, carries through into social thought. The problem with the notion of hybridity is that it implicitly projects the idea of the primordial as an abiding source from which all else is derivative, rather than an image of perpetual change and renewal which corresponds better to the nature and history of human group formation.

Neither notion is well adapted to capture the multiple ways in which culture relates to globality. While standardization is an important feature of certain technical preconditions for global cultural participation – in specifications for recording equipment, for instance, or in global competitive activities – it may thereby also provide for maximum diversity in the uses to which these are put. So while new forms may result from contact between artistic expressions of different ethnic traditions, as with jazz, it is equally the case that traditional forms may be sustained as never before through the ease with which exponents can remain in contact. The diminishing significance of physical distance means that diaspora may be as effective as a way of maintaining culture as resistance to change in a locality.

The result is that the multiplication and diversification of worlds rather than homogenization or hybridization better express the dominant forms of cultural relations under globalized conditions. It is a conclusion similar to the view expressed by Mike Featherstone when he writes of global culture as a trans-societal process giving rise to emerging sets of 'third cultures' (1990: 1).

7.3 The Relativization of Identity

*How identity can no longer be confused with group membership,
and the way each is negotiable*

The multiplication of worlds means that individuals can inhabit several
simultaneously, but secondly that each severally can only make a small
selection from the many which coexist. The result of a plurality of
individuals making their own selections is that each builds a different
repertoire, and its total scope is obscure to everyone else.

This has major consequences in every sphere of social life, in
particular for the state, which has to accept the competing and cross-
cutting allegiances of its citizens, up to and even including the point
where they are committed to other states. But it has had equally direct
consequences for individuals and the theorization of their relations to
society.

The problem of individual and society has moved away from what
used to be the central issue, agency and structure, to the problem of
identity, and this has increasingly been made the focus of contemporary controversy as so-called identity politics has detracted from old-
style class politics. Identity politics has centred on the relative positions
of groups whose very existence is problematized by processes of global
social change. Where the identity of the group is problematical, this
translates into difficulty in assigning membership of the group to individuals. The result is that identity politics becomes a matter of identity for groups and individuals equally.

This development is difficult for much of older modern theory to
handle. In particular, both political theory, with its emphasis on citizenship as the route to social recognition, and sociological theory, which
stresses the construction of individual identity through social interaction, tend to postulate unambiguous, defined social formations as a
precondition for the emergence of clear personal identity. This is
compounded by an implicit psychological theory which sees the
development of personality itself as damaged by an ambiguous or
conflict-ridden social environment.

The difficulties of old modern theory are well illustrated by its response to nationalism and fundamentalism. The prevalent interpretation of the former is that it marks a return to primordial roots as
the frame of the modern state is disrupted by the end of the Cold War
or by the weakening of national boundaries through globalization.
The latter is explained equally as an urgent grasp on certainties when
the world around has become increasingly uncertain. Both then are versions of a totalizing theory which explains contemporary movements in

terms of the human attempt to re-establish a firm structure after an earlier one had been lost. Both theories are compatible with an account of globalization which sees it both as a disruptive force and as a dissemination of Western images and ideologies. Effectively, in each case, theory offers an understanding based in old modern social scientific discourse. Both leave the victims of nationalism and fundamentalism without even intellectual consolation.

Neither account does justice to the dynamics of the phenomena under the conditions of the Global Age. In particular they neglect the transformations of structure which the multiplication of worlds has created. For a start we have to distinguish the identities individuals acquire by their membership of a multiplicity of groups, from their accounts of themselves and their ability to construct such narratives. Self-identity is constructed out of the experience of social life and group membership, not by assimilation to one or other unique group. Personal identity is forged out of individual experience of complex social life, and its public correlate is not membership of a particular group, or even set of groups, but the unique identifier to which every person in the world has a right. Identity is a unique particularity recognized in the universality of the right to be a distinct human being.

Under globalized conditions it becomes less and less easy for individuals to affirm their identity within the strict confines of nation, gender, age, or any other categorical distinction. Moreover the great majority of individuals do not want to do so.

The prevalence and media attention given to the extreme expressions of nationalism and fundamentalism, the massacres in Bosnia, the hounding of Salman Rushdie, should not blind us to the fact that the chanting crowds or gun-wielding youths are minorities vis-à-vis the larger minorities they claim to represent. For it is effectively not representation but intimidation through force and threats issued against their own people. Moreover the motives cannot be assessed by taking the slogans at face value. The fanatics are the dispossessed. They have lost the allegiance of the people which their forebears could take for granted. Their resort to force is not a measure of the frustrations of their people, but a sign of their weakened hold over them under globalized conditions, or else of a power vacuum where established state control has broken down.

Two questions arise out of this account of the place of extremism in the global world. The first is whether the state as we understood it in the modern era is in a position to respond, and we will look at that in the next chapter. The second is what the social configurations are which replace the older nation-state societies and which I contend provide the dominant ways today in which individuals find their identity. We will consider this now.

7.4 Reproducing Society

How in negotiating relationships people constitute social reality and
why children are metaphors of this process become literal

Nowhere have the consequences of the relativization of old identities
proved more controversial than in the area of sexuality and personal
relations. Here again we can identify two fundamental forces which
contributed to the simultaneous transcending and destabilizing of
traditional social relations in the modern period. The first was an
intensification of cross-cultural contact and the consequent comprom-
ises in customs between cultures, leading to the more general sense
of the relative nature of the relations between the sexes. The second
was the pressure from capitalist development, which has always
recognized culturally defined relations between the sexes for consumption purposes, but been ever ready to erode them in the production process.

In the late modern period the feminist movement has drawn strength
from these destabilizations and from the generalization of human rights
issues to campaign for women's rights on a worldwide basis. Against
this background, attempts by nation-states to maintain traditional
relations between the sexes have been contradicted by their own equal
rights legislation. Out of these contradictory currents an implicit general
code emerges transcending the conflicting parties.

Equality between the sexes makes sexuality equally a negotiable
part of their relations. In other words, sexuality is made dependent on
the wills of the two parties, and once severed from the legal necessity
to be confined to a particular authoritatively defined relationship called
marriage, sexuality has become an element for free determination, both
between members of the different sexes and between members of a
single sex. To that extent sexuality has been made both gender free
and a matter for individual exploration, alone or with others.

This implicit code does not mean that sexuality is not a fraught
area. On the contrary, it is contested, controversial and replete with
conflict as older definitions of right conduct compete with each other
and contest the new ethos. But the implicit code has the advantage of
crossing cultures and offering individuals freedom to explore where
older codes require restraint. Any disadvantages are discovered rather
than issued as threats. But the premium placed on knowledge, understanding and ability to learn from experience is correspondingly greater
for the individual, and the costs of mistakes fall on others too.

Sexuality becomes part of the exploration of the nature of relationships. But that means that the contingent nature of each in respect of the other as well their separate existence becomes a central issue. More concretely this directs attention to gender as the universal main classificatory device for organizing sexuality in social relationships and as one of the core sources of social identity.

Beyond the question of the search for the pure relationship, which undoubtedly is a subsisting element in contemporary social relations, is the search for the social frame for personal self-identity. In premodern societies, relations between men and women were defined as complementary. Long term male/female dyads embedded in extended kin relations spanned the greater part of the daily activities of each adult member of society. In modern societies the gendering of activities in the wider world persisted, while the dyadic relation retreated into sexuality and the home. Public and private spheres were created. But subsequent shifts in the gendered activities have consequences for the private dyadic relations. Sexual politics takes place in the household as well as at work.

At the same time, the commodification of domestic consumption has extended to sexuality through products which alternately use sexual signs and symbols and promise sexual gratification. While much commercialization of sex uses traditional gender stereotypes, the usual commercial pressures produce equally diversity and encouragement to try new products. The image of capitalism stabilizing traditional sexual relations is then a considerable underestimation of the way it persistently erodes established social order and promotes new social practices.

The steady displacement of gender as a structuring principle in the public sphere and the development of sexuality as a consumption good have each contributed to the destabilization of older identities constructed on the basis of the male/female difference and have led to the creation of dyadic relationships as fields for exploration of self and other.

But this is not simply a matter of discovering the pure relationship, since it is the more general field of relations between the sexes which defines the terms in which the parties to a relationship try to find themselves and each other. They still need to negotiate with those whom they wish to have acknowledge their relationship, as well as with each other, what it is to be a man or a woman, or gay or lesbian.

In this sense, people in relationships are always engaged in constructing new social fields. The significance of the gay and lesbian communities for self-exploration and definition is widely understood. The same processes occur in heterosexual relations but the issues are even more complex because of the cleavages in the feminist movement around the topic of sexuality.

In the Global Age, because of their always conditional and explor-atory nature, new temporal and spatial definitions arise to govern the relationships between the sexes. In building their careers, partners to a relationship may put that on a level where they live and work in differ-ent continents. At the other extreme, a partnership may be pursued briefly for the purpose of providing a child for one of them.

Relationships become a matter of the discovery of personal identity in the course of creating something which goes beyond the personal and becomes a constituent part of a wider social reality. In that sense the profound sense of the social under global conditions is of its self-generative qualities, so that what happens between people extends far beyond them in time and space, making them parties to a collective product which spans and impacts on the globe as a whole.

This conceptualization of society will have, and to some extent already has had, its greatest impact on the future in according a new place for children. Once the crescive, socially generative nature of social relationships is acknowledged, the aspiration to have a child in a relationship becomes a metaphor for it, and the child becomes not simply the outcome of sexual relations, but a product and repres-entative of the particular social relationship.

In the old nation-state society the child was 'socialized'. That term was no accident, for the contribution of the parents to the child's upbring-ing was subordinated to the need to fit the child to an authoritatively defined social order. In the Global Age the child is the representation of the parents' relations to the wider world, all the way to signalling even an appreciation of the world's population problems, by remaining the only child or by arriving as the first child late in the woman's child-bearing years.

This could appear an idealistic sketch if it were not for the fact that the problems posed by the new place of children in society require more complex collective solutions than were ever conceived at the high period of the welfare state. For the aspirations of parents fail as often as they succeed; relationships often do not last as long as the children they bear; and children born under anything other than the ideal conditions suffer relative and absolute deprivations which leave them far worse off than their welfare state predecessors. In the gap for children between ideal and reality grow the seeds of possible cata-strophe in the Global Age.

The future of society will in some part be bound up with the recog-nition of its self-creative nature in the activities of each and every human being. Where that awareness is lost there is the ever present danger of a reversion to relativism and nihilism. Gazing into the abyss of the consequences of that reversion itself provokes awareness, so no one should fear the loss of innocence which social theory brings with it. But, equally, awareness without the action to avert disaster can remain just idle speculation.

7.5 Community, Socioscapes and Milieux

Why those who lament the loss of community should not ignore new and labile forms of sociality which may afford people equal value

The eclipse and survival of community was a standard theme of old modern theory: both the impact of industrialization on traditional patterns of life and the maintenance of community under conditions ostensibly ill-suited to it, in cities or in shanty towns. Research was dominated by the idea of locality, neighbourhood and proximity. To this extent an administrative logic attached to it, in spite of the researchers' normal concern to be quite detached from official definitions. For the modern state the division of its territory into areas and sub-areas, working in conjunction with centrally defined and functionally co-ordinated tasks, has been an axiomatic principle of organization. Research which looks at bonds of locality effectively fits within that logic if it disregards the bonds which tie people to other social units.[4]

Territoriality distinguishes the state from churches, where as a principle it is subordinate to the *oecumene* of believers, though where there are state churches like the Church of England the parish has doubled up as a state and religious unit. T. S. Eliot (1939: 29) viewed the parish as an ideal unitary religious-social community, in which all classes were represented. Other organizations which seek a territorial basis, households, schools, farms, sports centres, find security only under the state's aegis and protection.

But the logic of capitalism has long left locality behind as a principle in the social organization of economic life. Separations of home and work took place early in the modern period. The modern state was therefore continually faced with the contradictions between its own and capitalist principles of organization, without ever being able to resolve them. Waves of reorganization persistently afflict state administration as it tries to accommodate the contradictory needs of stable local living conditions and the ever expanding spatial freedom required by production and consumption at the current level of capitalist development.

It is left to people of all kinds to develop their own responses to the situation the state can never succeed in managing. Moreover they do so by making whatever use they can of the facilities of new technology. Effectively, in all kinds of ways, social life has been deterritorialized, so that there is no longer any validity in many parts of the world in social scientists seeking to impute the coherence and integration of social activities to the local area where they take place. Locality loses any unequivocal significance in a social sense; rather it becomes a site for multiple coexisting worlds.

The social activities which transpire in any one area are disconnected from each other, but equally are parts of social worlds which may extend beyond localities and national boundaries to the globe as a whole. This applies not simply to the more obvious economic linkages, work for a multinational, or a retail outlet of a national firm, but equally to kin, friendship and special interest relationships. These can all be sustained actively at a distance, through telephone, letter and cheap transportation. David Harvey has summed up these developments as time–space compression (1989: 241).[5]

The image of the close-knit working-class urban community, sharing leisure time, intimately connected through marriage, with a common experience passing from parents to children of employment and motherhood, is now as much part of the mythology of modernity as the village community, with its shared customs and rooted experience of the soil, was to premodernity. In each case the image is at variance with reality but is sufficiently expressive of dominant tendencies to serve as a benchmark for comparative analysis. Even if the discordant reality were taken seriously, then the social critic would look to community within the state's borders. So Eliot spoke of the 'Community of Christians' within England (1939: 46).

In the Global Age there is as yet no equivalent dominant image of community, largely because inclusiveness characterized both rural and urban versions. The communities of the Global Age generally have no local centre. One type engages only segments of the lives of the individuals who adhere to them and is occupational, professional, educational, or based on an elective special interest. The use of the term 'enclave', as in Robert Bellah's 'lifestyle enclave' (Bellah et al. 1985: 71–5), is an effective way of conveying the way sociality may be configured in a way which is neither total, functional nor local and yet serves as a vital reference point for its adherents.

Where there are localized bases for community then they serve predominantly a special category of people, the retired and elderly, those with learning difficulties, a selective recruitment at odds with the inclusiveness of the old communities. Or else the cult or the sect may respond to the globalized world and offer a total way of life to its adherents, without succeeding in deflecting the course of the wider world, even if that is the explicit justification for its activities.

The Utopian localization of community is the opposite pole to the decontextualized activities taking place in increasing numbers of localities in the globalized world. In them the context of daily activities is obscure even to near neighbours. Such localities are sites for people each of whom will be part of a unique multiplicity of constituted frameworks of social relationships and interactions, only some of them being focused in the local area. People living in the same street will have fleeting relationships with each other, have widely differing lifestyles and household arrangements, and have a common interest only in the maintenance of certain shared facilities they take for granted. In fact the maintenance of those facilities is correspondingly more difficult given the weakness of the ties between people and between them and the area.

If we want to characterize these relationships between people living in the same area under globalized conditions, it might best be called disconnected contiguity. In the light of old modern theory, effort will be directed towards interpreting it as disorganization or anomie. But this is not an appropriate conceptualization. It concentrates on place rather than space. The lives of people in this situation are neither disorganized nor meaningless. On the contrary they are engaged in intense social construction generating connected activities whose geographical scope reaches as far as the globe (Budd and Whimster 1992). They inhabit spheres of social life which intersect at the locality they occupy for the moment without ever interfering with each other. This is why the image of the sphere is appropriate: sociospheres have orbits which cross in space but never touch. It is the polar opposite of the idea of the functionally integrated community. The only single overarching social unit to comprise them is world society itself. Their traces in any one locality may be virtually invisible.

An Asian woman from East Africa who lives in London visits India every year and talks to her sister in North America. A white professional who works in the City talks to the Far East four or five times a morning and attends a wedding in Madras. A retired woman who has lived all her life in one area of England writes to France and the United States and entered into correspondence with Terry Waite while he was a hostage in Beirut. A black community worker in England telephones Jamaica every week and visits every year. A young man, unemployed and black, born in London, only notices friends on the estate and a few outside troublemakers. They might live in one of any number of streets in London in the 1990s.[6]

Developing an idea of Appadurai (1990), we might characterize the social life of the locality as a socioscape: like a landscape the parts fit together, are viewed differently depending on one's position and interests, even provide an aesthetic experience, but the principles holding it together depend on factors far beyond the gaze of the beholder.[7] Just as in the landscape, rules of composition govern the distance between and integrity of its elements, so in the socioscape rules of everyday living, especially those summed up in Goffman's felicitous term 'civil inattention' (1972), govern the comings and goings of its occupants. Its existence depends as much on refraining from infringing the conditions of life for others as on any positive contribution to each other's welfare. 'Minding your own business' and 'not getting involved' are socioscape norms and sustain the freedom to participate in far-flung sociospheres.

Deterritorialization contributes to removing misplaced concreteness from sociological, and perhaps eventually also from administrative, concepts. The delinkage of community from place permits new theoretical formulations which emphasize the contribution of imagination to social reality. It contributes to a radical phenomenology which addresses the transformation of social life as much as eternal essence.

It is not possible to anticipate where such a theoretical turn will take us, but it always limps behind the real changes people have effected in their lives. For a start, once community and place are separated we are bound to ask whether disembedded community is actually what people now seek to construct, or whether there are not alternative directions implicit in the directions of their lives.

It may be that they seek as much as anything a familiarity in their surroundings and confidence in shaping the conditions of their lives as they discover the extent to which they can share values with others. It is a thrust effectively expressed in the contrast between 'personal milieux' and 'social structure', a distinction C. Wright Mills once called 'one of the most important available' (1956: 321).

When conceived crudely as the connection between individual and immediate environment, the milieu idea is easily absorbed into a positivistic view of social structure. When it is not reduced in this way, it conveys the way individual confidence in self and the world depends on the maintenance of familiar conditions to which a person contributes vitally (Grathoff 1989: 432).

The milieu concept therefore is well suited, in the way the community idea is not, to capture the importance of the abstract or far distant for everyday life. For the scholar, access to the US Library of Congress may guarantee her milieu even as she works in Toronto. For the trader in securities in London, the familiar e-mail contact with the Hong Kong dealer is equally intrinsic to the order of daily events. Milieux may be extended as far as is practicable in the globe; they may also be generalized, guaranteed by the anticipated familiarity of every international airport lounge even before the plane has touched down. The milieu then is distinct from locale.[8]

It is equally distinct from the emotional sociality implied in community. While the milieu involves people, it is entirely open about the nature of the relationships with them. And disruptions to personal milieux may involve far-flung or local events equally, a war in Kuwait or street repairs. For Erving Goffman, atomic weaponry effectively turned the world into 'one *Umwelt* which includes us all' (1972: 300).[9] In this sense, global threat effectively elides the distinction between international and personal security. Politicians concerned to tap the currents of the time for electoral support may therefore be better advised to consider aggregate satisfaction with personal milieux than the sense of lost community. They cannot assuage the latter, whereas they can make a recognizable contribution to enhancing the former.

7.6 Inequality and Stratification

Why stratification is a global phenomenon and people tolerate ever grosser local inequalities

The deterritorialization of social life, coupled with the disembedding of institutions from the nation/state society, means that the social configurations of the Global Age coexist as multiple worlds in the minds of people. As socio-economic realities they exist as a complex of stratifed spheres of varying extent and differential control over resources.

To link globalization with the often noted decline of class alignments in nation-state societies is therefore very likely to give rise to the spurious interpretation that there has been a decline of class inequalities in general. There is, on the contrary, every reason to propose that inequalities of wealth and life chances will continue to increase between individuals and between groups, but the distributional system of which they form a part is the world economy as a whole.

Thirty years ago it appeared that Marxist and conflict theories of class relations in modern societies were diametrically opposed. Marx sought to show how the political crises of the modern state arose out of the opposed interests of capitalists and workers. Conflict theorists like Dahrendorf (1959), taking a lead from Weber, emphasized the way power and authority relations structured the conflicts of both politics and the workplace. In historical perspective we can see now how their differing interpretations were of less importance than their common problem setting, the relations of class and the nation-state.

Both elements in that problem setting have changed. Whether one looks at the constitution of class in terms of an aggregate of positions in the productive process, or in terms of similar market position, or in terms of authority in the workplace, the development of capitalism has made it impossible either for analysts, or more importantly for actors themselves, to find locally or nationally based solidarities which carry any preponderant weight in national politics.

The struggles continue as the processes which set one group against another extend across the world. But the rich in rich countries can adopt several strategies. They can seek to align with the poor in their own country to resist or diminish the demands of the poor elsewhere in the world. Alternatively they can align with the rich in poor countries to resist the demands of their own poor. Those transnational options are always a source of potential cleavage for political parties when they seek to consolidate support among voters.

The problem becomes more complex where the parties can no longer hope to incorporate voters into the political process. Where life chances depend less on the outcomes of nation-state politics than on transnational ties of all kinds, we cannot expect solidaristic communities of political interest to emerge on a class basis.

But the decline of local and nationally based class solidarity is matched by the new-found expressions of common economic and political interest discovered by women, the elderly, ethnic minorities, homosexuals, the educationally disadvantaged. The decline of class as a factor in politics is then revealed as a decline in class community and the consequent unmasking of the segmented labour market. For class position does not belong primarily to individuals in the workplace but to structural categories of people, each of which have life chances dictated by legal and social discriminations deeply embedded in national traditions. Those are not local categories.

In so far as nation-states still control the legal status of minorities of all kinds, to this extent national politics is a salient arena for them. But since the old political parties were born out of modern class affiliations, they each offer competing attractions for minority groups. And in their mobilization, those groups draw on support from a transnational process of opinion formation. It is not simply a matter of applying ideas of human rights, though that is an important source of raised consciousness. It is also a question of recognizing that identity extends beyond national definition and that personal fates are linked to global conditions.

Contrary to many of the interpretations of globalization, the declining significance of nation-state societies in the organization of social life does not mean the end of stratification or the phenomenon of class, only that they cannot be equated with the social structure of a national entity. We considered the residents of our hypothetical London street as occupying differing sociospheres.[10] In that place they present themselves to participants and observers as a socioscape (Albrow 1996). It is a section, very limited in time and space, of the wider society and, as a section, severed from the wider society, it displays blatant juxtapositions of contrasts and disparities, a concurrent display of cultural diversity and traces of differing historical time-frames. It is in a place where social interaction reduces to everyday routines of passing the time of day, and common culture extends not much beyond parking routines and the corner shop.

But this local place is the area where hugely diverse sociospheres intersect. People pass without interfering with each other (hence the celestial imagery of spheres, nothing to do with shape but much with motion) and conduct their days as parts of networks of immensely varied size and dispersion, as members of families, firms, syndicates, associations, unions, churches, cults, parties, movements and conspiracies.

Residents then share in varyingly constituted social formations which have differing access to power and resources and require different types of personal engagement, including travel and distance communication. The huge expansion of transportation and communications technology vastly increases the possibilities of maintaining extended networks. Hence one of the characteristic forms which social stratification takes now is the extent to which individuals can move and communicate freely in the spheres which they occupy. Very broadly the space limitations on a person are linked to the resources which they can command in the spheres to which they belong. So stratification in general is a phenomenon of world society, incident upon localities, not a local phenomenon, like a peasantry, generalized into a class when external circumstances permit.

Social stratification, the hierarchical distribution of people according to characteristics such as power, money and status, is now not directly mediated by class but by membership of groups which command these goods and which are themselves ranked by their control of time and space. It is the groups which have the class position. If we consider the phenomenon of the power elite in the world today, it moves and communicates literally across continents with the most sophisticated information technology, air travel and multiple residences. It can preserve its past through accumulating artefacts, and guarantee its future through investment. Nationality is merely another life-chance factor and national boundaries calculable opportunities or hazards.

None of this is to say that the traditional working-class community does not still exist somewhere, just as the village community or even the preliterate forest dwellers may. But these are not the characteristic forms of social life for globality. The coexistence of these forms with vastly different histories poses its own problems, theoretical and practical. The problem for social scientists is that our theories have not yet accommodated the realities of the new age, and the uncertainties this brings have produced intellectual responses which substitute nihilism for the careful observation of the way people are making new social realities. The contemporary crisis is as much one for intellectuals as it is for people leading ordinary lives.

8

The Future State and Society

In the metaphysical view it is itself the sole guardian of moral worth. In the democratic view the sovereign state is already doomed, destined to subordination in a community of the world. In the metaphysical view it is the supreme achievement of human organization. For the truth let the present condition of Europe be witness.

Leonard Hobhouse, *The Metaphysical Theory of the State*

8.1 Recovering the Social

Why globalization brings back the social into the centre of concern for politicians

The Global Age means the emergence too of a new political order, though lagging behind the other changes we have surveyed. The slow pace of its development reflects the centrality of the national democratic state to modernity. Its crowning achievement was securing the union of state and society and the group which benefited most from that, the political class, finds it as hard as intellectuals to accept the transformation of the conditions which brought it into existence.

The delinkages of culture, community and relationships and their escape from the frame of the nation-state are constant sources of concern for politicians and commentators. They find it difficult to see them in any other way than as aspects of a general fragmentation of modern life. They undertake repair work with the rhetoric and solutions of the past. But it is a sign of the dated nature of their equipment when they advocate return to community, old values and modernization in the same breath.

The deeper, longer-term, historical diagnosis escapes them, namely that society and the nation-state have pulled apart. There are hints of this in talk about the rediscovery of civil society, although it is important not to allow the argument to stray into historical parallels. There is too much in current conditions which is novel. Our historical method is different. It requires us to understand the depth in time and scope across cultures of the idea of the social and then to identify the new conditions for its realization.

We can sum up our previous account of configurations of the Global Age by saying that essentially the social has been released by the impact of globalization on the inherent contradictions of modernity. A brief review of the organizing principles of nation-state society suggests how this happened. In that society, social relationships acquired a functional definition which suppressed the social. Relations became matters of business, contract, political power, delegation, marriage and so on. Institutional, and very frequently legal, definitions were held to constitute the core of the relationship and everything else amounted to random personal elements, allowing limited free play for tastes and emotion.

The purest theoretical expression of this was in a functionalist role theory which saw the dominant functions of society inscribed in role relations. Any activity which did not fall within these definitions became deviant and the sphere of the social *per se* was trivialized – crowds and chance encounters qualified but not much else. Paradoxically then, this idea of society differentiated into economic, political and cultural sectors suppressed the social nature of people.

Since the 1960s neither the many theoretical critiques of functionalism (with rare exceptions such as Touraine 1981), nor its managerialist elaborations have recovered the idea of the social.[1] We have had to wait for globality to impact on modernity and to release a side of it which always existed in tension with the nation-state, namely the transnational and the quest for experience. Globalization as a real process, not theory, has revivified the social.

It shows both in facts and theory. It is simply a fact that the nation-state has failed to confine sociality within its boundaries, both territorial and categorical. The sheer increase in cross-national ties, the diversification of modes of personal relationships and the multiplication of forms of social organization demonstrate the autogenic nature of the social and reveal the nation-state as just another timebound form. The reference to the global caps and reinforces this detachment from state definition.

In theoretical terms globalization is remarkable because it has cut a

swathe across disciplinary fields as widely dispersed as communication studies and geography, marketing and social theory. To that
extent it invites the question as to who are the bearers of the process.
The common feature of disciplines which, for clear intellectual pay-
offs, rely on rationalist or structuralist method is that they put people
out of bounds. Or, which comes to the same thing, they each bury a
distinctive, abstract idea of the social within their own discourse. Globalization then sweeps across as an extraneous process, as a contemporary historical reality which confronts disciplines with people in the
round. The social is much more then than its version in any one of the
analytical disciplines.

The reason we need now to return to the idea of the social is because
the relations which prevail between so many people under globalized
conditions can no longer be assimilated to old categorical schemes and
yet display both sense and sufficiently abiding qualities to take on a
real character. If the bond between a male and a female adult can no
longer be described simply as married or not married, or that between
two adults of the same sex simply as not married, then the quality of
the relationship becomes a central issue rather than an afterthought.
This gives them quite unpredictable political meaning. We can think
of the ineptitude with which contemporary politicians unsuccessfully
try to make capital by invoking categories like 'single mothers' which
no longer carry the message which they did in nation-state discourse.

Now the fact is that the old categorical schemes were never adequate
to depict social reality, but it took a strong act of intellectual will to
distance analysis from the self-descriptions of an age or a culture,
especially if they commanded authoritative force. The position now
is that self-descriptions take on such a rapidly changing and reflexive
character that they become standing candidates for empirical and
theoretical analysis. Government, since it can no longer determine
relationships, either falls back on old stereotypes, or, if it is wiser,
sponsors research to catch up with the changing social reality. But not
just any kind of research can make government wiser.

8.2 From Social Relations to World Society

How we can carry the social beyond presence as far as the world
can go

Research which has no guidance from theory easily runs into the sand.
The social theorists of globalization have already given us new pointers.
When Robertson (1992) points to the relativization of social relations

and collectivities, and Giddens (1991) theorizes the idea of the pure relationship, they lead us beyond modernity to questions of the universal
qualities of social relationships. The global reach of communication
emphasizes the reality of relationships at a distance and restores the
importance of absence, presence and frequency of contact to questions
of the strength and salience of bonds between people.

In the late modern period there has been an overriding emphasis
on the primacy of presence, on face-to-face and physical contact as
the fundamental constituent of social relationships. It has been the
counterpart of the myth of the primordial rural community contrasting with modern structures remote from human feeling. It has been
the basis of the dominant internal critiques of modern society. But
distance in time and space, discontinuity in presence and contact, is
constitutive of relationships in general and it is this which gives them
the abstract quality of being in the mind.[2] As we argued earlier (6.5
above) paradoxically the advance of global communication renders
relationships less rather than more abstract, but it does put the issue
of presence and absence into the foreground.

The necessarily abstract aspect of relationships is reproduced and
even more obvious in social formations larger than the dyad. It is a
crude misplaced concreteness which denies the existence of social
organization beyond the individual, from the mother and toddler
group, to the transnational enterprise, as far as society itself. This
scepticism about social organization gains strength, of course, in proportion to the increase of fluidity in contemporary forms of social
organization.

At first sight the relativization of social organization strengthens
the cause of those who would prefer to analyse the core meanings of
what the old modern structures contained: theology without believers,
game theory without players, wealth creation without workers. But
just because the old structures have declined does not mean people
have gone away. Rather their potentiality for combination, for movement, for individualized and collective responses to the world around
has been enormously amplified. There is now less chance than before
that abstract rational models of human behaviour, derived from first
principles, will be able to predict concrete outcomes in the real world.
There is simply less standardized behaviour about to serve as working
assumptions for the models.

Under conditions of indeterminacy there is a greater premium on
faith and commitment, and with globality a new source has arisen –
no longer transcendental values but the future of humanity on earth.
Globalism, all those values which focus on the condition of the globe
and the well-being of people in relation to it, has introduced a significant new dimension to universal values which, in the Modern Age,

had simply been expressed in abstract terms like justice, equality and freedom.

It is against this background that we need to review the idea of society. There has never been any difficulty since the ancient Greeks, or indeed in any other culture, in conceiving a general notion of the bonds between human beings, in other words a notion expressed in English as 'human society'. But this has no territorial reference. The main problem has always been in conceptualizing the barriers between ourselves and others. Once the nation-state determined that its people formed a society as opposed to others, the idea that there might equally be a world society became problematical. Indeed, for such a notion to be current, there had to be sense of the potential of ties crossing boundaries.

Although the idea of a world society is as old as political theory, it has never been seriously entertained as an immediate prospect, only as a tendency implicit in human political activity. Once human society was thought of as divided between nation-state societies, that prospect was seen in terms of the result of acts of political will. A world united by accident, like an empire obtained in a fit of absent-mindedness, was not predicted.

In fact the extent of transnational ties, of a non-state nature, makes the total set of relations spanning the world much more than the sum of nation-state societies. If we add two further elements, the recovery of the idea of the social and the positive evaluation of absence in social relationships, we can have no difficulty in attaining a concept of world society today.

The consequences of this unification for older concepts of society are radical. The categories, structures and boundaries of the old modern state appear now as problematical or alien to the organization of daily life for increasing numbers of people. As we have seen, social relationships have become an area for personal exploration rather than bureaucratic definition. Similarly, shorn of their purpose in the competitive power struggle between nations, the institutions of the welfare state no longer generate national solidarity but rather become the focus for distributive struggles around the state. The ways in which people come together outside the confines of the nation-state draw attention simultaneously to the universal and the personal in the construction of social life. In other words, world society exists not as a pact between nation-states but out of the ties which cross boundaries.

Whether this world society is yet, or could become, global society is a key question for social theory. World society is not yet something counterposed to the nation-state. It has emerged out of nation-state societies and could in some sense be said to parallel and be the social analogue of international trade.[3] Some of its operation is precisely in the form of the spanning of boundaries through family business alliances, family transfers of income across boundaries and migration for employment.

But, as we have explored already, the global is much more of a challenge to the old order than the international or the transnational. It is a direct alternative to organization based on nation-state boundaries and categories. From that point of view, global society has to be the structuring of social relations in a way which challenges nation-state definitions. It is the main challenge to the theory of the nation-state.

8.3 Beyond the Theory of the Nation-State

How late modern theory of the state developed to accommodate class divisions and why globalization as social transformation requires new theory for the state

The renewal of the idea of society means that the theory of the state has to be recast. The modern nation-state is neither the only possible form of state nor the crowning political achievement in human history. The conceptual frame which contained ideas of people, nation, society, state and government in an arbitrary territorial context was relative to a specific historical period. Locked in a modern thought-world, social theorists have often seen the distinction between those concepts as recent achievements. From outside modernity, the artificial elisions and conflations by which the nation-state sought to bind them indissolubly together look outdated. The bonds have now come apart.

In fact, throughout the modern period constant effort was exerted to bring reality and concepts to fit each other. From de Tocqueville (1854) onwards, through the rise of empirical social research and political sociology in the twentieth century, the theory of democracy responded to evidence of changes in power relations. So much so in fact that what was known as the theory of the state changed from being one of governmental institutions, of separation of legislature, executive and judiciary, to being one of legitimate control of those institutions. The concepts had to accommodate the realities of power.

Late modern theory of the state was concerned with two main problems in those realities. The first revolved around the question of consent, and the way a whole people could be persuaded to give up an original freedom to a collective body. The second tried to find a solution to the way freedom and welfare could be derived from a unitary body. The former was a theory of democracy and the latter a theory of rights.

Reflecting the shifting historical bases of modernity, the former issue has been associated primarily with the Anglo-Saxon world, the latter with continental Europe. In England and later in North America, until the twentieth century, freedom appeared to spring from local rights, either from time immemorial as in England, or from original power as in the United States. In Europe, on the other hand, power and right appeared more often to spring from the head of the prince who conferred dignity on his subjects.[4]

In each case, however, the issue became thorny because of the position of elites. Basically the American theory located the nation-state as the outcome of agreement between communities; it pictured a multitude of small (usually rural) communities whose representatives came to an accord to form a common identity as citizens of the United States. But where then was the federal state? The really disconcerting problem was to find that Washington was run by an elite without local roots – people with power, money and influence who owed nothing to local communities and everything to a different level of society which had no theoretical legitimacy.

The European theory equally came up against the problem of unrepresentative elites. It assumed that the central power holder would work with the best will through established institutions and rational principles. Right did not stem from the people, but from a fount of wisdom. But the problem which spoilt this vision was that the ruler required agents, and they so easily worked for their own selfish interests. Again a problem of elites, in this case the bureaucratic elite.

In other words, in both cases, which increasingly merged in the corporate state of late modernity, the problem centred on human agents, who did not fit a theoretical frame which supposedly represented the ideal way for a state to work. Basically the conceptual solution to discordant reality was found in the idea of the nation. From Hegel onwards in Europe the bureaucracy was conceived as the truly national class.[5] In the United States a power elite of fame, business and military connections equated their own success with the nation's ideal.

In this way the facts of class division in late modern society, following the rise of the working class and the welfare state, were squared with the ideals of equality of rights, citizenship and democracy. The rhetoric of equality of opportunity and service to the community legitimated the facts of inequalities of wealth, social hierarchy and concentration of elite power. The modern nation-state could even inherit the long tradition going back to Aristotle of seeing the unequal social division of labour as being inherent in the idea of the bounded national community.

But no sooner had the theory of the state solved the challenge of class division, by universal suffrage and then by democratic elitism and

corporatism, than it became apparent that new divisions were opening up. By the 1970s it became obvious that historic divisions of gender,
language, religion and colonial exploitation could have no legitimation in terms of a nation-state theory which had developed to accommodate class division. Patriarchy and the biological justification of
discrimination against women contradicted the clear messages from
the labour market that their participation in the workforce was more
important than child-rearing. Something other than capitalism, namely
historically rooted racism, worked against ethnic minorities. There were
no state mechanisms in place to defuse conflict on religious lines.

None of this meant that developments in capitalism were unimportant for the course of nation-state society, only that the shift in its
structure, technology and the international division of labour displaced
the focus on male industrial and white-collar workers on which the
old welfare state settlement was based. Economic globalization accentuated this shift, intensifying capital flows and shifts in the location of
production, while global communication raised the consciousness of
the groups released from the tight grip of nation-state conceptions.

There arose an increasing recognition that the boundaries of nation-
state society, in every sense of boundary, conceptual and territorial, are
the outcomes of historic power struggles which are reproduced and
reconstituted in every generation. The shape of the state as administration is the way in which these struggles become routinized in the
practices of daily life. But if those boundaries change so do the daily
struggles. Effectively the nation-state no longer contains the aspirations nor monopolizes the attention of those who live on its territory.
The separation of the nation-state from the social relations of its citizens
is by no means complete, but it has advanced a long way.

The crisis of the nation-state in the Global Age poses a considerable
task for ideology, namely making the new facts fit the old concepts,
and alternatively fitting new concepts to shore up old power relations.[6]
Even where commentators accept globalization as an empirically
ascertainable trend they tend to view it in the light of its implications for future government management of the economy.[7] None of
these arguments reaches the point of recognizing globalization as a
comprehensive social, rather than simply economic, transformation,
involving a shift in the total conceptual frame. The argument is largely
conducted in old terms which assumed an identity between nation,
state and government and a situation where internationalism reinforced nation-states.[8]

But it is no longer possible to equate increasing state activity with
greater governmental control, or more assertiveness by national governments with popular identification with the nation. What one commentator has called the 'nationalization of Britain' (Jenkins 1995), in the

course of which Conservative governments have vested local powers in central bodies, takes place against a background of disenchantment with government and politicians and the growth of regulation from non-national, especially European, sources.

When the state is a polycentric worldwide web of practices (see 3.4 above), where individuals assert their independent capacity to act as world citizens and national aspirations frequently reside outside established nation-states, then governments no longer control the fate of their populations. Where globalization is recognized as a social and cultural transformation, it is possible to see the underlying necessity for the reconceptualization of politics in the new conditions.[9] That recognition in the end will extend to a fundamental reappraisal of representative democracy and nation-state government.

8.4 World State

The state idea is only coercively backed activity for the common good. But whose activity and whose good?

The old pluralist theories of the modern state depended on the accommodation of class within the idea of the nation-state. Time–space social stratification jumps national boundaries, and class is no longer the dominant text for national politics. But at the same time the formation of the global managerial class transfers questions of class society to the global level. Just as late modern state theory was stimulated by class division in nation-state society, so the new global class puts the global state on the theoretical agenda. And just as national elites went about creating nation-state society, so we can expect the global managerial class to strive in the same direction for a global society. But is the idea of a global state to be the preserve of a global ruling class? This is the question which democratic theory in the Global Age has to answer. It can only do so if it realizes the advantages of having escaped from the iron cage of modern concepts.

The delinkages which globalization induces encourage us to restore to concepts meanings which modernity concealed. The postmodern world offers more than fragmentation; there is also the chance of retrieval and reconstruction. We can recognize a wider meaning of the state idea when nation-states, bound by the logic of their own administration, acknowledge law beyond their frontiers, state identity beyond particular governments, or the binding nature of interstate activities. State activities are therefore to that extent denationalized, polycentric and to a degree decentred, without central control.

The global shift leads necessarily to a reconceptualization of the state. It disaggregates the linkage of nation and state which national elites managed to effect and focuses attention on the development of institutionalized practices operating at the transnational level, and on the operation of global relevancies in the day-to-day activities of ordinary people. The delinking of the ideas of state and nation has been the most important aspect of the transition from the Modern Age to the Global. It clearly has its downside in the consequent release of suppressed nationalisms, but at the same time it reasserts the idea of state as distinct from the vagaries of the government of the day.

The idea of the state does not have quite the universality of the idea of society, but it has roots long before the modern period. In the later modern period the idea which has dominated has been Max Weber's, the idea of a body which can lay claim to the monopoly of the legitimate means of violence in a specific territory. This corresponds with one aspect of the modern nation-state, but it plays down the aspect Hegel stressed, namely the state as reason in human actions, in particular rational administration. At the same time it suppresses the extent to which there is always a residue of legitimate means of coercion left in the hands of individuals, even if only in the ideas of self-defence or passive resistance.

Premodern thought had no difficulty in conceiving the state in a much wider sense of an enduring collective activity for a common good, for which the use of coercion was one means among many, and that I would suggest is an abiding meaning beyond modernity. The rulers of the great Indian and Chinese empires over two millennia ago had available to them advice from Kautilya or Confucius which still speaks across the ages. They set out a vision of the state as orderly administration for the common good which the ruler had to tend with a fine sense for the limits of the use of force.

The most general problems of the state, ever since its idea was identified, have always been the following. Whose collective good? What is its scope? Who implements it? And how? Taking the early modern period, the main feature of the state's development was the incorporation of the feudal groups into its structure. The high modern period accommodated class, and in the late modern period the state has penetrated deep into the daily routines of the lives of ordinary people. If we take this time perspective, we can see that the state is manifested in and through the activities of all its people as much as those of a titular head or central organ of government.

In the Global Age the state is decentred, crosses nation-state boundaries, penetrates and is realized in the daily activities of ordinary people. In this sense a world state develops to parallel the growth of world society. Just as it is useful to identify world society as the sum total of social relations in the world, so we need an equivalent term for state activities. However, in this minimal sense the world state does not yet constitute an organized form of government and it is certainly not directed by the United Nations or any other world agency.

As the worldwide organization of humanity, the world state exists at the moment more as potential than reality. For instance, if we want to delimit its sphere in value terms from other state forms, then we have to say that it is defined by all those activities which take the good of humanity as a criterion for self-regulation. So the world state already exists where nation-states and their agencies regulate their bi- and multilateral relations by such criteria. But it would be starry-eyed idealism to imagine that such criteria dominate their concerns. Or again we would deceive ourselves if we imagined that all individual commitments to movements for peace and the world environment arose out of the highest motives. At the same time, if we close our eyes to the implicit reference to such criteria in state activity worldwide, we will completely misconstrue the changing place of the nation-state. World chaos does not ensue if we have no transfer date from the world of nation-states today to a ready-made New World Order tomorrow. The world state already has a place in the order of things.

However, it is vital to understand that the world state does not operate as the nation-state writ large. It originates out of quite different conditions – not from rivalry over territory and the insecurities of ruling classes, but in joint endeavours to control the consequences of technical advance for the environment, in shared interests in human rights and in a common fear of a nuclear catastrophe. It represents a new stage in the idea of the state, taking it beyond that configuration of monopoly of legitimate violence, nationality and territoriality. Their association with rationality and citizenship turns out to be historical, of the Modern Age, not intrinsic.

The world state, in comparison with the nation-state, reorders those elements, and itself is something other. It has not arrived in the way earlier generations expected. The transformation of communications, the practices of multinationals and the interests of nation-states between them have been far more important than a centrally imposed worldwide order. Moreover competitive nationalism extends its hold, is possibly more intense than ever, and can even threaten state order. Past visions of the future treated the linkage of state and society as such that a world order simply meant there would be a world state connected intimately with its corresponding social arrangements, universal values, harmony, basic human freedoms, even democracy.[10]

The new idea of the world state arises out of delinking the nation from the state. Once that delinking takes place then a whole series of disaggregations follows in quick succession. Violence is no longer the prerogative of the nation-state, human rights inhere in the relations between individuals and communities, welfare begins with households. Each one of these consequences generates a rhetoric, a horde of interpreters and libraries of books and papers.

In such a babel it would be all too easy to lose the idea of the state altogether. Indeed this is an ever present danger. For the dissociation of violence from the state can lead to its lodging in cliques, mafias, mercenaries and murderers. Detachment of welfare from the state can produce cardboard cities of the destitute. The apprehension arises that, delinked from the nation, the idea of the state could lose any appeal to the public-spirited. Throughout the Western world the political establishments fear the ebbing of interest in politics.

But the decline of the nation-state leaves intact its greatest achievement, the civic education of its populations, which have become not just the human resources of consumer capitalism but also the citizens of the world state. The decline of interest in national politics is paralleled by the rise of involvement in movements which seek to mobilize opinion on a worldwide basis on issues which nation-states have regarded as marginal to their own agendas.

For those movements, globality has become a key reference point and globalism a pervasive theme for values. In these respects they respond to and often become the antagonists of the global managerial class. They seek to bring influence to bear on whoever has work with a global remit or might have some aspect of the global fate of humanity as their responsibility. It is grass-roots mobilization on which Paul Ekins (1992) pins his hopes for a truly democratic new world order, and which Falk (1992) has called 'globalization from below'. We can go on to suggest further that it is where the most intense interaction and exchange on issues of globality takes place that the global state begins to crystallize. For the global state is both a variant of the world state and not yet realized in existing international institutions. We can see, incidentally, how vital it is to develop clear distinctions between the global, world and international.[11]

The United Nations and its agencies are the collective organization of nation-states, not a global organization. They cannot, either, achieve globally what the nation-states impose internally. For the internal organization of nation-states is vitally dependent on the construction of the 'other', non-citizens, foreigners, whereas a global state constructed on the basis of one nationality would have no 'other', unless it was to turn in on itself and find them in disfranchised, alien subgroups, a standing challenge to the order from within.

At the same time, in the management of globality, in the estimation of global forces and in environment, health and population, the United Nations has proved to be a free arena for the promotion of globalist values among its staff. Bodies like the World Health Organization, the Food and Agriculture Organization and the International Planned Parenthood Federation have as their main output the promotion of global criteria for a sustainable future and effectively provide the public forum in which states, capitalist organizations, and movements meet. As the global state emerges, it has not yet succumbed to the definitions of the global managerial class and there is no authoritative global social order. It is still open for the global state to take on a form which no state has ever yet had. But this depends on the qualities of its citizens.

8.5 Performative Citizenship

How the outcome of the state colonization of everyday life in a
global world is the ongoing renewal of the state by the people

A new realization of the idea of the state already inhabits the activities of multitudes of people worldwide. We only have to bring into the light of day a subterranean element below the consciousness of ordinary people and officials alike. The state is the most universal form of social organization for common need. It arises in both a recognition of, and capacity to impose, a solution to the most general practical requirements of living a life of common humanity. That 'recognition' and 'capacity to impose' is accomplished quite as much by ordinary persons in their daily lives as it is by the official of an international agency. In saying that, we affirm that the idea of citizenship has a vitality outside either representative democracy or the nation-state.

Again it is fundamental in appreciating this to relativize the modern achievement, to detach the idea of citizenship from modern discourse and to reset it in the longest and widest perspective. It is not difficult to do this as far as Western history is concerned, since citizenship was a key concept for the Greeks and Romans and their discussion of it had a profound influence on the moderns. I am going to suggest, against that background and towards that broader perspective, that we are experiencing the emergence of a new kind of citizenship, as opposed to the ancient and the modern.

If we take Aristotle again as the benchmark for the ancient discussion, his account makes the continuity of state structure depend on the activities of the citizen defined as 'a man who shares in the administration of justice and in the holding of office' (Aristotle 1946: 93). His account entrusts the state to citizens who are therefore its rulers – a possibility which was not entirely unrealistic, since the polis was small in size and only some men could be citizens. It is also an account which applies best to the polis with limited democracy and much less to states run by one person or narrow oligarchies. Fundamentally, then, Aristotle's citizenship is participatory, even if it is exclusive to a privileged group of men.

Modern citizenship began from a different starting point altogether, from the extension of centralized state power over populations which at the outset had rights far more limited than those Aristotle accorded to his citizens.[12] It therefore took its departure not from democracy, but from centralized and sovereign state power, and from that point took its meaning from the extent to which a wider population could benefit from and contribute to it. In other words, citizenship of the nation-state was a central feature of the Modern Project. It meant that the benchmark statement on the theme in the mid-twentieth century could quite unreservedly restrict itself to a citizenship which was 'by definition national' (Marshall 1964: 72).[13]

Effectively, then, the theory of modern citizenship has been a question of the relations between central power and citizens defined as beneficiaries and contributors, with rights and duties. The participatory aspect of citizenship, Aristotle's starting point, has never been primary because of the dominance of the centralized state within the Modern Project. Democracy has had to be representative democracy, only the least bad system, which the theory of the modern state has served by explaining why it cannot be any better. Aristotle's vision, where citizens were the power holders, has inspired Utopian and revolutionary thought in the modern period, but has never proved feasible for the nation-state.

Now those notions of citizenship, ancient and modern, do not exhaust the idea of citizenship, even in their own time. We are always talking of dominant types. There has also been an undercurrent throughout of an idea of world citizenship or, if one likes, of people ruling the world, but more precisely of the individual who takes on the welfare of humanity as a task to realize in daily life. It begins with Socrates, and we find it in medieval thought, in early modern, and up to the present. It is the counterpart of the idea of the state as the activity towards a collective good.[14] It is lively to this day in bodies like World Government for World Citizens.[15]

However, whenever the idea of the state is realized, it is under specific conditions which result in a variation on the basic theme. World citizenship is the counterpart of a world state without centre and there can be as many conceptions of it as citizens. Moreover the relation between world state and world citizen is entirely open and unspecified. That may appear an entirely negative message for a postmodern period. But it is not the end of the story.

Increasingly, and this is a mark of the Global Age, the activities of individuals, acting as world citizens, involve collective organization for global ends. It begins in their daily lives, is realized in everyday practices and results in collective action up to the level of the globe as a whole. The major historical antecedent for the global activities of the world citizen of today were the activities of the international working-class movement in the nineteenth century. But they were effectively domesticated in varying ways within capitalist and socialist nation-states. The global movements of today retain their independence from nation-states and even begin to negotiate with them almost as equal partners. They engage in debate with global agencies and draw on the expertise of the global managerial class.

Global citizenship is world citizenship focused on the future of the globe. Moreover it is developing distinctive forms of action which involve co-ordination on a global scale through open networking. Global citizens are not ruling the global state as Aristotle's citizens did, nor do they have a contractual relationship with it in the manner of modern nation-state citizens. In an important sense they are actually *performing the state*, creating it through practices which they have learned as the colonized and skilful citizens of the nation-state. This is where the penetration of the modern state into everyday life has pre-pared its citizens for a new and proactive role.

Basically Habermas's thesis of the colonization of the lifeworld assumes that the systems of the modern state and capitalism are successful in getting people to act out their requirements. Against that he counterposes communicative rationality working against the encroachments of a hegemonic state. In effect he combines Marxist alienation and Weberian iron cage themes with phenomenological ideas of everyday life. What he does not do is take forward the possibility that the encroachments of the modern state on everyday life have actually assisted in the empowerment of people, through education of course, but also in requiring participation in everyday bureaucracy.[16]

Individual rationality has never been defined exclusively by the state and to the extent that the state relies on the critical judgements of its citizens in a whole range of everyday matters, from health to road safety, from crime prevention to care for the environment, it is clear that it has its basis in their activities. At the same time, the colonization also involves the expansion of competence on the part of individuals, without which the modern state could not operate through their lives. To this extent the consequences of colonization of the lifeworld are the same as territorial colonization: the eventual acquisition of an independence, but one which depends on assimilating the colonial culture. In the Global Age, world citizens are turning to the task of building the global state and it is being made in and through their activities.

8.6 The Global State

How the global state is the contested terrain where people worldwide encounter the managers of globality

The global state is already operating in the activities of the millions of people who campaign to bring pressure on national governments in the interests of global issues, whether those be whaling, female circumcision or the waters of the Ganges. People work to influence existing global and national state institutions and their agencies, both educating and collaborating with officials. The official, sunk in the routines of state administration, requires constant re-education in order to remain in touch with the true practicalities of the state.

It is this individual state awareness which has been released by globality to engage with global problems in everyday life and at the level of globality itself. In the first instance it does not detract from the nation-state, merely supplementing its endeavours. Only later, in so far as individuals see the nation-state as part of the problem, does activity at the global level represent a genuine challenge to nation-state definitions.

The global state, then, exists at every moment when the individual takes account of and seeks to perform in the interests of a common interest spanning the globe. This is not to be confused with morality, which involves the rights and wrongs of interpersonal behaviour. It presupposes institutional arrangements for law and order, for enforcing human rights, for protecting the world environment, and it operates with those in mind. It is purposive and technical and not just the expression of values. Just as the nation-state, however far it is equated with the apparatus of government, is dependent on the goodwill, loyalty and discernment of the citizen who essentially is the mover and activator of state purpose, so the global state relies on the global consciousness of countless individuals. But in this case it is being constructed from below. The performative citizen is not acting out of some duty imposed by a statutory body but acts out of conscience and free commitment. And the shape of the new global state is emerging out of those activities, not as an imposed structure.

The new global state is coming into existence, not first of all through the United Nations, which was originally just that, nations united, but through the activities of all those who have responded to globality by making the globe the criterion for their active engagement in common purposes. In this sense it is very different from what T. S. Eliot said about the League of Nations on the eve of the Second World War.

He called the idea of someone owing a loyalty to it a chimera which few could even imagine (1939: 54).

The idea of common purpose in political thought has never had an easy passage because the structure of the modern state has depended so obviously on division of authority. Hegel's state embodied rational purpose, but it needed social animators, the bureaucrats as a class. Ortega y Gasset saw the modern state sucking out the spontaneity of social action (1932: 88). The state as constituted in the nation-state was an impediment to people acting out a purpose for the community as a whole. Moreover the modern state as organized with its administrative machine, when linked with a common social purpose, became the totalitarian nightmare.

In this respect the most instructive example and original antecedent of potential commitment to collective good beyond the nation-state has to be that of the religious believer acknowledging the universal church beyond national boundaries. Eliot held that the 'universal church', by which he meant no single hierarchy, always had a prior claim on the individual compared with any national church. That distinguished religious from state structures, where the League of Nations could never claim the same priority. It is a principle which since the 1970s has inspired transnational movements of all descriptions, not simply religious.

What is different now is that globality has effectively led to that sense of active common purpose attaching to the state itself, not the national state, but the state in general, in the mode of concern for globality. It brings out what earlier theories of the nation-state variously ignored, suppressed or distorted, namely that the idea of state action is power for the general good and that each person is capable of asserting that. The universality of the idea has finally surfaced as the global reference point for individual and collective action and has increasingly impressed itself on governments and business corporations.

The global state idea does not disavow the importance of power and force. But what it does is break with the Weberian tradition which stipulates that it is the linkage between the monopoly of legitimate violence and the support of government by the people which guarantees the state. This legitimation theory has helped all types of nation-states, whatever their ideological presuppositions to find a theory which supported each in their respective claims on individuals. It now looks increasingly dated.

For a start it depends on an estimation of the significance of violence, compared with other forms of coercion, which has less validity in a world where control of information and material resources is more important for administration and civil order than control of weapons. It minimizes also the importance of legitimate (variously in popular, legal and moral terms, though not all at once) force which is not in nation-state hands (self-defence, protection of minors and property, liberation movements).

Above all it neglects the power which arises out of taking charge of events, the facticities created by action, everywhere used by the exponents of non-violent protest. For it is this kind of action which reveals the limitations of violence as a means of state action. It is the basis of Greenpeace actions, for instance, which represent the sharp end of the facticities of action performed by citizens concerned for the environment. Let no one suppose that this is not coercive power, and it is successfully winning legitimacy at the expense of nation-states. This mobilization of power for collective ends may be enlisted by the nation-state ('please don't use your cars this weekend in the hot weather'). But when opposed by governments in the courts, the legal judgements are often finely balanced and not necessarily against the protestors. Increasingly governments have been forced to recognize that the public good is determined in public discourse and not by themselves alone.

The global state has none of the territorial, national and military baggage of the nation-state. It is now more than pure potential, although certainly the potential still very greatly exceeds the actuality. At the same time its institutional features are confused and multiple. It is open to every form of new organizational intervention by a vast number of collectivities – people in every combination using whatever new techniques and technology are available to further common purpose.

8.7 Democracy and the Future of the Nation-State

Why national governments have increasingly to content themselves with modest subsidiarity

Two elements of the old modern state's structure and functions remain, not exclusive to it but none the less still mainly associated with it, namely the predominant control of the means of violence in a territorial area and the organization of collective expressions of will. They correspond to law and order and political community and citizenship.

Neither is inherently related to the nation-state as now constructed. Indeed the huge variety of nation-state sizes for a start makes a nonsense of the idea that any particular state formation is technically the ideal arrangement for the exercise of these powers. Any single state structure therefore requires legitimation on non-technical grounds, and these are in the broadest sense cultural: historical identities, appeals to common ethnicity, community of religion or language.

The erosion of the common purposes of the old modern state makes appeals to common roots more strident. The steady decline in political participation at the nation-state level by individuals, coupled with value commitments which are defined outside national politics, leaves the older political communities of the nation-state with a legitimation deficit which politicians seek to rectify by intensifying the symbolic appeal of national identity or by emphasizing their control of legitimate violence.

Both courses of action are equally dangerous. Nationalism as a cultural phenomenon cannot be contained within nation-state boundaries and mobilizes precisely those groups which historically have been excluded, alongside those who have been included, especially since globalization assists in the maintenance of cross-boundary ties. Secondly, the state's control of the means of violence leads to the ready association of nationalism with force.

In any case, neither feature of the state is costless to maintain. The rhetoric of nationalism brings consequences in its train which can well overstretch the forces of law and order and risk policies which result in retaliation. Expenditure by the state is limited by its legitimation deficit, for it is not simply the masses who resist paying higher taxes: elites have disproportionate access to residence abroad and overseas investment. They have less at stake in any particular country and have less to gain from state expenditure.

The political uses of culture fail to fill the vacuum left by the end of the modern state project. The citizen voter in the Western state does not find a compelling project at the national level in which to make sense of civic responsibility. The collective will at that level is too weak to shape individual responsibility, which is far more exercised by the erosion of local control than by the decline of the nation-state. This is the key problem and source of weakness of the so-called communitarian movement. It has been conceived by Etzioni and others as a revitalization of the nation-state, 'the reinvention of American society', and shares the old modern belief that there is a hierarchy of concerns rising from families through nations to 'the long imagined community of humankind' (Etzioni 1994: 266). Yet in the Global Age there is no intrinsic reason why actions at local level should reinforce national consciousness, and many reasons why they might run counter both to nation-state requirements and to each other.

Indeed the exercise of citizenship, a sense of responsibility for events in the world, is expressed as much now through support for global movements and their initiatives at local level as it is in working through representative democracy. The problem is that representative democracy as a principle operates in areas which appear to have less relevance to individual people, while on those issues where their lives are involved and are affected by outside forces, representative democracy has little purchase.

Parliamentary government still oversees a huge amount of administrative detail, but increasingly the room for major shifts of policy is limited by technical complexity and the constraints which the international and transnational institutional framework imposes. When national government is not making rhetorical gestures it lapses into routine administration.

This does not mean that citizenship and democracy in the nation-state are dead as notions, rather that their scope and application need serious re-examination. The notions of rights and responsibilities in the state of today go far beyond a vote in a territorial jurisdiction, since the technicization of the state involves all residents and visitors in any area. The complexities of permissions, licensing, taxation, regulations and inspections make a naïve acceptance of the conditions of life impossible. There is a general assumption of competence in civic responsibility irrespective of participation in the representative institutions in the local or national state.

In political theory a shift is taking place to reflect the new transnational loci of power and a grass-roots participation which no longer looks simply to the nation-state. For instance, David Held proposes the development of democracy on a cosmopolitan model as a response to these fundamental changes (Archibugi and Held 1995: 112), and has outlined a comprehensive set of action targets towards that overall objective. Far from the global order being remote from individuals, the new interpenetration of global/local relations puts participatory democracy on the agenda again (Held 1995: 278–83).

In the new state, globally, nationally and locally alike, democracy will work best at the point where the knowledgeable user of the institution can bring experience to bear on the decisions which affect him or her. As the producer democracy of the old trade unions declines, the new consumer democracy correspondingly will grow: councils of registered users of services, whether schools, roads, water or medical care. Use and contribution, rather than birthplace or residence, will need to be a qualification principle both for voting and for being elected as a representative for bodies governing these public services.

The germs for this development already exist, though it is often stifled as the territorial state perceives the threat to its own existence. In Britain the resistance to user democracy takes the form of transfers of control to appointees of the ruling political party. It is a spoils system operating in secret and correspondingly irresponsible. Its democratization would, however, be far more effective in legitimating national party politics and could serve to reinstate respect for central state government. At the same time it is an implicit recognition of the growth of performative citizenship.

Representative user democracy will not be restricted to the territorial frame at national level. Once the national frame ceases to monopolize democratic practice, then there is no territorial limit to its extension. There is equally room for its extension globally, to reinforce or supplement the legitimacy of the United Nations. There is no reason why representative democracy should not be extended to the World Health Organization, or to international telecommunications, the law of the sea or the regulation of carbon emissions. Globality requires new democratic forms and the social technology of the Global Age is as adequate for this task as it is for air flight tickets, credit card transactions or trading in foreign exchange. All this can make more realistic what Ralf Dahrendorf in the mid-1970s said was both a matter of basic survival and a precondition for justice, namely the renovation of the international system (1975: 89–91).

But where does this leave the nation-state? Broadly, in the context of globality and with the development of the global state, we can envisage the nation-state coming to terms with a position of modest subsidiarity. The institutional developments which matter will take place across its boundaries, while the framework for people's lives will conform less and less to purely national definitions. As far as political leaders of nation-state governments are concerned, the choice will be between summoning up old identities, with all the risks that involves, or concentrating on the competence needed to manage advancing social technology.

For the global citizen it will be reassuring if leaders of the nation-state can guarantee the train timetable without asking for patriotic pledges in return. National culture may then be returned to people without states, with good examples to be found in those nations which for centuries have maintained identity without statehood. The alternative of a proliferation of new sovereign nation-states is, on the basis of the recent past, an ugly prospect.

9

The Global Age
Hypothesis

Is there anyone in the world, Meletus, who believes in human
activities, and not in human beings?

Socrates, in Plato's *Apology*

9.1 Narrative and Science

Why the poetics of present history cannot do away with the need for
theory and research

If the thesis of this book is valid, then there is already a widespread
intuition that the modern has lost its hold on the contemporary
imagination. But it still holds on to our language and prevents intuition from gaining full expression. Hence the 'Global Age' is not yet
common currency. Even the main sign of a loosening grip, the idea
of postmodernity, is still homage to the success of the Modern Age
in persuading people that it alone secures the foundations of society.
'Postmodernity' raises the spectre of the end of history, or of society
as such as the only alternative to modernity, and incites the faint-
hearted to cling to the past even more strenuously.

This book has been concerned to bring our language into a closer fit
with our experience of the present. It has challenged the dictum that
the only alternative to modernity is disintegration and has highlighted
the timebound limitations of the modern attachment to rationality. I
have argued that the onset of the Global Age provides us with ample
illustration of newly emergent social forms and forces which enable us

to see the Modern Age as a past historical period, and modernity as ephemeral and not as a permanent, ever renewed human condition.

My method of argument has been critical and exemplificatory rather than experimental, persuasive rather than conclusive. That is in the nature of the changes which we experience. They are not housed in a laboratory, nor can they be run as a set of equations. But experience of what is happening is a prime source of knowledge, even if the appreciation of its meaning arrives at different times for different people.

This means that my own perception will not be shared by everyone, or initially even by many. Clearly this flouts the common view that at any one time the majority perception must be right and the minority wrong. Indeed, when it comes to detecting changes in the world around us, the initial recognition is bound to be a minority view. On the other hand, no one could urge that every minority view will turn out to be right over time. Were that the case the world would have ended many times over already this century. Consequently the claims of this book require tests more exacting than merely other supporting views.

Equally I am making a larger claim than merely asserting the right to my viewpoint. In alluding to majority and minority views I am not suggesting that the shift from modernity is simply a matter of differing perspectives. Rather, one view or the other will turn out over time to be warranted. There is nothing peculiar about this as a cognitive problem. None of us can be absolutely sure of the direction of events. The first speculations about global warming were isolated reports initially. As time goes on the evidence mounts and eventually we shall know one way or another. But if we wait for certainty, it will then be too late.

The perception of global warming itself is, of course, a significant feature of the shift to the Global Age, both in its own right and as an example of the way global forces now enter into the calculations of individuals and agencies of all kinds. To that extent there is a temptation to use the easiest argument for the Global Age thesis and leave it to the test of time. It will be proved right or wrong over a decent lapse of, say, twenty years. The test would be a strong one. If in the vernacular and in expert views there is widespread acceptance of the existence of the Global Age in twenty years' time, then this would be proof enough of what this book has sought to show.

However, it is not unreasonable to ask for something more convincing at this moment in time. Taking the global warming example again, mere prophecy, ungrounded in scientific evidence, is not going to persuade most people. Even with the evidence it is hard enough, but a far greater number of people will be open to persuasion if it is treated as a hypothesis, related to theory, for which evidence can be gathered and evaluated.

Let us then consider the Global Age as a hypothesis. In doing so we can first review the accumulation of arguments and illustrations so far and then consolidate them with further argument and evidence focusing on the main hypothesis. There have been three broad aspects of the Global Age hypothesis which we explored in turn, although each is dependent on the other, and we could have taken them in any order.

After making the case for a return to epochal theory in chapter 1, chapters 2 and 3 involved a reassessment of the Modern Age, at an acquired distance from it. To do this we had to reassert historical narrative as a genre in its own right, not reducible to any other special science, and thus to gain distance from the self-images of the age, including its self-styled rationalities, and above all from the definitions of the nation-state. This was a task of deconstruction made possible first by retention of concepts with a transepochal scope and secondly by the immanent actual dissolution of links between the factors which gave the Modern Age its identity.

The second aspect in chapters 4 and 5 involved examining the discourse of late modernity to find in it the intimations of a more general epochal theory. In the literature on globalization we detected a thwarted appreciation of the immanence of epochal change, unable to recognize itself through its attachment to the modernist conceit that the modern embraces all that is new, and that all that is not new is doomed to be supplanted. At root the arguments about globalization relate to questions of narrating and accounting for historical change which we experience in our own time.

The third aspect in chapters 6–8 took some of the configurations which constitute the Global Age on their own terms. I sought to show why what modern discourse represented as disorganized, abstract and anomic might in the new global discourse signify variously the social experience of new identity in relations at a distance, or the reappropriation of environment into human existence, or the reconstitution of the social.

Now the cross-referencing between these three aspects of the argument arises in large part out of the concern which the reader will have detected throughout to affirm the possibility of communicating across ages and cultures. The historical and cross-cultural imagination must seek to find what is special and unique in the experience of different times and peoples and simultaneously discover the means of making that communicable to all. I have called this pragmatic, as opposed to logical, scientific or religious, universalism because it relies on universal communicability only as a working assumption, not as deduced, discovered or revealed truth. It is the working assumption on which common humanity is asserted, but the extent and limits of that commonality are continually being revised in the light of experience.

As an example of the way this working assumption operates, we have both identified the social as being a possible universal idea and at the same time shown that it has undergone transformations which have almost entirely concealed its underlying continuity and abiding relevance to the human condition. Indeed one of the guiding ideas in this book is that a distinctive masking of the social can prevent one age or culture from recognizing itself in the other. But are we sure there is something behind the mask? This is the question which haunts every attempt to understand other people and yet prompts it to be tried again and again.

So the three aspects of this narrative are interwoven in this way, that the break-up of the modern reveals the continuities and similarities with the pre- and non-modern, while the advent of the global suggests the possibility of a new, but non-modern, form of social existence. Epochal theory thus permits us to escape the comprehensive hold which an age, or indeed any age, exerts over contemporaries. It is a theory which allows us to grasp epochal change not as collapse, but as yet another extension of human experience. It permits us then to conceptualize our time in its own terms as the Global Age and simultaneously affirm our affinities with humanity in all ages.

Now it will not escape the critic that the interlocked nature of my argument is not in itself a strength, unless there is independent corroboration for each part. If it is only the advocate of the Global Age thesis who identifies modernity with the Modern Project, who affirms the decline of the nation-state, who sees globalization as qualitatively different from the unification of the world, and who sees them as implying each other, then the chances are that this is a highly idiosyncratic reading of the trends of our time.

In fact it is the weight of opinion and evidence in favour of each of these developments *taken independently* which encourages me to link them through the Global Age hypothesis. Equally there is no denying the enormous amount of argument and accumulated evidence which remains to be reviewed. The vastness of the task is apparent if we only consider the variety and scope of the discourses in which 'modern' lodged itself as undisputed marker of mood, style, method, approach, assumptions and paradigm. By the beginning of the twentieth century every sphere of life, from theology to music, from architecture to philosophy, from personality to politics was qualified as 'modern', with its own intricate refinement of what that might mean for what was acceptable or even recognized.

It is this comprehensiveness of the discourse of modernity which justifies speaking of the Modern Age, and it is its breakdown which justifies us in talking of epochal shift. But that very comprehensiveness means that we can potentially (and the doubting Thomas will require us to) search in every life sector to test the Global Age hypothesis, a task beyond the abilities of any one scholar, or even a whole university of researchers. I make no apology for leaving it to theologians, and lawyers, and designers, and art critics to decide whether globality is the key to understanding the overarching change which displaces modern as the key marker in their own discourses.

But we can also assess the overarching change itself as a total social transformation, impacting on every sphere of life. In the next three sections of this chapter we will consider evidence of that change drawn from three areas: the uses of analytic social theory; empirical social research on value change; and the changing expressions of ethnicity and nationalism. Most of the references (apart from work of colleagues and myself in London) arise from work which is within the thought-world of a late modernity. It is a re-evaluation which leads us to detect the Global Age in data which have hitherto been seen as late modern or postmodern.

But we must not discount contributions which arise out of modernity, either. It is no part of the Global Age hypothesis that we can discount the contributions of other epochs. On the contrary, it seeks to appreciate all through each, and we are close enough to modernity to be intimate with its achievements while rejecting its presumptuously exaggerated claims. Epochs are not hermetically sealed from one another. A characteristically modern social research method like the survey is still capable of having some purchase on the Global Age.

Older accounts of periodization were also alert to the problems of overlaps, borrowings and cultural lags. Marxists, for instance, were always alert to medieval and feudal survivals and their importance in modern capitalist societies. But in the Global Age the contemporaneity of the past and the co-presence of different cultures are pervasive features. It is a period of co-presence of periods, anticipated in Foucault's rejection of 'totalitarian periodization' (1974: 148), where everyone would have to say the same thing at the same time.

9.2 Analytic Theory and Epochal Change

How contemporary transitions are encoded in shifts in the use of concepts and the project as organizing idea is displaced

One aspect of the Modern Project was the theoretical analysis of human action to identify its basic elements and then to explore the potential of combining these in different ways. Lawyers, economists, philosophers, psychologists and sociologists have all contributed to this enterprise. It has found application in spheres of life as various as education, business, politics and social policy.

Such analytical schemata have been put to prolific use in seeking to understand the distinctive nature of modernity. Max Weber's (1921) basic concepts revolved around the extension of rationality in social life. Talcott Parsons (1951) sought a frame which contrasted modern and traditional societies. Equally the enterprise could serve to promote modernity. Herbert Simon (1947) developed concepts as tools for the rationalization of organizational behaviour.

This duality of analytical concepts, both diagnostic and propaedeutic, part of the double hermeneutic of social science, is widely recognized. Less frequently acknowledged, though a main focus of the work of Foucault, are the limits on their use and their embeddedness in the discourse of a period. But if we do acknowledge this, we can equally treat analytical concepts as historical phenomena, ideas as facticities.

This was the burden of our earlier remarks about the Modern Project, which suggested that its power derived from the way individual lives were bonded into the overall scheme of the nation-state, with rationality as the bonding substance. The project, or projects, depended on setting goals, determining means, finding resources, motivating participation, developing and utilizing skills, defining relations with other projects, determining membership, establishing routines and procedures for settling disputes, etc. This is modernspeak and the identification of these elements and the theorization of their relations were a major aspect of modernity.

Underpinning modern discourse was the assumption that there were rational ways to determine optimum arrangements of the elements and that these necessarily integrated the spheres of individual and state activity and all the intermediate instances of social activity, such as family, firm and community. The principle of hierarchy appeared in numerous ways, in decision-making trees, in relations of authority, in levels of abstraction or of jurisdiction.

In highlighting the 'project', as such, as the characteristic frame of life for modernity, we are not pointing to some particular Modern Project distinguished from a medieval or ancient one. For the mark of modernity is the effort to put every aspect of life into some determinate relation to a human project and to relate each project to an overarching project. There was no 'ancient project' and no Hindu or Chinese project. Of course, the antecedent to the Modern Project may have been the divine project of the Christian God, but the shift from the divine to the human plan was itself a major epochal change. The project, both as concept and social reality, became a fundamental aspect of modernity and we can even date the highpoint of its recognition in the eighteenth century (see 2.1 above).

The epochal shift from the Modern to the Global Age in analytical terms clearly involves the dislocation of the relations between the old elements. So the sequencing known as 'career' breaks down, norms which link sexuality with marriage are loosened, values of loyalty are detached from hierarchy and so on. It is these dislocations which feed the postmodern imagination and provide the justification for theorizing postmodernity. But something more profound is happening. It is not just a matter of dislocation and disjuncture. A new configuration is emerging. Some terms may lose their unquestioned use for analysis and become redundant, although in the process they may for a time acquire heightened significance precisely because we have to face the consequences of their loss.

It is in this way we can interpret the course of the concept of values in modern discourse from its origin in the 1860s to its hypertropic use in the 1980s. The appeal to the idea of values in general as a transcendental justification of action arises precisely when the goal-oriented projects fail or when they conflict with each other. It is very difficult to deduce any precise course of action from an abstract value position, but this is the very pointer to the rhetorical use of values: used in this way, they permit an ostensible, often specious, harmonization of disparate and conflicting courses of action and personal positions. So even when our projects fail or we disagree on their conduct, we can comfort ourselves in the belief that we still share the same values.

Politicians therefore make frequent reference to values to maximize appeal under conditions of fragmented electorates and failed policies. The counterfactual nature of values, pointing as they do to unrealized states of affairs, makes them an ideal rallying call when real conditions fall short of values. Indeed this gap between values and reality may even be a requirement for this appeal to work. So rises in crime which reflect failed policy projects produce appeals to the values of law and order by those responsible for the projects. As I have suggested elsewhere (Albrow 1990b), the rhetoric of values from 1980s politicians could be seen more as a sign of the failure of the welfare state than its revitalization. At the same time, the call to faith in 'modernization' is characteristic of the late modern leader of a Western political party.

Analytical social theory in its modern guise provides the starting point for postmodern theory when the old relations no longer hold. It is also a resource for the abstractions of the contemporary nation-state politician seeking to hold together the old modern vehicles of political power in the face of disintegration. For many, the contest between these two aspects of late modernity is the real narrative of the present. The position of this book is that they are symptomatic only of a new age. The contest between them becomes more strident and carries less conviction as time goes on because they lack the diagnosis of the new configuration which underlies them both.

Rather than simply producing disintegration and repair, let us suppose that the lifeworld and systems under conditions of globality between them generate new forms of human living and with them new analytical concepts. Suppose the 'project' no longer compels admiration or mobilizes masses. Perhaps 'values' rings hollow. If the world is different, then many such concepts will lose their salience, older ones will reassert themselves and new ones arise. It is transformation and not reconstitution, and in the period of transition we can expect greater use of higher order abstractions as we seek to bridge the mutual incomprehension between the discourses of the two epochs.

The idea of culture has been one of the most popular higher abstractions which has bridged (or masked) the transition from the Modern to the Global Age. It has developed to express the unlimited variety of human expression. Its very abstractness is the sign of late modernity seeking to accommodate this diversity. But within its ample scope it has been possible to effect conceptual change and explore alternative ways of living. For the idea of culture relativizes the notion of rational action, recognizes its irrational anchorage, and at the same time allows for the non-rational. We can see this in different modes of social organization.

If we take individual behaviour, then we can, following Dick Hebdige (1979), recognize the way style becomes the distinctive life expression of the subculture. The pursuit of style provides a quite different pattern of living from the organizational career. Investment, leisure, qualifications, training are all concepts belonging to the career; let style displace career in the organization of a person's daily life, then performance, preparation, initiation, credibility become key concepts. Nor is this a question of rebellion against career, or of counterculture, each locked in conflict with the other. Rather the shift may be one in which career is simply dislodged from its dominant place. This is clearly marked by the emergence of Bellah's 'lifestyle enclaves' (Bellah et al. 1985), people who seek mutual support and find affinities with others who share the same style. Again this is not a question of 'opposition' but of 'transformation'.[1]

We can see the way 'culture' has also provided the cover for the profound shift in organizational practice over the last twenty years. It has expressed the institutional embeddedness of organizational rationality and thus encouraged the exploration of alternatives to older hierarchical arrangements. The complex networking of the delayered organization, with multiple channels of communication, upward, downward and lateral, combined with the flux of changing boundaries, produces individual orientations to work which owe as much to lifestyle as to career. Organizational purpose is delinked from structure to be ever renegotiated by parties to transactions in which they reaffirm their competence again and again. We can call this postmodern organization (Clegg 1990: 180; Parker 1992; Bergquist 1993), but that is to understate its place within the much wider transformation which is the Global Age.

For it is the way that globality enters into the frame of world society and state which displaces modernity as the dominant ordering principle of contemporary life. As we have explored at length earlier, the unification of the world, which happens as an outcome of the Modern Project, signals also the project's termination. Moreover the unification which has occurred is not as the project designed it, but arises as much from the limits of the world in which it was situated. The examination of these paradoxes is vitally important to dispel illusions about what a new world order may mean.[2]

If the Modern Project invited its participants to dream of a united world, which it did, the result of the invitation was very different from the dream. It resembles the outcome of an invitation to a party in a faraway place, where, because the routes converge on one narrow road, the host finds the guests have been forced together before they even arrive at the venue. A social occasion takes place very different from the host's intention. So, yes, unification occurred, and wouldn't have happened without the invitation. But it was not pre-planned or even intended in the way it happened.

Globality promotes the recognition of the limits of the earth but is profoundly different from modernity in that there is no presumption of centrality of control. The unification of the world which was the outcome of the Modern Project generates the common recognition that the project has ended. No one has to issue a declaration to that effect. For with the end of the project the controllers have lost control. Globality is open to appreciation and response by anyone or everyone. One of the odder linguistic turns in late modernity was to talk of geocentricity. There is no centre to the globe and globality has no directing agency.

This is a justification for the link which Ulrich Beck (1986/1992) made between globalization and risk. In modernity the accumulation of wealth could serve as an expansive project around which society was organized. Risks along the way could always be covered by further expansion, until the global level was reached. Indeed the expansion of states and capitalist firms in modernity could be seen as the progressive assimilation of risks. But each expansion generates a new field of risk, up to the global level.

The globality of risk forces recognition that response to it may need to be something very different from further expansion, that a new way of life may be required. It is the impact of globality on the Modern Project as a comprehensive way of life and conduct of affairs in the world which ultimately underpins the displacement of modernity in the nation-state, in the organization and in personal lives.

This account is intended to be more than rhetorically persuasive. It draws attention to real changes which require research. It points to options which face those who seek to manage globality or order the world. We could set up a scenario where the Global Age finds its own project, for instance either in the form of the exploration of space (which, however, may be so far-reaching as to take us into another age[3]), or alternatively in a programme to combat global warming. Either could serve as a dominant goal. But it is implausible to imagine that either could take on the shape of the Modern Project, dependent as it was on the expansion of the nation-state. Each would involve the networking of material, information and social technology to form a quite distinctive configuration.

9.3 Researching the Shift

We may look for empirical evidence of epochal change in the way people live

This argument from the shift in analytical concepts and the facticity of their application is persuasive at one level, namely in suggesting counterfactual theoretical possibilities. In other words, it indicates that ways of living alternative to the modern can be conceived and that new concepts will be generated as a result. In fact those possibilities have already been realized. The correlation of changing concepts with changes in ways of life has been noticed many times before, not counterfactually, but in relation to Western history (MacIntyre 1967)[4] or to non-Western cultures (Winch 1958).

But the problem with applying the argument to the present day is precisely that for those imbued with modernity it may *appear* counterfactual. In other words, it is all very well to suggest that theoretically modernity could pass away, and equally it may be easy to accept that alternative ways of life have existed, or even survive to this day in other parts of the world; but this in itself will not demonstrate for the sceptic that modernity is in decline. It is no good asserting that globality displaces modernity if the modern sees the global as its culmination.

What kind of empirical evidence can then have a bearing on the hypothesis? The strongest requirement might be that we need worldwide survey data on ways of life, coupled with surveys of representative holders of power positions worldwide and case studies of organization and decision-making processes in national and international organizations, states and corporations. Over time I have little doubt that many will undertake such research. It has, after all, firm antecedents, although it has to be conceded that the nation-state provided funds for such research out of its interest in the outcome.

But, irrespective of nation-state motives, earlier research on modernization was often a model of open sociology and provides both empirical and theoretical indications of the kind of work which could test the Global Age hypothesis. The main exponent of research into individual modernity, Alex Inkeles, insisted on defining modernity in such a way as to be able to test empirically just how far people could be judged modern, how many there were[5] and how likely modernity was to be enduring. But it was no part of his research to suggest that everyone, or even a majority of people, was becoming modern worldwide. Indeed he pointed out that under current conditions of population growth, while absolute numbers of 'moderns' were growing, proportionately they were declining (1983: 319).

This in itself draws attention to the fact that the Modern Age has never depended on a majority of the population of the world holding modern views or behaving in modern ways. The dominance of modernity in the Modern Age has not depended on numbers. At the same time it points both to the survival of so-called 'traditional' ways of behaving and to the open possibility of a person being neither traditional nor modern. In the words of Inkeles, the individual modernity of today might become a 'historical anachronism no longer appropriate to the structural features of some as yet unimagined future society' (p. 321).

In fact, even on Inkeles' account, a 'postmodern man' was emerging, although on terms which suggested the continuing hold of modern concepts. For Inkeles the postmodern seeks mystical experience, drugs or violence, unlike the bicycle-riding gardener of organic health food who remains quintessentially modern. It becomes apparent, just from the haste with which the issue of the ecological movement is dismissed, that it posed a problem for the future of modernity. Inkeles passes it by without reference to the most interesting empirical work on changing Western values, the Eurobarometer surveys and Ronald Inglehart's 'silent revolution' (1977), which suggested that environmentalism is part of a more far-reaching cultural shift.

In work beginning in the 1970s, Inglehart hypothesized that a major shift was under way in Western values from what he called materialism to postmaterialism. Through to the 1980s, time series of data on values have shown a consistent trend towards increasing numbers of people espousing postmaterialist values, so that the ratio of materialists to post-materialists, which was 4:1 in six European countries in 1970, was only 4:3 by 1988 (Inglehart 1990b: 105).

The questions which were originally asked arose very much out of interest in the balance of political forces and reflected economic and psychological hypotheses about the impact of prosperity on value preferences. So 'maintain order in the nation' served as an indicator of materialism, and 'protect freedom of speech' was a postmaterialist item. Although postmaterialism suggested post-industrial society, reflecting increased prosperity, this was still the 'post-ism' of modernity. But as the time series lengthens the suspicion grows that something more fundamental is occurring.

Although for making cross-cultural and longitudinal comparisons the basic measuring instrument (a set of attitude items) necessarily remains constant and effectively timebound, Inglehart has correlated the data with other areas to disclose the link between the shift in values and more far-reaching change. He thus begins in 1990 to speak of 'global change' in 'advanced industrial society' as well as post-industrial society (Inglehart 1990b). In effect he is supplying data which are increasingly supportive of the Global Age hypothesis.

In the 1980s environmentalist causes were beginning to attract majority approval in twelve European Community countries, and active support for these was six times higher among postmaterialists. Secondly, postmaterialists were only half as likely to declare themselves very proud of their nationality as were materialists, and in six countries for which there were data between 1970 and 1983 there were striking declines in pride in nationality.

Inglehart is concerned to use the values data to illustrate the importance of cultural change. At the same time he is drawn towards a wider range of explanation as time goes on. For us the most interesting new suggestion is that decline of pride in nationality is directly related to the declining economics of imperialism (Inglehart 1990b: 121). It no longer pays nation-states to wage wars, a point similar to the one made by John Mueller (1989) that new norms make major wars unacceptable. Both writers then find the changed position of nation-states and the values of their populations intimately related to each other.

But we can equally add that the loss of warfare as an element of the national project weakens its hold on individual interests as well as on values. At the same time, active campaigning is increasingly directed towards values with a non-national reference point, the environment. Over time that is likely to generate attachment through interests as well as through values. The environmental movement is developing its own human and intellectual capital resources which far outstrip its puny physical and financial capital.

The evidence mounts for the case that the change of our time, rather than being a simple one of changing values, or new technology, or a single world market, is a transformation in every sector, in systems and the lifeworld. It is the kind of historical change which we have been able and accustomed to identify for the past as epochal change, but which in the present we have not yet become used to acknowledging.

The survey data are not yet conclusive. They have after all been gathered on the basis of conceptualizations of modernity. The kinds of questions which would detect the rise of new patterns of life, and individual profiles of attitudes and values have not been systematically explored. Similarly, case study material for the transformation is still sparse, although Robert Bellah and his colleagues (1985) have provided suggestive indications of the way new values have penetrated daily life in the United States.

But the research can and should be done. Even at this stage, however, we can be sure that it will not generate a point-for-point contrasting profile to the characteristics of individual modernity as Inkeles developed them. The reason it was possible to point to a dominant type of modern individual was the concerted stress in all the institutions of the modern state to produce such people. There is no similar project for the Global Age, and the main effort from the nation-state is still to put redoubled emphasis on reproducing modernity. We should not expect therefore that globality will generate a dominant 'global person', and because of the indeterminacy and openness of globality (see above) as a factor for shaping lives we may rather expect a whole variety of responses.

The pilot work which my colleagues and I have done in one area of London support this expectation (Albrow et al. 1994a). The way globality enters into the ways of life of people living in one area of London varies greatly according to a range of factors, but especially depends on the maintenance of contact with people outside the area and on the length of residence. In our study we identified two kinds of 'cosmopolite', for instance. One businessman was in daily work contact with countries all over the world and maintained what he called a 'total international social network'. If he spoke of 'local' he meant belonging to the UK. At the same time he insisted there could never be a one-world community, because 'the difference between the races in the world is so vast'.

In contrast, a 'local cosmopolite', while maintaining contacts worldwide and appreciating past experience of travel, seeks to settle in an area and find a local part of a globalized world. We labelled another type 'the Western elite enclave dwellers' because they and their neighbours share the assumption that their social network extends from

Europe to the United States and that it can be maintained through regular visits. As often as not the enclave will contain a transient population of the Western elite. But that kind of transnational social network is not exclusive to the white elite. We also identified the 'diasporic familist', a member of a group which maintains ethnic identity across boundaries and who works for the reproduction of family ties across the seas on a long-term basis.

We called none of these people a 'globalist', that is someone who guides their daily life by globalist values, and yet each in their way is deeply affected by globality and their varied responses to it are often at odds with the assumptions of modernity. For instance, a young person we met who particularly values multicultural contact *per se* as an enrichment of personal experience, rather than as a strategy for pluralist social order, simply wishes to keep on the move. In another case, an elderly long-term resident, apparently quintessentially a local, took up regular contact in writing with the global celebrity of a hostage crisis (see also 7.5 above).

9.4 Ethnicity in the Global Age

In the longest historical perspective, contemporary nationalism is no longer an assertion of modernity

We can argue that it is 'globality' rather than 'modernity' which opens up and poses the most significant choices for people in their lives today, and even though the old dichotomous choice of modern and traditional was always an oversimplification, the new diversity of possible orientations and lifestyles as a result of the impact of globality is vastly greater than modernity allowed. It is this, of course, which also allows critics of accounts of globalization to deny that any significant change has taken place, precisely because one cannot identify anything as equivalently dominant to take the place of the modern person.

It is also always possible to point to dissonant and contradictory tendencies which have no clear direction, and as a result to deny the significance of globalization. As we have seen, to the extent that the literature suggests that globalization has a clear direction simply as the continuation of modernity, this scepticism is justified. But up to now the critic has had nowhere else to go except into the shapelessness of postmodernity, or to reproduce the essential unity of modernity. In each case this involves missing the transformative impact of globality and the way it is generative of new diversity. For that reason globality means a break with the totalizing discourse of modernity.

Nationalism has often been one of the reference points for those who hold to modernity or postmodernity. For some theorists it can represent a modern creation, and for others a postmodern primordialism. The case for seeing nationalism as a feature of the Modern Age is reinforced if attention focuses on its association with nation-state societies. The nation-state certainly sought to use and promote nationalism when it served its purposes. To that extent then the multiplication of new nation-states as a result of the break-up of the Soviet empire can appear as the further extension of modernity. It seems to represent the achievement of statehood by aspirant nations without a state and a consequent advancement of the nation-state idea.

But in order to understand the dynamics of the state–nation relationship we need a much longer perspective than the events of the last five years, and a much wider one than simply the relatively local area of the former Soviet empire. The difficulties arise if we stay exclusively with a conceptualization of state in terms of nation and nation in terms of state, in other words if we accept the particular historical conjunction emphasized by the modern nation-state. In the broadest and longest perspective, the state in Greek, Roman, medieval or non-Western forms has not required the nation. Equally there has never been a time in recorded history when it has not been possible to identify human groups wider than the kinship group, internally related and distinguished from others through collective experience and culture. Whether we call these 'a people' or '*Volk*' or '*ethnie*', as in Western languages, the concept is ubiquitous.

In Anthony Smith's words, the first nations were formed 'on the basis of premodern ethnic cores', for which he prefers the French '*ethnie*' (1991: 21). It is a formulation which prepares the way for a historically grounded definition of 'nation' which links it with the territorially based population of citizens of the nation-state. It allows for both the state appeal to ethnicity to create 'nations', and the aspirations of ethnic groups to become nations. At the same time it acknowledges the way modernity has produced the Janus face of nationalism, the inculcation of enthusiasm for the nation by the state, on the one hand, and the aspiration of nations without states to statehood, on the other.

It is out of these correlated definitions of state and nation that we can see how both the artificial imposition by the colonial powers of state boundaries on Africa, irrespective of indigenous ethnic divisions, and the division of Europe on ethnic lines are equally modern. But in either case the number of ethnic groups, or even nations without nation-state status, vastly outnumbers those with it. Nor is it plausible to imagine that the 300 or more tribal groups in Nigeria, or the speakers of the fifteen official languages, let alone the 1,500 mother tongues, in India will at some point acquire nation-statehood (Oommen 1986: 64).

This observation draws our attention to premodern and non-modern ethnicity, not as some preliminary stage to the nation-state but as another form of sociality, in tension with the nation-state idea and often an alternative to it. Indeed it is studies of non-Western movements, ethnic and religious, which compel us to recognize that other group identities are not inherently preliminary or thwarted kinds of nationhood.[6] The nation-state which pursues a multicultural policy, allowing for ethnic identities to flourish on parallel lines, is accepting both the autonomy of the social and the deracination of the state, in the sense of uprooting (but with that apt assonance of 'de-racing').

The occasional establishment of new nation-states and an increase in their number are not the main thrust of the Global Age. Eric Hobsbawm argues that nationalism is less important now than in the period of nation-building and that the global infra- and supranational restructuring subordinates nations. He cites how in Canada the question of the future of Quebec generates endless debate about the meaning of 'nation', 'state', 'people' and 'society' (1990: 190). In the argument of this book this is a necessary debate and corollary of the actual disaggregation and decentring of the state at the end of the Modern Age. 'Nations' no longer need to look to statehood. It is not so much a question of the subordination of nations to statehood, but of the delinkage of the one from the other.

We can therefore go beyond Hobsbawm's argument. In the Global Age nations may become less than, but also more than, nation-states. The rhetoric of 'black nation' or 'Islamic nation' is an assertion of a group identity transcending nation-state boundaries, not in an old modern imperial sense of a claim to territory, but as an abiding independence from the confines of nation-states. It is a consciousness beyond land which Paul Gilroy (1993a) aptly finds in the oceanic idea of the Black Atlantic.

It applies to small nations as much as large. They are able to locate themselves and assert a cultural identity more obviously and effectively in relation to supranational state organization than in a modern world in which too often the alternatives have appeared to be statehood or extinction. In part, nationalism has long sought to legitimate itself by reference to the wider world: in Mazzini's words, 'We are seeking not merely the emancipation of a people, but the emancipation of peoples' (1835/n.d.: 42). But in the Global Age this takes on a new aspect.[7] Nationalism escapes the frame of nation-state structures into a cultural space defined in terms of globality rather than territory.

It follows that diaspora ceases to represent the thwarted nationalism of the Modern Age. On the contrary it is likely to become the dominant mode of ethnic sociality in the Global Age. Global communication technology makes it easier both to sustain links at a distance and to sustain and affirm cultural identity within the global cultural space. Indeed the strength of that identity may give the freedom to travel to any part of the globe, more than to seek a return to a homeland. Changed political conditions in Poland have not led to a massive return by Poles from abroad, nor do Irish, Welsh or Scottish emigrants flock back to their country of origin, even if they retain a pride and interest in it.

9.5 Conclusion: Out of Nostalgia

The new political movements need to explore tolerance and
individual freedom beyond the imagination of modernity

Ethnic identity then becomes yet another focus for social life in the Global Age, freed from state definition in the same way as gender, religious, linguistic or stylistic bases for group formation. It does not prevent, and in some ways provokes, a reaction from those who hanker after a return to modern structures. But they run the risk of lapsing into 'nostalgic anachronism'.[8] Along with 'values', 'community' and 'nation', this constitutes the characteristic political programme of modernity. But the constant repetition of 'new' only re-emphasizes the traditional character of the package.

The precise problem for the politician seeking to reinvigorate the old structures and institutions of nation-state societies is that the appeal to the new is the same old theme in a context where those structures are steadily but surely losing their hold on people. The decline of political participation and of faith in political institutions has proceeded in both the United States and Europe without real interruption now for over fifty years.

The most significant political experiment of the period, the forging of the European Union, is itself largely detached from the interests and enthusiasms of individual voters and proceeds on the basis of a bureaucratically engineered project. One of the reasons for promoting European Monetary Union by ardent Europeans is the sense that it is in the attainment of projects *per se* that integration is achieved. This is the last great expression of the authentic Modern Project, namely that it is the travelling towards the goal, no matter what the goal might be, that alone can guarantee the perpetuation of social order.[9]

In contrast to the European project – the pure representation of modernity in all its facets, from constructing the European nation to guarding external boundaries and regulating lives – we have at the other extreme the new constellations which are gradually coming to challenge nation-states for the loyalties of their citizens. In part their significance is not fully recognized because they are not nation-states, but they represent potent alternative foci for communal action. They are the expressions of concern for public good, depending on constructed identities beyond the nation-state. They are the outcome of what I called above 'performative citizenship'.

There is a set of similarities between the diasporic Black Atlantic culture, Greenpeace, the idea of the Islamic nation and the feminist movement. None of them depends on a single project, each is multi-faceted and polycentric, each depends on the reflection and communication of a global condition in the lives of individuals, each in its way resists the univocal ordering of the nation-state. However aggressive their stance is towards the older structures, these new social configurations are still fundamentally responsive and reactive to a world which they have not made. They seek to create space for themselves within the world, rather than shaping the whole world into which others will fit.

Such an emphasis on the openness of different futures from the standpoint of alternatives to the modern state may be an affront to all who have seen in the modern liberal nation-state the ultimate expression to date for individual freedom and tolerance. But they should remember what Aristotle once claimed for the Greek polis, and how the glories of Greek citizenship depended on the subjection of slaves and women.

The alternative movements represent a challenge to old nation-state definitions of politics because they do not meet them head-on. In part this has been reflected in the on-going debates among their memberships as to how far they should form conventional political parties. In general, and this looks to be the final outcome, the arguments for non-conventional organizing and application of pressure have won the day. This is apparent in the green and women's movements.

It also applies to black power, which arises out of the strength of the diversity of small acts.[10] Recognizing the global nature of the black diaspora is intrinsic to this shift away from direct confrontation with the nation-state and at the same time creates new social and political arenas. The same reconstitution of political activity took place when the women's movement achieved globality, through self-conscious international networking (Morgan 1984). Fed back into the context of the nation-state, it takes feminism out of fringe politics and reshapes the discourse of existing political parties.

In the modern context, the beneficiaries of the Westernized nation-state were largely confined to those white adult middle-class males who could claim citizenship of a wealthy state. In the global condition, other groups lay claim to those values of tolerance and freedom of expression in challenging that privileged status. Moreover, in their challenge they often appear even to overturn those values, sometimes resorting to strident attacks and even violence. But that ought not to detract from the overall thrust of these movements towards the pluralization of access to power and self-esteem. Intolerance should no more be regarded as central to them than we should regard fascism as the characteristic expression of the modern nation-state.

If political leaders take this analysis seriously, it will help them to avoid some of the risks involved in treating Islamic fundamentalism as in some sense the essential nature of Islam, presenting a threat which can only be met by military means. This is one view being expressed at the moment in the debate about the future of European security, Islam being seen as the replacement for the Soviet threat. But fundamentalism and resort to violence are no more sanctioned by the Koran than by the Bible. Indeed historically Islam has been a polycentric religion based in a popular intellectualized religiosity. Those features of it which resonate with male dominance and violence reflect more the inherited social and economic conditions of Islamic people than the core of religious belief.

But then we have to extend our tolerance and not decry the historic contribution of the nation-state. Whatever displaces it in the Global Age, modernity's achievement was to keep alive the transhistorical values of democracy, tolerance and individual freedom which it developed out of the classical heritage. Globality does not require novelty, expansion, bureaucracy, male or white domination. But the vitality, richness and variety of the Global Age depend on the care with which its citizens preserve and tend the other more valuable achievements which were to the credit of the old modernity.

Notes

Chapter 1 Resuming the History of Epochs

1 Allan Megill calls on historians to 'confront the fictionality implicit in all works of history' (1995: 172) but at the same time to address theories from other disciplines. I would argue that the universality of historical accounts derives from the experience of common humanity and that provides its own theoretical perspective.

2 Bryan Turner (1990a: 1) has pointed to the 'great difficulty of finding an adequate periodization of modernity and postmodernity'.

3 Edmund Husserl (1937/1970: 65–6) made the same point in relation to Bossuet's contemporary philosophers, in particular Descartes. Husserl attributed to the 'founders of the modern age' a belief in the increasing control of both natural and social worlds through knowledge. Unlike him I shall suggest that the origins of modernity have far more than simply intellectual origins.

4 Just as you know geographical spaces by the main towns, Bossuet argued that you ordered times around key events: 'This is what is called an "epoch", from a Greek word for "stop", because you stop as in a resting place to consider everything which happened before or after, and you avoid anachronisms in this way, the sort of mistake where times are confused' (Bossuet 1681/1887: 4).

5 Friedrich Meinecke (1959: 82–3) judges that Bossuet gave Voltaire the impulse to invert and secularize the Christian view of history. Backing a new cultural ideal with a new interpretation of universal history then represented 'a new era for the Western mind' and after Voltaire it was not possible to promote a new ideal without providing a comprehensive historical foundation. As Meinecke says, the danger then was that the history was contaminated by the ideology. Writing about the Global Age is equally hazardous.

6 Jacob Burckhardt's classic study *The Civilization of the Renaissance in Italy* (1860) adopted Möser's principles and applied them to the emergence of the modern world. He marked that time off from the previous period of

medievalism by its individualism, by the cultivation of excellence which transcended old differences in birth and by the rediscovery of ancient literature. Burckhardt insisted that the Renaissance possessed a coherence in which every aspect of life was connected, from fashion to festivals, from language to zoology. Social life as a whole had a characteristic stamp in sharp contrast to medievalism (Burckhardt 1860/1944: 217).

7 The passage occurs in the Economic and Philosophic Manuscripts of 1844 where Marx explains the bitterness existing between landowner and capitalist. Möser was the type of writer who served the landowner's self-image by stressing noble lineage, the poetry of recollection, romantic disposition and political importance, and depicted the capitalist as heartless, trading community away and lacking honour, principles or anything else. Marx put Saint-Simon, Ricardo and Mill (among others) in the opposite camp. With Möser he brackets the Swiss economic romantic Sismondi.

8 Marx applied his theory in a very direct way a year after the *Communist Manifesto* was published when he spoke in his own defence in court in Cologne on a charge of incitement to revolt. He challenged the legality of a demand to pay taxes on the grounds that the legislature, the United Diet, had no legitimacy, representing as it did big landed property, 'the foundation of medieval, feudal society. Modern bourgeois society, our own society, on the other hand, is based on industry and commerce' (Marx and Engels 1977: 326). He was acquitted.

9 Spengler and Weber met for a special debate staged by students in Munich city hall just four months before the latter's death in 1920. Weber responded sharply to Spengler for deriding Marx's predictions. Spengler had no means of verifying whether any particular fact represented the flowering or decay of a culture. His predictions were no better than saying, 'The sun is shining now, but you can be sure that one day it will rain.' Marx, on the other hand, could come back and find the world much as he expected (Baumgarten 1964: 554). It was a telling encounter. Weber's own intellectual course had taken him in a direction of comparative cultural studies which could superficially have suggested an affinity with Spengler. Clearly he was keen to avoid this. At the same time, the way he distanced himself from Marx left him locked into a frame of thought which appeared to leave virtually no alternative futures.

10 For the significance of the idea of intensification in Weber's work see Albrow (1990a: 238). As with so much else in his thought, its source is in Goethe (Meinecke 1959: 569).

11 Umberto Eco's *The Name of the Rose* (1983) has since reversed Collingwood's procedure by turning the detective story into fictional historical narrative.

12 David Carr (1986) has effected the union of phenomenology and historiography in arguing that awareness of the past is an unthematized background to all experience. Historical narrative then becomes an intrinsic ingredient of human existence, not an additive, and the professional historian simply thematizes this background. In other words history writing is embedded in the distinctive nature of human reality, a view very different from the approach to narrative adopted by Hayden White (1987), who stresses its artefactual and arbitrary nature.

13 Turner (1990a: 6) maintains that Weber's account of rationalization is still the best way to approach a theory of modernity.

14 Goethe said in 1827 that the 'world event' occurred with the conjunction of underlying tendencies which had hitherto been at work silently and independently (quoted by Meinecke 1959: 559).

15 The historical approach to conceptualizing an epoch which is closest to the one adopted here is that of Arnold Toynbee (1939–61). His focus on challenge and response kept human achievements and failures in the centre of the narrative and avoided the pitfalls of organicism, evolutionism and determinism. Each of his civilizations had therefore a unique history and their trajectories could not be predicted from any formula. The fact that one critic called him a positivist (Collingwood 1946: 159) and another a mystic (Tainter 1988: 74–86) suggests he may have got the balance about right, although 'positivistic mysticism' is not unknown (Rudolf Steiner, for instance, and obviously Spengler).

16 Norbert Elias made extensive use of 'configuration' to refer to patterns of social relationships (see especially Elias and Scotson 1965). Earlier the cultural anthropologist A. L. Kroeber (1944: 844) adopted the term to refer to the specific relationships in space and time between elements of a culture. He was influenced by historians of art and style and tended to use 'pattern' as a synonym. But it is easy to slide from pattern to system with the consequences that brings in Talcott Parsons's work (1951). Toynbee in turn borrowed the term from Kroeber, regretting that he adopted it so late in his work (1939–61, vol. 12: 77, 602).

17 From its first use 'modern' has retained the meaning of 'the present time' as opposed to a previous time. Talk of the 'Modern Age' therefore implicitly always assimilates the ever moving present to the past and erases the possibility of a new age.

18 Richard Price (1990) contests the tendency to let the modern period slip forward in time by challenging the way recent English historians have regarded Victorian England as the axis of modernity and calls for renewed recognition of the stretch of the modern period back to the seventeenth century. Toulmin (1990) would only be satisfied by returning to the Renaissance.

19 Hans Gumbrecht's (1978) very useful article on modernity notes that the first use of 'modern' is in a letter of Gelasius in AD 494/5 ('admonitiones modernae'). He follows Nathan Edelman (1938) in dating the earliest uses of terms equivalent to the Middle Ages, 'media tempestas' (1469), 'media aetas' (1518) and 'medium aevum' (1604), with the beginning of the Modern Age.

20 Joseph Schumpeter criticized Max Weber's account of the rise of capitalism because it confused the use of abstract systems concepts for analytical purposes (ideal types) with the requirements of historical explanation, which are supplied by the right amount of factual detail (1954: 80). He equally criticized Marx and his followers for allowing theory to limit historical causes to particular categories (p. 144).

21 This is why Niklas Luhmann's attempt to apply systems theory to social life through the idea of 'the reduction of complexity' leaves so many questions open. Every time the complexity of the world is reduced by some institutional mechanism, that in turn generates a new set of complexities. His favourite example of law is particularly double-edged in this respect (Luhmann 1985).

Chapter 2   The Construction of Nation-State Society

1 Quoted in Becker (1932: 39–40). Acton (1952: 469–70) pointed out that this scheme anticipated the idea of a European confederation, and its machinery bears a striking resemblance to the European Union today. This bears out

the Abbé's own dictum that things have to be repeated many times to be remembered.

2 Ortega y Gasset explored the idea that the transition from one epoch to another would be felt as a crisis by those who experienced it. The collapse of belief in a world system would result in disorientation, feelings of being lost, with new enthusiasms beginning in the world of art. This was what happened with the ending of the Middle Ages (Ortega y Gasset 1962: 88–9). It was also what was happening in the modern period, a loss of faith in reason, a 'crisis of foundations' (Ortega y Gasset 1984: 200).

3 These paragraphs deliberately echo the language and style of Max Weber's introduction to his sociology of religion (published in English as the introduction to *The Protestant Ethic and Spirit of Capitalism*, (1920/1976: 13–31)), where he sets out his theory of rationalization.

4 For extensive discussion of this aspect of Max Weber's work see Albrow (1990a: esp. 186–9); and more generally on rationality and irrationality in social thought see Alan Sica (1988). None the less the view persists that Weber neglected the irrational consequences of rationalization. For instance Beck says that his concept no longer grasps the late modern reality of the incalculable consequences of technology (1986/1992: 22). It is true that he was not alert to environmental threats, but the idea that the rationalization of one sphere of activity inevitably produced conflict with others is central to his characterization as a conflict theorist which is the preferred view of many commentators.

5 Modernity had also many outstanding examples of success in the combination of opposites. Goethe was the supreme literary exponent of the competing claims of individual and national and human destiny in a setting where the nation-state effectively dictated the terms of the bargain. His probing of individual experience, the unpredictabilities of relationships and the demonics of the quest for knowledge tested the boundaries of rationality and irrationality even while he served as the highest bureaucrat in a small German state.

6 Immanuel Wallerstein (1974: 50–1) has pointed to the various ways in which the motives of different groups, younger sons and merchants, intertwined with monarchs in the early modern European explorations. The later growth of bureaucracy found other ways of incorporating career motives into state structure.

7 The centrality of the nation-state to the Modern Age was axiomatic for the great vista of modernity which Lord Acton planned, *The Cambridge Modern History*, 13 vols, 1902–11. In his 'Introductory Note' Bishop Creighton declared that 'the two main features of modern history are the development of nationalities and the growth of individual freedom' (Creighton 1902: 3). He was fully aware of their interdependence: 'The strength of national life depended upon the force of the individuals of whom the nation was composed. International competition implied a development of national sentiment, which needed the aid of each and all' (p. 2). It was this which marked off the modern from the medieval period.

8 In this respect the true founder of sociology was Georg Simmel (1908), since all his work revolved around the paradoxical dualities of the hermetic idea of the social and he alone managed to cross national boundaries into the newly established training schools in the United States, Europe, Asia and South America at the beginning of the twentieth century.

9 A point made effectively by T. D. Weldon when he said that confusions arise in questions concerning the state because of the mistaken quest for

real meanings (1953: 46). With that precaution we can still seek to convey meanings of abiding relevance with aptly chosen language.

10 A curious common assertion has arisen in this century that the ideas of the social and society are recent inventions of the modern period. One author oddly attributes the distinction between man as social being and man as citizen to Adam Ferguson and John Millar: 'The traditional doctrine knew only the state' (Stark 1958: 198). We are bound to attribute such a misreading of the history of ideas to the limited self-understanding of modernity itself.

11 Arnold Toynbee argued that it was characteristic of the age of the Great Powers that they sought to be universes in themselves and 'aspired to be a substitute for Society' (1939–61, vol. 1: 10).

12 For one writer 'the invention of the social' came about after the disillusion of the French people with the political process after 1848, when the social became the sphere to which passion was attached (Donzelot 1984: 21). For another, 'society' took on its meaning as an object with its own nature and laws only in the early nineteenth century (Rabinow 1989: 11).

13 L. Winterer, a deputy in the German parliament and pastor and canon in Mulhausen, Alsace, provided a vivid account of how that crisis was perceived by the ruling class:

> We offer the reader a new instalment of our studies on contemporary socialism. When we began these in 1878 leading statesmen still denied the existence of a social problem. It's a position no one holds today. The social problem confronts us everywhere, its existence demonstrated by a series of events which unroll with uncanny speed. Increasingly they dominate public life. Will there be a peaceful solution or will a terrible catastrophe intervene? That is the big problem which faces us at the end of the nineteenth century. Socialism asserts that it has the solution to this problem. It summons the proletariat of the whole world to combine and is making unbelievable efforts to assume the leadership of the mighty movement which has gripped the whole world of the working people. (Winterer 1890: iii)

14 The formal similarities between structural functionalism and Marxist structuralism were often noted. Perhaps that was a reason why the keenly awaited debate between Parsons and Althusser at the 9th World Congress of Sociology in 1978 in Uppsala never took place. Neither appeared at the advertised time.

15 For a recent indictment of professional and academic economics, which emphasizes how far the discipline has moved from social reality, see Paul Ormerod (1994).

16 'Double hermeneutic' in Giddens's sense (1984) of exchange between the language of society and the language of social scientists so that each feeds back into the other.

17 I shall make extensive free adaptation of this idea especially in chapters 7 and 9. For a recent account see William Outhwaite, *Habermas: a Critical Introduction* (1994).

Chapter 3 The Decay of the Modern Project

1 Brenda Maddox (1994) has vividly portrayed the way Lawrence explored in practice and in writing German theories of sexuality through his relationship with his wife Frieda and her circle of German intellectuals, which included Freud's erstwhile favourite pupil Otto Gross and also Max Weber.

2 Daniel Bell pointed out that the attack on sexual repression of the cultural avant-garde of the 1960s was prefigured in the voluminous works of Charles Fourier (1772–1837), who 'builds his whole social system on the primacy of passions' (Bell 1968/1980a: 99).

3 There was one obvious sign that Nietzsche could not break completely with the modern. Such was Goethe's hold on German culture that Nietzsche could never bring himself to denounce this particular icon. He contented himself with declaring that he was following his true intentions. It was manifestly untrue. Goethe found Kant forbiddingly theoretical but acknowledged his stature. Nietzsche dismissed him with a hatred only possible for someone who had been brought up by and rejected a Protestant father.

4 Gianni Vattimo sees philosophical postmodernity as born with Nietzsche's work (1988: 164). The culmination of the modern appears to represent its denial and decline. We should be cautious about this. The lauding of power and the freeing of the individual from the shackles of rationalist ethics are modern themes, a play with the oscillation along the rational/irrational dichotomy which characterizes Western culture. Only when Nietzsche intimates possibilities outside that frame can we see him as a genuine forerunner of an age beyond the modern.

5 Martin Green has located the beginning of the counterculture in the intense intellectual experimentation of the succession of artists and intellectuals who gathered in Ascona between 1900 and 1920. Peter Kropotkin, D. H. Lawrence, Carl Jung, Herman Hesse and Isadora Duncan were just a few who visited the Swiss village. But he rightly stresses the political ambiguity of the counterculture. It even fed in part into Nazism. The most telling point about its relation with modernity is that the ideas current among the Asconans achieved transformational potential when Gandhi assimilated them to Hinduism (Green 1986: 246). In other words the addition of non-Western elements was needed to destabilize the enduring structure of contradictions in modernity.

6 In fact Roszak (1970: 2) hit incidentally on the decisive transformation underway when he noted the international dimensions of the youthful rebellion. But his account remained at the level of critique, without drawing out the implications of this key sociological fact for epochal change. As others have observed, the problem with the idea of technocratic society is the way it locks analysis into an enduring modernity (Kumar 1978, Webster 1995).

7 If Marx was right to point out in 1844 that from a political point of view the state was the structure of society, it was because that view was achieving hegemonic power (Marx and Engels 1975a: 197).

8 As Aristotle explained, for the purposes of trade it is in everyone's interest for citizens and foreigners to be treated alike everywhere and as trade increases it becomes generally more advantageous to conform to a universal model of commercial law.

9 'The most perfect example of the modern state is North America' (Marx and Engels 1976a: 90). This dictum from *The German Ideology* referred to the pure identity of interests between the state and private property owners in the United States which was still hidden in Europe by the survival of feudal estates. The view here is that the Modern Project involved equally the creation of national community, and in this respect too the United States was the most modern nation.

10 See the narrative accounts of the conquest of the Indians, whether the attitude was malevolent, as with the Spaniard Cortes, who termed them 'barbarians without reason' (quoted in Sinclair 1977: 24), or benevolent as

with Montaigne, who spoke of them as 'governed by natural laws and very little corrupted by our own' (1580/1842: 89).

11 Munsterberg's study *The Americans* (1904) read like a litany of the Modern Project:

> Such is the America which receives the immigrant and so thoroughly trans-
> forms him that the demand for self-determination becomes the profoundest
> passion of his soul. . . . Neither race nor tradition, nor yet the actual past
> binds him to his countryman, but rather the future which together they are
> building. It is a community of purpose, and it is more effective than any
> tradition, because it pervades the whole man. (1904: 5)

12 In an interview immediately after his election with Trude B. Feldman of the *New York Times* (*Guardian* 4 Nov. 1992, p. 17).

13 *Guardian*, 4 Nov. 1992.

Chapter 4 Globalization: Theorizing the Transition

1 There was an early intimation when Machiavelli advised his prince that the best way to secure territories acquired by conquest was to plant colonies in them – they 'cost nothing, are more faithful, and give less offence' (1517/n.d.: 8). World empire was not his stated goal, but the logic of the state required conquest and expansion. If the state maintained its momentum, the outcome eventually had to be world empire, even if it was a relatively benign colonization.

2 We can find a representative example in an essay by the French philosopher Paul Ricoeur entitled 'Universal Civilization and National Cultures' (1965: 271–86). He depicts mankind as on the brink of a single, universal world civilization. He finds five attributes of universal world civilization: abstract rationality, which unifies humanity not because of its Greek and European origin but because of its universality; a de facto universality through technology; a universal rational state structure, inescapably democratic; a rational, universal economy; and a standardized culture of consumption (pp. 271–4). He was profoundly ambivalent towards this outcome of modernity – the human masses enter on the historical scene with access to dignity and autonomy but there is a worldwide imposition of a mediocre consumer culture. But this simply repeats the dilemma of mass society for modern intellectuals.

3 Even the refugee from modernity, Henry Thoreau, in his forest retreat, felt like a citizen of the world when the freight train rattled past carrying palm leaves for New England heads (1854/1927: 103).

4 David Hume, whom Spengler quotes, wrote an essay 'Of Public Credit' attacking public borrowing for creating an 'unnatural state of society' with a stockholding, rentier class with no hereditary authority:

> These are men who have no connections with state, who enjoy their revenue
> in any part of the globe in which they choose to reside, who will naturally
> bury themselves in the capital, or in great cities, and who will sink into the
> lethargy of a stupid and pampered luxury, without spirit, ambition, or enjoy
> ment. (Hume 1741–2/1903: 363)

The intrinsically stateless and free-floating nature of money and the people who live from its management and manipulation has been a constant theme to this day. For Spengler only the race and the sword were more powerful.

5 Stephen Toulmin's *Cosmopolis: the Hidden Agenda of Modernity* (1990), which is highly critical of received notions of the nature of modernity, and in particular of the centrality of Cartesian rationality, goes only part of the way in recovering the full potential of theory because his concern is to salvage a hidden modernity, locating it in the Renaissance. But if we acknowledge the contribution of the premodern and the non-Western we are better able to offer a positive conceptualization of an age after the modern.

6 For a recent critique of the technological determinism inherent in so many accounts of modernity see Frank Webster (1995).

7 Ferrarotti (1985: 159) speaks of an epoch of 'vertical imperialism' and the peculiar significance of the entry into history of peoples and nations who had previously been excluded. He also stresses the 'openness of history' (p. 18). But he does not yet draw the consequence that modernity might have lost its dominance.

8 Gianni Vattimo (1988) has specifically addressed the question of the end of modernity as the end of history in such a way as to shut off the possibility of speaking of a new epoch.

9 These requirements echo the sentiments expressed by Berger, Berger and Kellner in their classic *The Homeless Mind* (1973: 19–25), where they called for the systematic description of the constellations of consciousness which characterize modernization. They did this specifically in part to answer the question of just what alternatives there might be to existing forms of modernization. Significantly they saw the countercultural movements of the time as demodernization, with inherent limits in the technological and bureaucratic requirements of modernity. There was no intimation of a future alternative to modernization.

10 He acknowledged that his total phenomenological attitude and the *epoché* belonging to it seek 'a complete personal transformation, comparable in the beginning to a religious conversion' (Husserl 1937/1970: 137).

11 A recent enquiry for a volume in the Economists' Bookshop in London revealed that they listed 134 books as available for sale with the word 'global' or its derivations in the title.

12 The *Oxford English Dictionary* documents the extension of the term 'global' for the first time in the Supplement of 1972. Previously it had recognized the sense of 'global' meaning 'pertaining to the totality of a number of items'. It dates the first usage of the term in the sense of covering the earth in 1892, oddly enough by a Frenchman, because *Larousse* (1979) still only recognizes 'global' in the sense of *pris en bloc*, presumably there being a perfectly good word, *mondial*, for the newer English meaning. Sir Ernest Gower in the second edition of *Fowler's Dictionary of Modern English Usage* recommends the use of 'mondial' in English as an alternative to 'global', which he objects to because: 'seeking wider fields [it] has now established itself, unnecessarily but firmly, as a synonym for what we use to call world-wide' (1965: 229). This was soon after McLuhan's popularization of the term which the *OED* cites. In sociology a benchmark was established by Wilbert Moore (1966) with his paper on 'global sociology', but even among sociologists the term global was still being used primarily in the sense of 'total' as late as 1976, when several papers were given on 'global society' to the Uppsala World Congress by Soviet sociologists referring to a total perspective on a single society.

13 Jeremy Rifkin (1992) documents the comprehensive and global enclosure of airspace, sea and earth and the way it is associated with their commercial exploitation.

14 For an example of this umbrella expansion of urbanization see Amos Hawley's (1981) discussion where the term covers the expansion of human interrelationships in a habitat.

15 Anthony McGrew (1992: 77) has also pointed to and documented complexity and ambiguity in accounts of globalization in a diversity of authors. The task here is to disentangle complexity from ambiguity, which is the purpose of an analytical approach.

16 The earliest explicit discussions of globalization arose in the study of international politics among those who advocated a transnational point of view in their study with a focus on the world as a whole rather than the nation-state (see Modelski 1972). Keohane and Nye also introduced a widely used collection of essays on transnational politics with a definition of 'global interactions' as 'movements of information, people, or other tangible or intangible items across state boundaries' (1971: xii).

17 There is an incisive account of the cross-currents in the debate on the impact of globalization on culture and identity in Hall (1992).

18 Robertson (1992: 173–4; 1994). The problem with this concept is that it focuses the discussion of the global/local on a question of local adaptation of a global product or practice. What I have called elsewhere the 'Mecca effect', where one place appears to be the focus for the whole globe, as with Hollywood for films or Silicon Valley for computing, involves the local siting of a global institution (Albrow 1995). Different again is the global division of labour which involves a network of specialized local sites for global economic activity. Finally Roehampton sociologists have drawn attention to aspects of individual orientations in local settings which could perhaps best be rendered with the idea of microglobalization (Albrow et al. 1994a, 1994b).

19 See Marjorie Ferguson (1992) who seeks to expose talk of globalization as an ideology to justify the expansion of global capitalism. My view (Albrow 1994) is that emphasis on the mythical features of globalization should not deflect attention from the realities of change.

20 This is exemplified in a recent good account of a number of theories of globalization where the author points to the globality of a common social environment as their common element, and then goes on to say in successive sentences, without comment on the obvious paradox, that 'globalization theories assume a salient discontinuity' between past and future and that they are an 'extension and reformulation of modernization themes' (Beyer 1994: 7).

Chapter 5   Historical Narrative for the New Age

1 Popper rejected both the idea of historical laws and historical periodization: 'Historicism claims that nothing is of greater moment than the emergence of a really new period' (1957: 10). He also attributed to historicists the view that there are no circumstances which cross periods (p. 6). In fact a central task in historical work is to identify those circumstances that do and those that don't. See my comments in the last section of this chapter on the 'test of time'.

2 There are strong similarities between Popper's account of the way history should be written and Collingwood's (1946). Both emphasize situational logic and the solving of problems. Both are scathing about history written in terms of periods. Neither has anything to say about writing history as

opposed to doing historical research. We might suggest that after the Second World War the feeling was that science could solve problems (end wars, for instance) and fresh starts could ignore the legacy of the past (e.g. forget Hitler). There was a loss of a sense of history.

3 About such factors Toynbee, who was one of the first to use the term 'postmodern', wrote with some foresight of a 'process of deracination' (1939–61, vol. 12: 276) for what later writers have called 'disembedding', and also of a future 'breakthrough' of 'non-Western elements' (p. 673). It is in this respect, rather than in his discussion of the unification of the world, that one can speak of him anticipating globalization.

4 Joseph Schumpeter used this argument from the contingency of material circumstances to illustrate the difference to capitalist development made by the unexpected torrent of precious metals released by the conquest of South America (1954: 144).

5 Toynbee (1939–61, vol. 12: 524) wrote 'The year 1949 opened a new era in human history' because the Soviet Union acquired atomic weapons. He was very flexible in his dating of new eras.

6 The economist Richard Norgaard (1994) has called the process whereby multiple factors interacting with each other are subject to adaptation and evolution the process of 'co-evolution' and equally sees them as having reached a point where 'the modern project of development has come to a halt in most of the world' (p. 3). What distinguishes this viewpoint from older multiple factor theories such as Max Weber's is the awareness of transformation rather than cumulative development.

7 Sam Whimster (1992: 314–15) observes how no recent paradigms have done justice to the transformations of the last two decades. His account of the changes which produced the 'yuppies', which rests on tracing changed meanings over time, itself implies that the paradigm which would serve this end would be a history of the present.

8 Krishan Kumar (1978: 237) pointed to the incongruity involved in Bell's derivation of a new age from the concepts modern social theorists employed to interpret modernity.

9 Nietzsche 1878/1910, Spengler 1919–22, Toynbee 1939–61, Bell 1973, Lyotard 1979, Vattimo 1988. An excellent survey of concepts of the postmodern and post-industrial is to be found in Margaret Rose (1991).

10 For an example see Benjamin Barber (1992), who expresses a characteristic modern fear for the future of democracy by identifying two 'axial principles' for our time, 'tribalism and globalism'.

11 Sociology and history are combined in C. Wright Mills's dictum: 'All sociology worthy of the name is "historical sociology" ' (1956: 146).

12 McLuhan invoked William Blake's poem 'Jerusalem' to justify employing 'a mosaic pattern of perception and observation' for his text *The Gutenberg Galaxy* (1962: 265).

13 The reader will have found 'human society', 'world society' and 'global society' used variously in the text. They are not meant to be equated. 'Human society' is an abstract concept of the ways human beings relate to each other. 'World society' is the aggregate of those relations on earth. 'Global society' is a particular configuration of human society in which global scope is an aspect of social control and social stratification. Nation-state societies are in different forms of tension with each of these.

14 Barrie Axford (1995) has sought to retain the use of the idea of system in an interdisciplinary approach to globalization; but he can only do so by simultaneously making it subject to 'the interpretative practices of agents',

who remake the conditions of their existence (p. 219). Given that he also rightly emphasizes the open nature of global futures, there isn't much work left for the system idea. The term effectively becomes a labelling device to enable reference to several things simultaneously. To that extent there is the chance that it may operate in practice not so differently from my 'configuration'. The problem is that it is virtually impossible to use 'system' in this anodyne way any more given its past heavy theoretical loading, both Marxist and non-Marxist.

15 Leslie Sklair's 'global system' is global capitalism and to the extent that his analysis reveals its systemic elements his terminology is warranted. But, as he rightly points out, the classes linked to global capitalism 'are not simply effects of the system, for they embody their own histories, cultures and practices, and they can turn the developmental strategies of global capitalism to their own purposes, and even, on occasion, challenge those who wield central power in the system' (1991: 238–9). So he concludes that history 'has hardly begun'. The reference to history and the open potentialities of social formations exactly illustrates the limitations of the system concept.

16 It is common to represent the social consequences of globalization as simultaneous immigration and unemployment, thus converting it into a social problem for the nation-state. But it could never have operated on the public psyche in the way it did during the American presidential campaign (see 3.7 above) if it had not encoded deeper fears, namely the intrusion of the foreign and the decay of national identity. Globalization sets up new poles of attraction for social relations, which threaten older forms of social cohesion. It therefore represents the innovative forces of sociality. As I have put it elsewhere: 'In this way globalization is the generalization of the problem that Marx and the international proletariat posed. It is the most generalized threat to prevailing forms of social organization ever to have existed' (Albrow 1994: 5).

17 Andrew Janos (1986: 149–50) proposed first that the 'globalization of the systems concept' was akin to Kuhn's paradigm shift and required a changing theory of social change. He also suggested that we had to revert to ideas dear to the historian, like the Zeitgeist to grasp the new transnational flows of knowledge and assumptions. One may judge the tension between the ideas of Zeitgeist and system to be a good reflection of the early difficulty faced by pioneers in moving from the one paradigm (the modern) to another (the global).

18 Keynes was eloquently misleading when he minimized the influence of vested interests: 'Madmen in authority, who hear voices in the air, are distilling their frenzy from some academic scribbler of a few years back' (1936: 383). The choice is not simply between ideas and interests.

19 This accords with MacIntyre (for example 1971: ix), who has consistently argued that philosophical concern for 'analysis' has masked the historical nature of concepts.

20 This is one of the implications of Foucault's account of the history of ideas when he disclaims any attempt at a 'totalitarian periodization' which would mean that 'for a certain time, everyone would think the same way' (1974: 148). The converse is that at any one time there are thoughts which have varying time-spans, durabilities which range between the passing moment and millennia (see also Sheridan 1980: 109).

21 Critics may notice that 'experience' serves for me much the same function as Pierre Bourdieu's (1977) 'habitus', a deep ground for practice. Foucault wrestled with the same problem of providing scientific concepts for a

preconscious and non-ideal ground for human discourse which will also render cultural and historical variety (1974: 56–63). But he rejected traditional humanistic methods in favour of the 'lived body' (see Dreyfus and Rabinow 1982: 70, 160–7). The intellectual strategy in this book is different. The situatedness of practices is relative to time and place. The reasons people can't give a good account of what they do lie not in their bodies but in the remote and unknown origins of the practices in which they engage. But they are *varyingly* remote. We apply the test of time. Some span epochs and civilizations, e.g. property, incest taboo; others are localized, e.g. Eton wall game, Ceaușescu's destruction of Transylvanian villages. But some practices are more transhistorical and transcultural than others, and it is to those with the greatest transitivity that theory most often attaches. Thus, associated with 'society' and the 'social' are ideas which (at least hypothetically, open for research) have been rendered everywhere at all times in any language, not because of the nature of thought, but because of the human condition.

22 David Lyon's account of postmodernity concludes by opening the possibility of a relativization of both modernity and postmodernity, and like Gray's (1995) hints at a future mysticism ('Age of Aquarius'). But this relativization equally allows him to acknowledge a premodern Judaeo-Christian heritage (Lyon 1994: 86).

Chapter 6 Configurations of the Global Age: Systems

1 We follow Robertson (1994: 35) here in stressing the importance of referring to globality as distinct from globalization when we want to avoid the connotations of process.

2 In the nation-state the struggle between institutional areas has been resolved at some time in the past in favour of one or the other, hence the frequently observed fact that lawyers dominate German institutions and accountants British. Where there are areas of dispute, elected politicans decide. There are no equivalent mechanisms at the transnational level. Each agency is largely free to develop its own conception of collective welfare and to follow the interests and values it judges appropriate.

3 International experience becomes a mark of distinction (difference and higher esteem) for all national elites and care is normally taken to ensure that it is transmitted to children. Roger Goodman (1990) has shown how this is true even for the Japanese managerial elite with the emergence of an 'international youth'. The big issue in terms of the formation of a global managerial class is whether these national internationalisms will give way to an overriding attachment to globalist values.

4 I am grateful to John Toulmin for sending me his Bishop Memorial Lecture at the University of Michigan (1994), which came to me after this section was written. His call, in the light of a 'new worldwide legal profession' which did not exist in 1965, for a 'vigorous assertion of those values which are important for the functioning of the legal system' exemplifies my argument exactly at this point.

5 One household name corporation in the United States, which has only approximately 10 per cent of its sales overseas, none the less seeks to attract graduate recruits by offering participation in a 'Global leadership development programme'. In fact the global elements in the programme are no more than proportionate to the foreign sales. The noteworthy fact

is that the corporation cannot afford not to headline 'Global'. It increases the status and attractiveness of the programme even for a firm with products of a non-luxury, non-prestige type for a domestic market.

6 A personal informant in one global corporation tells me that it uses the new information technology to shadow all work tasks throughout its management. There is no item of work which does not appear as equally the responsibility of two people. He keeps in touch by modem and lap-top computer with his shadows from any point in the world. In one government department staff are still coming to terms with the fact that decades of conventions on forms of address and internal communications protocol disappear overnight when anyone can send a message to all others on internal e-mail.

7 Kees Van der Pijl (1984) identified an 'Atlantic ruling class'. The global elite is still dominated by the descendants of the white imperial ruling class and crosses the Atlantic often enough. But developments in the last ten years provide enough indication that neither the historical origin nor the geographical base of the activity of the elite remains still. There is a shift to the Pacific both in activity and influence, while the Hungarian billionaire financier George Soros is only the most prominent example of the way money markets cross the boundaries of history and geography.

8 This has interesting consequences for the adaptation of national cultures. Hideichiro Nakano (1984) has attributed the success of Japan in the new global economy not to Japanese moral imperatives but to a pragmatism which is well suited to the shifting contingencies of world markets.

9 This is the interpretation which Andrew Marr (1995) gives for the enthusiasm Margaret Thatcher and the Conservatives have had for deregulation, which for him has been more of a threat to national independence than anything emerging from Brussels.

10 This effectively continues old modern political debate. There are both right-wing and left-wing globalizationists and anti-globalizationists. So in Britain we find, predictably, a right-wing advocate of the free market like the contender for the Conservative Party leadership, John Redwood (1994), lined up against a left-wing sceptic about globalization like the *Guardian* economics editor, Will Hutton (1995). On the other hand, the left-wing Martin Jacques (1993) and the free-market *Economist* agree on globalization as a fact of life and disagree fundamentally on its consequences for national governments (for the position of the *Economist* see 'The Myth of the Powerless State', *Economist*, 7–13 Oct. 1995, pp. 15–16).

11 The head of tax at Coopers & Lybrand, Peter Wyman (1994), has explained that national tax systems require accounting firms like his to go global to give the requisite advice for their multinational customers. Hence the Big Six accounting firms have 3,600 offices in 130 countries.

12 An Indian columnist, Sanjaya Baru (1993), has argued that the failure of Indian companies to market a successful brand name abroad, as compared with South Korea, is attributable to a negative image of India as such. The implication is that nation building and the global dissemination of a national image are the priority before there can be successful corporate images and brand names.

13 Steve Coll (1994) reports how trade in waste was worth 90 billion US dollars in 1991 and turned local pollutants into a global disposal problem. John Vidal (1995) reports on the worldwide doubling of demand for water every twenty-one years and the vicious circles of industrial farming, over-extraction and desertification.

Chapter 7 Configurations of the Global Age: People

1 These facilities are equally available to religions from the older world civilizations. The milk-drinking Ganesh miracle which happened in a Delhi
  temple on Thursday morning, 21 September 1995, and spread throughout
  India was reported worldwide next day. The *Guardian* of 23 September
  reported it as 'probably the first example of global religious fervour pro-
  pagated by mass telecommunications'. My colleague Jörg Durrschmidt was
  invited the same day to observe the milk-drinking in the home of an Indian
  family in London.
2 To this extent Greenpeace then equally becomes a potential ally in interstate politics. The German government opposed Britain on the policy of
  deep-sea disposal of waste and gave support to Greenpeace in the dispute
  over sinking the derelict Brent Spar oil rig in the Atlantic. It had the added
  incentive that 80 per cent of German public opinion was against the sinking (*Guardian*, 21 June 1995, p. 6).
3 Jameson holds resolutely to the classic Marxist insistence on deriving
  the movement of the times from a non-human logic of capitalism, in the
  case of the present time from 'late capitalism'. The supreme agent is then
  'multinational capital' (1991: 408). He freely acknowledges that this employs
  the old base–superstructure imagery. He is particularly paradoxical in
  suggesting a 'logic' to postmodernism. There probably never has been a
  time when the influence of culture on capitalism has been greater, and
  there is precious little logic to it.
4 This may happen with the best of motives. Young's and Willmott's Institute of Community Studies work (e.g. 1957) from the 1950s onwards sought
  to influence government policy and for that reason worked within the
  frame of loss of community. But it led to a systematic neglect of questions
  about ties beyond locality. Even Elias and Scotson (1965), who sought to
  alert British community studies to questions of migration, effectively produced a model where 'outsiders' were assimilated to a structural feature
  of community. It was only when Rex and Moore (1967) introduced questions of colonialism and immigration that the non-local came to be recognized as an essential aspect of local studies. For further elaboration on this
  point see Albrow (1996). The Roehampton Local/Global studies (Albrow
  et al. 1994a) treat ties extended as far as the global as intrinsic to the study
  of locality.
5 Harvey dates these new ways in which we experience space and time
  quite precisely as beginning around 1972 and as being central to the culture of postmodernism. But he resists the idea of epochal change since he
  sees all these as simply surface accompaniments of underlying capitalist
  accumulation.
6 The examples are real, drawn from the Roehampton Local/Global studies
  (Albrow et al. 1994a, Albrow 1996), but they do not actually live in one
  street. However the diversity in any one locality of social class, ethnic characteristics and types of housing occupancy in large parts of South London
  makes that entirely possible.
7 Appadurai argues that the state of the 'new global cultural economy'
  is inadequately captured by older models drawn from political economy
  (1990: 296–7). He advocates thinking in terms of flows and suggests that
  the suffix '-scape' can express both the perspectival nature of our 'imagined
  worlds' and their fluid, irregular shape. He thus proposes ethnoscapes,

mediascapes, technoscapes, finanscapes and ideoscapes. But his ethnoscapes are categories of persons, which he contrasts with 'relatively stable communities and networks'. I would wish to stress the relative fluidity of these 'stable units' as compared both with earlier periods and with previous theoretical accounts, hence 'socioscapes'. 'Socioscape' has also been used independently by Axford (1995: 213).

8 For an introduction to the concepts of extended and generalized milieux, see Albrow et al. (1994b). I am much indebted to Jörg Durrschmidt for his intensive work on these ideas.

9 The *Umwelt* is the region surrounding an individual in which alarm signals of a threat to security can be registered.

10 'Socio-sphere' was used by Alvin Toffler (1981: 42) to refer to social organization. 'Sociosphere' is used here with more specific connotations of extension through and separation between people.

Chapter 8 The Future State and Society

1 When Touraine (1984: 37) wrote of the weakening of the representation of social life because of the 'decomposition' of the ideas underpinning so-called modern society, namely modernity and the national state, he was drawing attention to the way those ideas had monopolized the image of society.

2 We can also find modern understandings of these universal qualities. Montaigne's essay 'Of Vanity' (1580/1842: 450–1) included an extended consideration of the interplay of absence and presence (1842: 450–1). (The *Oxford Dictionary of Quotations* dates the saying 'Absence makes the heart grow fonder' from 1602.) Max Weber recognized the inherently abstract aspect of any relationship when he said that for it to 'exist' one would point to the *possibility* of something taking place, not its actuality (1921/1974: 28). We can gloss this by reflecting on the question of whether a relationship exists between two lovers. We are more likely to be persuaded of its existence if they embrace after they have been *apart*. If they do not part, neither they nor anyone else can have confidence that a relationship exists. Conversely, long periods of constant proximity can put intense strain on a relationship because of the lack of absence. The projection of the intense nature of the requirements in early years of life for bodily presence on to adult life, or even on to community and society, is a literal immaturity lodged in the discourse of modern social theory.

3 World society as a concept is as inchoate as world market. We can think of many world societies, as we do in talking of the 'Islamic world' and the 'Christian world'. They have no territorial limits, they create a world of their own for their adherents. Even discounting or denying multiple worlds, 'one world society' is not the same as global society. It is simply the sum total of transnational relations without any global reference, just as the world market is simply the sum total of markets.

4 However, we can exaggerate these differences. Even within the two traditions the other strand appears. So, from English thought, Thomas Hobbes was eagerly received by conservative thinkers in Europe, while radicals throughout the Western world found Rousseau an inspiration. The point is that the top-down, bottom-up contrast represented an unresolved tension in modernity, characteristic of it, and therefore the focus for the theory of the state.

5 The bureaucracy was a class which sank its particular interests in the general interests of the state. It alone corresponded with the idea of state because it consisted of individuals acting 'only by virtue of their universal and object-ive qualities' (Hegel 1821/1991: 314), that is beyond their membership of any partial group. Those individuals together made up the collectivity. 'The nation state (*das Volk als Staat*) is the spirit in its substantial rationality and immediate actuality and is therefore the absolute power on earth' (p. 366).

6 John Gray (1994), reviewing John Redwood's book (1994), complained that the rhetoric of globalization was preventing Britain from following policy options such as those of the French in protecting their film industry or of the Japanese in maintaining lifetime job security. Will Hutton (1995) equally sees globalization as a myth, promoted by the right to justify government inaction in the face of internationalization.

7 Geoff Mulgan (1995) takes the view that economic globalization is here to stay but that it by no means implies an end to government, rather a chal-lenge to it. Paul Hirst (1993) argues that economic globalization is an ideal-typical concept and unlikely to be realized.

8 Just one sentence from a leading article, 'The Myth of the Powerless State', in the *Economist* provides a clear example of the persistence of older nation-state discourse (7–13 Oct. 1995, pp. 15–16): 'Start with the simplest gauge of the state's involvement in the economy – the fraction of a country's income which the government spends.' The equation of state with govern-ment may be the national government's dream but is far from the realities of power. Governments are constrained at every turn in what they spend. The state is power, and the 'powerless state' is a contradiction in terms. Hence equating government with the state acquires rhetorical force beyond any realistic analysis of the powers of government. On this kind of analysis we can't entertain the possibility of the coexistence of powerful state and weak government; hence Italy will always have strong govern-ment! This is quite aside from the use of 'state' to mean 'national state'.

9 As does Jacques (1993) who speaks of a crisis of politics and democracy.

10 In the words of a Polish historian working in the United States, democratic government and national self-determination will have to be 'federated in an efficient world organization' for the world to be really one (Halecki 1950: 191).

11 We are engaged in a conceptual task akin to the one Goethe assumed in conceptualizing the idea of world literature. He wrote in 1827 that national literature had little meaning and that an epoch of world literature was at hand (Strich 1949: 349). For him a world literature transcended national literatures but did not absorb them. It provided a universal frame through which nations could understand each other. The distinction between world state and national state is roughly parallel. But the distinction made here between global state and world state is of equal importance. There was no equivalent distinction to make in Goethe's time.

12 Carl Brinkman's brief essay on citizenship (1930: 471) points out that the personal concept of citizenship precedes the territorial everywhere. So it is not simply a contrast of ancient and modern. The Roman *civis* was based on personality, not domicile. The main point to recognize is that a historical and comparative grasp of citizenship beyond modernity makes it possible to recognize a suppressed substratum to the idea. Brinkman is therefore able to go on to imagine more far-reaching notions of citizenship.

13 Marshall's account was delivered as the (Alfred) Marshall lecture in Cambridge in 1949.

14 J. G. Fichte sought to elaborate this universal idea of citizenship beyond the nation-state in his science of rights. In an account of international and comparative law he located the idea of the state in the right of an individual to compel another to enter into a legal relation: 'If neither is as yet a resident of a state, both unite to form at least the beginnings of a state.' This for him is proof that the state is 'not an arbitrary invention but is established by nature and reason' (Fichte 1869: 473–4). This right is not beyond community, it is established in interaction with others (p. 160), but the state as such is returned to being the outcome of the active engagement of people with each other, rather than being a fixed entity encircling or imposed on them. At the same time, the exercise of control and constraint is also vested in individuals.

15 The doyen of world citizens, Garry Davis, in a transmission of 19 August 1995 (http://www.together – org/orgs/wcw/wcninter/ntml), encourages Internet users to say 'Hello, fellow Net Citizens. I am a sovereign World Citizen.' He declares that the possibility of communicating with others worldwide permits world citizens to affirm a global social contract. For him citizenship implies self-policing, not government. Essentially it is Fichte for the Global Age. (I am indebted to Neil Washbourne for his net search.)

16 Even a theorist like John Dryzek (1990: 21, 220), who seeks to take communicative rationality beyond the limitations imposed on it by Habermas's system/lifeworld dichotomy and to extend the idea of discursive democracy into what he calls the enemy's camp, is reluctant to extend it to the state and bureaucracy. If, however, we recognize state and bureaucracy as discursive formations, we have equally to acknowledge that the discursive democracy of social movements is engaged in constituting an alternative kind of state. Organizational problems do not disappear with discursive democracy.

Chapter 9   The Global Age Hypothesis

1 The importance of the difference between opposition and transformation is highlighted by Hebdige's brilliant account of youth subcultures. When it was written it was still possible for him to incline to the view that 'what they express is, in the last instance, a fundamental tension between those in power and those condemned to subordinate positions and second class lives' (1979: 132). Althusserian structuralism, almost the last pure expression of modernist social theory, provided an anchorage, but it left the author uncomfortable with his own admitted kind of romanticism which stressed transformation (p. 138). By now it is clear, from the ravers through to what Ted Polhemus (1995) has called 'the gathering of the tribes' and 'the supermarket of style', that cultural transformation is not limited to struggles beween the dominant culture and subcultures. It arises now out of negotiating a way through multiple culture contact.

2 John Naisbitt (1994) has sought to interpret globality by focusing on contemporary paradoxes and this is clearly instructive in managerial writing. We should not, however, be lured into thinking that the Global Age is peculiarly paradoxical. The relation of contradiction to structure is a fraught and difficult area of social theory and needs more discussion than is possible

here. My position is that every epoch has its characteristic contradictions, which stabilize over a period of time until a new factor unsettles their coexistence. This avoids the rationalistic prejudice of seeing the epoch deriving from some overarching axial principle (see 5.2 above). The point is that the paradoxes of the Global Age are different from those of the Modern Age and this forces them on our attention.

3 I owe this suggestion to Neil Washbourne.

4 'Moral concepts change as social concepts change. . . . Moral concepts are embodied in and partially constitutive of forms of social life' (MacIntyre 1967: 1).

5 The actual numbers would depend of course on just how stringent the researcher was in the initial definition. In a sample of Pakistani men, for instance, Inkeles could find anything between 0 per cent and 14 per cent 'modern' depending on the stringency of the definition (1983: 333).

6 T. K. Oommen (1990: 13) stresses the historicity of movements in India, for instance, and points to them as reminders of the social creativity of human beings.

7 Jordi Pujol calls for the affirmation of Catalonia through the combination of 'a global life-style and the strengthening of its own cultural identity' (Guibernau 1995: 15).

8 In this respect the current state of the British Labour Party is instructive for the dilemmas faced by nation-state politicians. 'Modernization' is the watchword and brings with it the terminology of the old modernity. The only surprising thing about a leaked internal memorandum which spoke of the need for a project and centralized management was the surprise which greeted it. Written in April 1995 by Philip Gould, campaigns and strategy consultant to Tony Blair, it called for 'a political project that matches the Thatcher agenda of 1979' with 'economic modernisation/renewal to be a priority' ('Leak Hits Blair on Eve of TUC Speech', *Guardian*, 12 Sept. 1995, p. 2).

9 This characteristically modern conjunction was well expressed in the 1995 Anglo-Italian Pontignano conference, where the three themes spanned institutions, monetary union and the dangers of new inequalities, i.e. structure, project and threatening chaos.

10 Gilroy has eloquently expressed the way 'pluralization of black identities' has fatally undermined 'the idea of a common, invariant racial identity capable of linking divergent black experiences across different spaces and times' (Gilroy 1993b: 2).

References

Where two dates occur for an entry, the publication details and page references refer to the later edition. Where no English-language editions are given, translations of quotations in the text are mine.

Acton, Lord 1906: *Lectures on Modern History*. London: Macmillan.
Acton, Lord 1952: *Essays on Church and State*, ed. Douglas Woodruff. London: Hollis and Carter.
Albrow, Martin 1970: *Bureaucracy*. London: Macmillan.
Albrow, Martin 1987: 'The Application of the Weberian Concept of Rationalization to Contemporary Conditions'. In Scott Lash and Sam Whimster (eds), *Max Weber, Rationality and Modernity*, London: Allen and Unwin, 164–82.
Albrow, Martin 1990a: *Max Weber's Construction of Social Theory*. London: Macmillan.
Albrow, Martin 1990b: 'Values, Strategic Planning and the Welfare State: the Collapse of Social Policy', *Annals of the International Institute of Sociology*, New Series, 1: 87–98.
Albrow, Martin 1994: 'Globalization: Myths and Realities', Inaugural Lecture, Roehampton Institute London.
Albrow, Martin 1995: 'Globalization'. In Robert J. Brym (ed.), *New Society: Sociology for the Twenty-First Century*, Toronto: Harcourt Brace, ch. 15.
Albrow, Martin 1996: 'Travelling beyond Local Culture: Socioscapes in a Global City'. In John Eade (ed.), *Living the Global City*, London: Routledge.
Albrow, Martin, John Eade, Graham Fennell and Darren O'Byrne 1994a: *Local/ Global Relations in a London Borough*. London: Roehampton Institute.
Albrow, Martin, John Eade, Neil Washbourne and Jörg Durrschmidt 1994b: 'The Impact of Globalization on Sociological Concepts: Community, Culture and Milieu', *Innovation* 7: 371–89.
Alleyne-Dettmers, Patricia 1996: ' "Tribal Arts": a Case Study of Global Compression in Notting Hill Carnival'. In John Eade (ed.), *Living the Global City*, London: Routledge.
Althusser, Louis 1971: *Lenin and Philosophy and Other Essays*. London: New Left Books.

Ankersmitt, Frank and Hans Kellner (eds) 1995: *A New Philosophy of History*. London: Reaktion Books.

Appadurai, Arjun 1990: 'Disjuncture and Difference in the Global Cultural Economy'. In Mike Featherstone (ed.), *Global Culture: Nationalism, Globalization and Modernity*, London: Sage, 295–310.

Aquinas, St Thomas 1954: *Selected Political Writings*, ed. A. P. D'Entrèves. Oxford: Blackwell.

Archer, Margaret 1988: *Culture and Agency*. Cambridge: Cambridge University Press.

Archibugi, Daniele and David Held (eds) 1995: *Cosmopolitan Democracy*. Cambridge: Polity Press.

Aristotle 1909: *The Art of Poetry*, tr. Ingram Bywater. Oxford: Clarendon Press.

Aristotle 1946: *The Politics*, tr. Ernest Barker. Oxford: Clarendon Press.

Aron, Raymond 1967: *Peace and War: a Theory of International Relations*. New York: Praeger.

Axford, Barrie 1995: *The Global System: Economic, Politics and Culture*. Cambridge: Polity Press.

Bacon, Francis 1620/1857–90: 'Novum Organum'. In *Collected Works*, ed. James Spedding, R. L. Ellis and D. D. Heath, London.

Bacon, Francis 1626/1857–90: 'The New Atlantis'. In *Collected Works*, ed. James Spedding, R. L. Ellis and D. D. Heath, London.

Barber, Benjamin R. 1992: 'Jihad vs McWorld', *Atlantic Monthly*, March: 53–63.

Barnett, Carole K. 1992: 'The Global Agenda for Research and Training in the 1990s'. In Vladimir Pucik, Noel M. Tichy and Carole K. Barnett (eds), *Globalizing Management: Creating and Leading the Competitive Organization*, New York: John Wiley, 319–39.

Bartlett, Christopher A. 1986: 'Building and Managing the Transnational: the New Organizational Challenge'. In Michael E. Porter (ed.), *Competition in Global Industries*, Boston, Mass.: Harvard Business School, 367–401.

Baru, Sanjaya 1993: 'Indian Brands Abroad: Country's Positive Image is Critical'. *The Times of India*, 29 Oct.: 8.

Baudrillard, Jean 1988: *America*. London: Verso.

Bauman, Zygmunt 1989: *Modernity and the Holocaust*. Cambridge: Polity Press.

Bauman, Zygmunt 1992: *Intimations of Postmodernity*. London: Routledge.

Baumgarten, Otto 1964: *Max Weber: Werk und Person*. Tübingen: Mohr.

Beck, Ulrich 1986/1992: *Risk Society: Towards a New Modernity*. London: Sage.

Beck, Ulrich, Anthony Giddens and Scott Lash 1994: *Reflexive Modernization*. Cambridge: Polity Press.

Becker, Carl 1932: *The Heavenly City of the Eighteenth-Century Philosophers*. New Haven: Yale.

Bell, Daniel 1968/1980a: 'Charles Fourier: Prophet of Eupsychia'. In Bell, *Sociological Journeys*, Cambridge, Mass.: ABT Books, 91–104.

Bell, Daniel 1968/1980b: 'National Character Revisited: a Proposal for Re-negotiating the Concept'. In Bell, *Sociological Journeys*, Cambridge, Mass.: ABT Books, 167–83.

Bell, Daniel 1973: *The Coming of Post–industrial Society: a Venture in Social Forecasting*. New York: Basic Books.

Bell, Daniel 1976: *The Cultural Contradictions of Capitalism*. London: Heinemann.

Bell, Daniel 1980: *Sociological Journeys: Essays 1960–1980*. Cambridge, Mass.: ABT Books.

Bellah, Robert, R. Madsen, W. M. Sullivan, A. Swidler and S. M. Tipton 1985: *Habits of the Heart*. Berkeley, Ca.: University of California Press.

Berger, Peter L., Brigitte Berger and Hansfried Kellner 1973: *The Homeless Mind: Modernization and Consciousness*. New York: Random House.

Bergquist, William 1993: *The Postmodern Organization*. San Francisco: Jossey-Bass.

Beyer, Peter 1994: *Religion and Globalization*. London: Sage.

Bossuet, Jacques-Benigne 1681/1887: *Discours sur l'histoire universelle*. Paris: Charpentiers.

Bourdieu, Pierre 1977: *Outline of a Theory of Practice*. Cambridge: Cambridge University Press.

Brainard, Robert 1993: 'Globalization and Corporate Identity'. In OECD, Special Issue on Globalization, *STI Review* 13: 163–86.

Brinkman, Carl 1930: 'Citizenship'. In *Encyclopaedia of the Social Sciences*, vol. 3, New York: Macmillan, 471–4.

Brogan, Denis W. 1944: *The American Character*. New York: Knopf.

Brundtland, Gro Harlem 1987: *Our Common Future*, report of the World Commission on Environment and Development (Brundtland Report). London: Oxford University Press.

Brunner, Otto, Werner Conze and Reinhart Koselleck (eds) 1972–: *Geschichtliche Grundbegriffe: Historisches Lexikon zur politisch-sozialen Sprache in Deutschland*. Stuttgart: Klett.

Budd, Leslie and Sam Whimster 1992: *Global Finance and Urban Living*. London: Routledge.

Burckhardt, Jacob 1860/1944: *The Civilization of the Renaissance in Italy*. London: Phaidon.

Burke, Peter 1987: *The Italian Renaissance: Culture and Society in Italy*. Cambridge: Polity Press.

Burnham, James 1941: *The Managerial Revolution*. New York: John Day.

Burnham, James 1947: *The Struggle for the World*. New York: John Day.

Carr, David 1986: *Time, Narrative and History*. Bloomington: Indiana University Press.

Clegg, Stewart R. 1990: *Modern Organizations: Organization Studies in the Postmodern World*. London: Sage.

Cohn, Norman 1957: *The Pursuit of the Millennium*. London: Secker and Warburg.

Coll, Steve 1994: 'Global Economy Faces the Global Dump', *International Herald Tribune*, 24 Mar.

Collingwood, R. G. 1946: *The Idea of History*. Oxford: Oxford University Press.

Council on Environmental Quality and the Department of State 1982: *The Global 2000 Report to the President: Entering the Twenty-First Century*. New York: Penguin.

Creighton, Mandell 1902: 'Introductory Note'. In *The Cambridge Modern History*, vol. 1: *The Renaissance*, London: Cambridge University Press.

Dahl, Robert A. 1961: *Who Governs? Democracy and Power in an American City*. New Haven: Yale University Press.

Dahrendorf, Ralf 1959: *Class and Class Conflict in Industrial Society*. London: Routledge.

Dahrendorf, Ralf 1975: *The New Liberty*. London: Routledge.

Dante 1312/1954: *Monarchy and Three Political Letters*, tr. Donald Nichol. London: Weidenfeld and Nicolson.

Descartes, René 1637/1912: *A Discourse on Method*. London: Dent.

Dicken, Peter 1992: *Global Shift: the Internationalization of Economic Activity*. London: Paul Chapman.

Donzelot, Jacques 1984: *L'Invention du social*. Paris: Fayard.

Dreyfus, Hubert L. and Paul Rabinow 1982: *Beyond Structuralism and Hermeneutics*. Brighton: Harvester.

Dryzek, John S. 1990: *Discursive Democracy: Politics, Policy and Political Science*. Cambridge: Cambridge University Press.

Durkheim, Émile 1893/1933: *The Division of Labor in Society*. Glencoe, Ill.: Free Press.

Durkheim, Émile 1895/1982: *The Rules of Sociological Method*. New York: Free Press.

Eade, John (ed.) 1996: *Living the Global City*. London: Routledge.

Eco, Umberto 1983: *The Name of the Rose*. London: Secker and Warburg.

Edelman, Nathan 1938: 'The Early Uses of Medium Aevum, Moyen Age, Middle Ages', *Romanic Review* 29: 4f.

Ekins, Paul 1992: *A New World Order: Grassroots Movements for Global Change*. London: Routledge.

Elias, Norbert 1978: *The History of Manners*, vol. 1 of *The Civilizing Process*. Oxford: Blackwell.

Elias Norbert 1982: *State and Civilization*, vol. 2 of *The Civilizing Process*. Oxford: Blackwell.

Elias, Norbert and Scotson, J. L. 1965: *The Established and the Outsiders*. London: Frank Cass.

Eliot, T. S. 1939: *The Idea of a Christian Society*. London: Faber.

Etzioni, Amitai 1994: *The Spirit of Community: the Reinvention of American Society*. New York: Touchstone.

Falk, Richard 1992: *Explorations at the Edge of Time: the Prospects for World Order*. Philadelphia: Temple University Press.

Featherstone, Mike (ed.) 1990: *Global Culture: Nationalism, Globalization and Modernity*. London: Sage.

Ferguson, Adam 1767/1782: *An Essay on the History of Civil Society*. London and Edinburgh: Cadell, Creech and Bell.

Ferguson, Marjorie 1992: 'The Mythology about Globalization', *European Journal of Communication* 7: 69–93.

Fernandez-Armesto, Felipe 1995: *Millennium*. London: Bantam.

Ferrarotti, Franco 1985: *The Myth of Inevitable Progress*. Westport, Conn.: Greenwood.

Fichte, J. G. 1869: *The Science of Rights*, tr. A. E. Kroeger. Philadelphia: J. P. Lippincott.

Foucault, Michel 1967: *Madness and Civilization*. London: Tavistock.

Foucault, Michel 1974: *The Archaeology of Knowledge*. London: Tavistock.

Foucault, Michel 1977: *Discipline and Punish*. London: Allen Lane.

Foucault, Michel 1979: *The History of Sexuality*. London: Allen Lane.

Fukuyama, Francis 1992: *The End of History and the Last Man*. New York: Free Press.

Giddens, Anthony 1984: *The Constitution of Society*. Cambridge: Polity Press.

Giddens, Anthony 1990: *The Consequences of Modernity*. Cambridge: Polity Press.

Giddens, Anthony 1991: *Modernity and Self-Identity: Self and Society in the Late Modern Age*. Cambridge: Polity Press.

Gifford, Don 1990: *The Farther Shore: a Natural History of Perception 1798–1984*. London: Faber and Faber.

Gilpin, Robert 1971: 'The Politics of Transnational Economic Relations'. In R. O. Keohane and J. S. Nye (eds), *Transnational Relations and World Politics*, Cambridge, Mass.: Harvard University Press, 48–69.

Gilroy, Paul 1993a: *The Black Atlantic: Modernity and Double Consciousness*. London: Verso.

Gilroy, Paul 1993b: *Small Acts*. London: Serpent's Tail.

Gilson, Étienne 1948: *Dante the Philosopher*. London: Sheed & Ward.

Ginzburg, Paul 1982: *The Cheese and the Worms*. Harmondsworth: Penguin.

Goffman, Erving 1972: *Relations in Public: Microstudies of the Public Order*. Harmondsworth: Penguin.

Goodman, Roger 1990: *Japan's International Youth*. Oxford: Clarendon Press.

Gore, Al 1992: *Earth in the Balance*. New York: Houghton Mifflin.

Gower, Ernest (ed.) 1965: *Fowler's Dictionary of Modern English Usage*. Oxford: Clarendon Press.

Gramsci, Antonio 1957: *The Modern Prince and Other Writings*. New York: International Publishers.

Grathoff, Richard 1989: *Milieu und Lebenswelt*. Frankfurt/M.: Suhrkamp.

Grau, Andrée 1992: 'Intercultural Research in the Performing Arts', *Dance Research* 10: 3–29.

Gray, John 1994: 'Against the World', *Guardian*, 3 Jan.

Gray, John 1995: *Enlightenment's Wake: Politics and Culture at the End of the Modern Age*. London: Routledge.

Green, Martin 1986: *Mountain of Truth: the Counterculture Begins. Ascona, 1900–1920*. Hanover and London: University Press of New England.

Guibernau, Montserrat 1995: 'Catalan Nationalism and Nations without a State', unpubl. paper.

Gumbrecht, Hans Ulrich 1978: 'Modern, Modernitat, Moderne'. In Otto Brunner et al. (eds), *Geschichtliche Grundbegriffe*, Stuttgart: Klett, 95–131.

Habermas, Jürgen 1981: *Theorie des Kommunikativen Handelns*, 2 vols. Frankfurt: Suhrkamp. In English as *The Theory of Communicative Action*, vol. 1: *Reason and the Rationalization of Society*; vol. 2: *Lifeworld and System: a Critique of Functionalist Reason*, tr. T. McCarthy, Cambridge: Polity Press, 1986, 1989.

Habermas, Jürgen 1983: 'Modernity: an Incomplete Project'. In Hal Foster (ed.), *The Anti-Aesthetic: Essays on Postmodern Culture*, Port Townsend, Wash.: Bay Press, 3–15.

Halecki, Oscar 1950: *The Limits and Divisions of European History*. London: Sheed and Ward.

Hall, Stuart 1992: 'The Question of Cultural Identity'. In Stuart Hall et al. (eds), *Modernity and its Futures*, Cambridge: Polity Press and Open University Press, 273–316.

Hall, Stuart and Martin Jacques (eds) 1989: *New Times: the Changing Face of Politics in the 1990s*. London: Lawrence and Wishart.

Hall, Stuart, David Held and Tony McGrew (eds) 1992: *Modernity and its Futures*. Cambridge: Polity Press and Open University Press, 61–102.

Harvey, David 1989: *The Condition of Postmodernity*. Oxford: Blackwell.

Hawley, Amos H. 1981: *Urban Society: an Ecological Approach*. New York: Wiley.

Hebdige, Dick 1979: *Subculture: the Meaning of Style*. London: Methuen.

Hegel, G. W. F. 1821/1991: *Elements of the Philosophy of Right*. Cambridge: Cambridge University Press.

Held, David 1995: *Democracy and the Global Order*. Cambridge: Polity Press.

Himmelfarb, Gertrude 1995: 'Preface'. In Digby Anderson (ed.), *This Will Hurt: the Restoration of Virtue and Civic Order*, London: Social Affairs Unit.

Hintze, Otto 1942: 'Der moderne Kapitalismus als historisches Individuum'. In Hintze, *Zur Theorie der Geschichte*, Leipzig: Koehler und Amelang, 71–149.

Hirst, Paul 1993: 'Globalization is Fashionable but is it a Myth', *Guardian*, 22 Mar.

Hobhouse, Leonard 1918: *The Metaphysical Theory of the State*. London: Allen and Unwin.

Hobsbawm, Eric 1990: *Nations and Nationalism since 1780*. Cambridge: Cambridge University Press.

Howe, Irving (ed.) 1967: *The Idea of the Modern*. New York: Horizon.

Hume, David 1741–2/1903: *Essays: Moral, Political and Literary*. London: Grant Richards.

Husserl, Edmund 1937/1970: *The Crisis of the European Sciences and Transcendental Phenomenology*. Evanston: Northwestern Press.

Hutton, Will 1995: 'Myth that Sets the World to Right', *Guardian*, 12 June, p. 17.

Ibn Khaldun 1958: *The Muqaddimah: an Introduction to History*, tr. Franz Rosenthal. London: Routledge.

Inglehart, Ronald 1977: *The Silent Revolution*. Princeton: Princeton University Press.

Inglehart, Ronald 1990a: *Culture Shift in Advanced Industrial Society*. Princeton: Princeton University Press.

Inglehart, Ronald 1990b: 'Changing Values: the Human Component of Global Change', *Annals of the International Institute of Sociology*, New Series, 1: 99–132.

Inkeles, Alex 1983: *Exploring Individual Modernity*. New York: Columbia University Press.

Jacques, Martin 1993: 'Politicians Stand Still While the World Moves On', *The Times*, 4 Oct.

James, Henry 1907/1917: 'The Energies of Men'. In James, *Selected Papers on Philosophy*, London: J. M. Dent.

Jameson, Fredric 1991: *Postmodernism, or, The Cultural Logic of Late Capitalism*. London: Verso.

Janos, Andrew 1986: *Politics and Paradigms: Changing Theories of Change in Social Science*. Stanford: Stanford University Press.

Jaspers, Karl 1955: *Vom Ziel und Ursprung der Geschichte*. Frankfurt/Main: Fischer.

Jenkins, Simon 1995: *Accountable to None: the Tory Nationalisation of Britain*. London: Hamish Hamilton.

Keohane, Robert O. and Joseph S. Nye (eds) 1971: *Transnational Relations and World Politics*. Cambridge: Harvard University Press.

Kerr, Clark, J. T. Dunlop, S. Harbison and C. A. Myers 1960: *Industrialism and Industrial Man*. Cambridge: Harvard University Press.

Keynes, John Maynard 1930: *A Treatise on Money*, vol. 2: *The Applied Theory of Money*. London: Macmillan.

Keynes, John Maynard 1936: *The General Theory of Employment, Interest and Money*. London: Macmillan.

Kornhauser, William 1957: *The Politics of Mass Society*. Glencoe, Ill.: Free Press.

Kroeber, A. L. 1944: *Configurations of Culture Growth*. Berkeley: University of California Press.

Kuhn, Thomas S. 1962: *The Structure of Scientific Revolutions*. Chicago: Chicago University Press.

Kumar, Krishan 1978: *Prophecy and Progress: the Sociology of Industrial and Post-industrial Society*. London: Allen Lane.

Lash, Scott and John Urry 1987: *The End of Organized Capitalism*. Cambridge: Polity Press.

Levitt, Theodore 1983: 'The Globalization of Markets', *Harvard Business Review*, May–June: 92–102.

Lobkowicz, Nicholas 1967: *Theory and Practice: History of a Concept from Aristotle to Marx*. Notre Dame, Ind.: University of Notre Dame Press.

Locke, John 1690–1706/1961: *An Essay Concerning Human Understanding*, 2 vols. London: Dent.

Luhmann, Niklas 1985: *A Sociological Theory of Law*. London: Routledge.

Lyon, David 1994: *Postmodernity*. Milton Keynes: Open University Press.

Lyotard, Jean-François 1979: *La Condition postmoderne: rapport sur le savoir*. Paris: Éditions de Minuit. In English as *The Postmodern Condition*, Minneapolis: University of Minnesota Press, 1984.

McGrew, Anthony 1992: 'A Global Society'. In Stuart Hall et al. (eds), *Modernity and its Futures*, Cambridge: Polity Press and Open University Press, 61–102.

Machiavelli, Niccolò 1517/n.d.: *The Prince*. London: Frowde.

MacIntyre, Alasdair 1967: *A Short History of Ethics*. London: Routledge.

MacIntyre, Alasdair 1971: *Against the Self-Images of the Age*. London: Duckworth.

McLuhan, Marshall 1962: *The Gutenberg Galaxy*. Toronto: Toronto University Press.

Maddox, Brenda 1994: *The Married Man: a Life of D. H. Lawrence*. London: Sinclair-Stevenson.

Mann, Michael 1993: *The Sources of Social Power*, vol. 2: *The Rise of Classes and Nation-States*. Cambridge: Cambridge University Press.

Marcuse, Herbert 1955: *Eros and Civilization*. Boston: Beacon.

Marcuse, Herbert 1964: *One-Dimensional Man*. Boston: Beacon.

Marr, Andrew 1995: 'The Real Enemy is the Money Market', *Spectator*, 9 Sept., pp. 20–1.

Marshall, Alfred 1890/1920: *Principles of Economics*. London: Macmillan.

Marshall, Alfred 1923/1965: *Money, Credit and Commerce*. New York: Kelley.

Marshall, T. H. 1964: *Class, Citizenship and Social Development*. New York: Doubleday.

Marx, Karl and Frederick Engels 1975a: *Collected Works, Volume 3, 1843–44*. London: Lawrence and Wishart.

Marx, Karl and Frederick Engels 1975b: *Collected Works, Volume 4, 1844–45*. London: Lawrence and Wishart.

Marx, Karl and Frederick Engels 1976a: *Collected Works, Volume 5, 1845–47*. London: Lawrence and Wishart.

Marx, Karl and Frederick Engels 1976b: *Collected Works, Volume 6, 1845–48*. London: Lawrence and Wishart.

Marx, Karl and Frederick Engels 1977: *Collected Works, Volume 8, 1848–49*. London: Lawrence and Wishart.

Mathew, David 1946: *Acton*. London: Eyre and Spottiswode.

Mazzini, Joseph 1835/n.d.: 'Faith and the Future'. In Mazzini, *Essays*, ed. William Clarke, London: Walter Scott.

Meadows, Donella H., Dennis L. Meadows, Jorgen Randers and William W. Behrens 1972: *The Limits to Growth*. New York: Universe Books.

Megill, Allan 1995: '"Grand Narrative" and the Narrative of History'. In Frank Ankersmitt and Hans Kellner (eds), *A New Philosophy of History*, London: Reaktion Books, 151–73.

Meinecke, Friedrich 1959: *Die Entstehung de Historismus*. Munich: Oldenbourg.

Mills, C. Wright 1956: *The Power Elite*. New York: Galaxy Books.

Modelski, George 1972: *The Principles of World Politics*. New York: Free Press.

Montaigne, Michel de 1580/1842: *Complete Works*, ed. William Hazlitt. London: Templeman.

Moore, Wilbert E. 1966: 'Global Sociology: the World as a Singular System', *American Journal of Sociology* 71: 475–82.

More, Thomas 1516/1970: *Utopia*. New Haven: Yale University Press.

Morgan, Robin 1984: *Sisterhood is Global*. Harmondsworth: Penguin.

Mueller, John E. 1989: *Retreat From Doomsday: the Obsolescence of Major War*. New York: Basic Books.

Mulgan, Geoff 1995: 'Myth of Withering Government', *Independent*, 15 May, p. 18.

Munsterberg, Hugo 1904: *The Americans*. New York: McLure, Phillips.

Naisbitt, John 1994: *Global Paradox*. London: Nicholas Brealey.

Nakano, Hideichiro 1984: 'Japan's Internationalization: Becoming a Global Citizen'. In Edward A. Tiryakian (ed.), *The Global Crisis*, Leiden: Brill, 114–22.

Nietzsche, Friedrich 1878/1910: *Human All Too Human*, tr. Helen Zimmern. London: Foulis.

Norgaard, Richard B. 1994: *Development Betrayed: the End of Progress and a Co-evolutionary Revisioning of the Future*. London: Routledge.

OECD (Organization for Economic Co-operation and Development) 1993: Special Issue on Globalization, *STI Review* 13.

Ohmae, Kenichi 1985: *Triad Power: the Coming Shape of Global Competition*. New York: Free Press.

Oommen, T. K. 1986: 'Insiders and Outsiders in India: Primordial Collectivism and Cultural Pluralism in Nation-Building', *International Sociology* 1: 53–74.

Oommen, T. K. 1990: *Protest and Change: Studies in Social Movements*. New Delhi: Sage.

Ormerod, Paul 1994: *The Death of Economics*. London: Faber.

Ortega y Gasset, José 1932: *The Revolt of the Masses*. London: Allen and Unwin.

Ortega y Gasset, José 1962: *Man and Crisis*. New York: Norton.

Ortega y Gasset, José 1984: *Historical Reason*. New York: Norton.

Outhwaite, William 1994: *Habermas: a Critical Introduction*. Cambridge: Polity Press.

Parker, Martin 1992: 'Post-modern Organizations or Postmodern Organization Theory', *Organization Studies* 13: 1–17.

Parsons, Talcott 1951: *The Social System*. Glencoe, Ill.: Free Press.

Polhemus, Ted 1995: *Streetstyle*. London: Thames and Hudson.

Popper, Karl 1945/1962: *The Open Society and its Enemies*, 2 vols. London: Routledge and Kegan Paul.

Popper, Karl 1957: *The Poverty of Historicism*. London: Routledge and Kegan Paul.

Porter, Michael E. 1986a: 'Competition in Global Industries: a Conceptual Framework'. In Michael E. Porter (ed.), *Competition in Global Industries*, Boston: Harvard Business School, 16–60.

Porter, Michael E. (ed.) 1986b: *Competition in Global Industries*. Boston: Harvard Business School.

Porter, Michael E. 1990: *The Competitive Advantage of Nations*. London: Macmillan.

Price, Richard 1990: 'Does the Notion of Victorian England Make Sense'. In Derek Fraser (ed.), *Cities, Class and Communication: Essays in Honour of Asa Briggs*, London: Harvester, 152–71.

Pucik, Vladimir, Noel M. Tichy and Carole K. Barnett (eds) 1992: *Globalizing Management: Creating and Leading the Competitive Organization*. New York: John Wiley.

Rabinow, Paul 1989: *French Modern*. Cambridge, Mass.: MIT Press.

Redwood, John 1994: *The Global Marketplace: Capitalism and its Future*. London: HarperCollins.

Reich, Robert 1991: *The Work of Nations*. New York: Knopf.

Rex, John and Robert Moore 1967: *Race, Community and Conflict*. London: Oxford University Press.

Richter, Philip 1996: 'Charismatic Mysticism: the Toronto Blessing'. In Stanley E. Porter (ed.), *The Nature of Religious Language*, Roehampton Institute London, Papers 1, Sheffield: Sheffield Academic Press.

Ricoeur, Paul 1965: *History and Truth*. Evanston, Ill.: Northwestern University Press.

Rifkin, Jeremy 1992: *Biosphere Politics*. San Francisco: Harper.

Robertson, Roland 1992: *Globalisation: Social Theory and Global Culture*. London: Sage.

Robertson, Roland 1994: 'Globalisation or glocalisation', *Journal of International Communication* 1: 33–52.

Rorty, Richard 1980: *Philosophy and the Mirror of Nature*. Princeton: Princeton University Press.

Rose, Margaret A. 1991: *The Post-modern and the Post-industrial: a Critical Analysis*. Cambridge: Cambridge University Press.

Rosenau, James N. (ed.) 1969: *Linkage Politics: Essays on the Convergence of National and International Systems*. New York: Free Press.

Roszak, Theodore 1970: *The Making of a Counter Culture: Reflections on the Technocratic Society and its Youthful Opposition*. London: Faber.

Sachs, Wolfgang (ed.) 1993: *Global Ecology: a New Arena of Political Conflict*. London: Zed Books.

Said, Edward W. 1975/1978: *Beginnings: Intention and Method*. Baltimore and London: Johns Hopkins University Press.

Sassen, Saskia 1991: *The Global City: New York, London, Tokyo*. Princeton: Princeton University Press.

Scaff, Lawrence 1989: *Fleeing the Iron Cage*. Berkeley: University of California Press.

Schumpeter, Joseph A. 1954: *History of Economic Analysis*. London: Allen and Unwin.

Schumpeter, Joseph A. 1976: *Capitalism, Socialism and Democracy*. London: Allen and Unwin.

Schutz, Alfred 1932/1972: *The Phenomenology of the Social World*. London: Heinemann.

Sheridan, Alan 1980: *Michel Foucault: the Will to Truth*. London: Tavistock.

Sica, Alan 1988: *Weber, Irrationality and Social Order*. Berkeley: University of California Press.

Simmel, Georg 1908: *Soziologie*. Leipzig: Duncker und Humblot.

Simon, Herbert 1947: *Administrative Behavior*. New York: Free Press.

Sinclair, Andrew 1977: *The Savage: a History of Misunderstanding*. London: Weidenfeld and Nicolson.

Sklair, Leslie 1991: *Sociology of the Global System*. London: Harvester Wheatsheaf.

Smart, Barry 1990: 'Modernity, Postmodernity and the Present'. In Bryan S. Turner (ed.), *Theories of Modernity and Postmodernity*, London: Sage, 31–44.

Smith, Adam 1776/1868: *An Inquiry into the Nature and Causes of the Wealth of Nations*. London: Nelson.

Smith, Anthony 1991: *National Identity*. Harmondsworth: Penguin.

Spengler, Oswald 1919–22: *Der Untergang des Abendlandes*, 2 vols. Munich: Beck. In English as *The Decline of the West*, 2 vols, New York: Knopf, 1926–8.

Stark, Werner 1958: *The Sociology of Knowledge*. London: Routledge.

Strich, Fritz 1949: *Goethe and World Literature*. London: Routledge and Kegan Paul.

Tainter, Joseph A. 1988: *The Collapse of Complex Societies*. Cambridge: Cambridge University Press.

Thoreau, Henry 1854/1927: *Walden or Life in the Woods*. London: Chapman & Hall.

Tiryakian, Edward A. 1984a: 'The Global Crisis as an Interregnum of Modernity'. In Edward A. Tiryakian (ed.), *The Global Crisis*, Leiden: Brill, 123–30.

Tiryakian, Edward A. (ed.) 1984b: *The Global Crisis: Sociological Analyses and Responses*. Leiden: Brill.

Tocqueville, Alexis de 1854/1956: *L'Ancien Régime*. Oxford: Blackwell.

Toffler, Alvin 1981: *The Third Wave*. London: Pan.

Toulmin, John 1994: 'Our Worldwide Legal Profession', *University of Michigan Law Quadrangle Notes*, Summer: 46–53.

Toulmin, Stephen 1990: *Cosmopolis: the Hidden Agenda of Modernity*. Chicago: University of Chicago Press.

Touraine, Alain 1981: *The Voice and the Eye: an Analysis of Social Movements*. Cambridge: Cambridge University Press.

Touraine, Alain 1984: 'The Waning Sociological Image of Social Life'. In Edward A. Tiryakian (ed.), *The Global Crisis*, Leiden: Brill, 33–44.

Toynbee, Arnold 1939–61: *A Study of History*, 12 vols. Oxford: Oxford University Press.

Turner, Bryan S. 1990a: 'Periodization and Politics in the Postmodern'. In Bryan S. Turner (ed.), *Theories of Modernity and Postmodernity*, London: Sage, 1–13.

Turner, Bryan S. (ed.) 1990b: *Theories of Modernity and Postmodernity*. London: Sage.

Van der Pijl, Kees 1984: *The Making of an Atlantic Ruling Class*. London: Verso.

Vattimo, Gianni 1988: *The End of Modernity: Nihilism and Hermeneutics in Postmodern Culture*. Cambridge: Polity Press.

Vidal, John 1995: 'The Water Bomb', *Guardian*, 8 Aug.

Voltaire 1751/1926: *The Age of Louis XIV*. London: Dent.

Wallerstein, Immanuel 1974–89: *The Modern World System*, 3 vols. New York and San Diego: Academic Press.

Waters, Malcolm 1995: *Globalization*. London: Routledge.

Weatherford, Jack 1988: *Indian Givers*. New York: Fawcett Columbine.

Weber, Max 1920/1976: 'Author's Introduction', in *The Protestant Ethic and the Spirit of Capitalism*. London: Allen and Unwin.

Weber, Max 1921/1974: *Economy and Society*, 2 vols, ed. Guenther Roth and Claus Wittich. Berkeley: University of California Press.

Weber, Max 1948: *From Max Weber*, ed. H. H. Gerth and C. W. Mills. London: Routledge.

Webster, Frank 1995: *Theories of the Information Society*. London: Routledge.

Weinstein, Deena 1989: 'The Amnesty International Concert Tour: Transnationalism as Cultural Commodity', *Public Culture* 1: 60–5.

Weldon, T. D. 1953: *The Vocabulary of Politics*. Harmondsworth: Penguin.

Welsch, Wolfgang 1993: *Unsere Moderne Postmoderne*. Berlin: Akademie.

Whimster, Sam 1992: 'Yuppies: a Keyword of the 1980s'. In Leslie Budd and Sam Whimster, *Global Finance and Urban Living*, London: Routledge, 312–32.

White, Hayden 1987: *The Content of the Form: Narrative Discourse and Historical Representation*. Baltimore: Johns Hopkins University Press.

Whyte, William H., Jr 1956: *The Organization Man*. New York: Simon and Schuster.

Winch, Peter 1958: *The Idea of a Social Science and its Relation to Philosophy*. London: Routledge.

Winterer, L. 1890: *Der Internationale Sozialismus von 1885 bis 1890*. Cologne: Bachem.

WOMAD Festival 1994: Official Programme. Reading Borough Council.

Wyman, Peter 1994: 'Tax in the Global Village', *The Times*, 10 Feb., p. 31.

Young, M. and P. Willmott 1957: *Family and Kinship in East London*. London: Routledge and Kegan Paul.

Index